Travelling Jack

Fifty-two weeks in the country

Travelling Jack

Fifty-two weeks in the country

Ian Valentine

Quiller

Dedication
For my Father

Copyright © 2008 Ian Valentine

First published in the UK in 2008
by Quiller, an imprint of Quiller Publishing Ltd

British Library Cataloguing-in-Publication Data
   A catalogue record for this book
   is available from the British Library

ISBN 978 1 84689 040 6

Printed in China

Quiller

An imprint of Quiller Publishing Ltd
Wykey House, Wykey, Shrewsbury, SY4 1JA
Tel: 01939 261616 Fax: 01939 261606
E-mail: info@quillerbooks.com
Website: www.countrybooksdirect.com

Contents

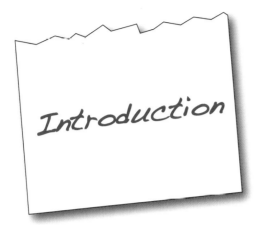

Introduction

'What size choke do you use?' asked the thirteen-year-old boy sat on the hay bale next to me. He had been told by his father to show his score card from a clay pigeon competition to the *Shooting Times* journalist, in the hope I might include it in the article.

I hadn't the first clue what he was talking about. 'What size choke?' he repeated, in response to my blank stare. 'You know, on your shotgun? I have a full choke on my twelve bore because it gives me a tighter pattern. Look, I scored forty-nine out of fifty.'

'Not bad,' I lied, implying I would not have missed any. In reality, I would have been chuffed if we had got fifty between us.

It was my first assignment as staffwriter for the weekly magazine *Shooting Times* and I wasn't going to be shown up by a teenager half my age who came up to my shoulder. My editor had sent me to the north of Norfolk, a region that boasts many of the greatest shooting estates in England, to interview a gamekeeper who had won a prize for conservation of grey partridges. His estate was hosting an open day to demonstrate these successes and many of the top keepers in the region had come to lend their support. Only the day before, I had learned there were two species of partridge in Britain, the English grey and the French red leg. I was in deep over my head.

How on earth had I got the job you may be wondering and it's a fair question. While I was not an experienced country sportsman, I had been brought up on a farm in Scotland where shooting, dogs, guns and game were a regular occurrence. I had been working as a journalist in London for three years previously, so I was a confident writer. For the record, I also played football with the editor. But within just one hour with dyed in the wool shooting folk, it was clear how little I knew about my new subject and how much there was to learn.

As a boy, my father had given me every opportunity to become a shooting man, but I had always resisted it. There had been good memories as a beater on the grouse moors and in the pheasant woods around Loch Tay, but with gun in hand I was a failure. I couldn't hit a cow's backside with a banjo. And when you are so woefully bad at a sport, it is almost impossible to enjoy it.

I am sure it was partly this ignorance that appealed to then editor of *Shooting Times* Robert Gray. At the time, the magazine was largely written by silver-haired gentlemen who had been there and seen it all. While they still wrote beautifully, their articles tended to be full of 'what they knew' rather than 'what the readers were doing'. Robert wanted someone young and fresh to charge about the countryside finding stories, recording events and talking to the readers. My brief was very simply to get out there and at 'em. Expenses would cover most trips within reason, as long as it returned a story full of action, quotes and insight. In short, it was a young feature writer's dream job.

Over the next four years, I like to think I fulfilled my brief. The choke incident taught me a sharp lesson that there was no point bluffing. If I didn't know something, I needed to ask. And there was so much I knew nothing about! I made a mental list of the country sports activities that I needed to tick off, and while I am not there yet, these fifty-two chapters represent a considerable step in the right direction. Of course, they were not all undertaken in the same calendar year, but across the four years since arriving at the magazine. A couple were covered a year earlier when I worked for the *Country Life* website.

In that time, I have managed to escape from London to the Cotswolds, from where it is much easier to reach the extremities of Britain and beyond. The job has taken me to almost every county on the mainland and several times to Europe. I have learned to shoot a bit straighter, so the idea of joining a team of Guns or a stalker on the hill no longer fills me with dread. If I was to revisit that north Norfolk shoot, I would now hold my own in a shooting conversation. But above all, I have experienced the enjoyment of the shooting field that my father had been so keen to share with me.

I hope you enjoy the book. I have certainly enjoyed researching it down the years. Throughout the text you will see reference to an individual called PQ. I also use 'we' regularly. Wherever I visited, more often than not the *Shooting Times* photographer Paul Quagliana was there with me. PQ was once a top class clay pigeon shooter and his quick eye serves him well in the field. More than anyone else, he has taught me about the shooting world and he has baled me out on numerous occasions when struggling for the right question. His excellent photography has made my writing that much easier. Our job necessitates hours on the road, staying in hostels of varying standards and sharing countless meals along the way.

Paul Quagliana, the photographer

We have probably watched more sunrises and sunsets than your average married couple. But there have been few cross words, plenty of laughs and I think we have perfected the most important tool for long journeys: comfortable silence! Thanks, Paul, you've helped make the last four years the best of my life.

Ian Valentine

JANUARY

FEBRUARY

MARCH

APRIL

MAY

JUNE

JULY

AUGUST

SEPTEMBER

OCTOBER

NOVEMBER

DECEMBER

1.
Falconry

The alarm on my mobile phone began to ring at 4 a.m. It was a Saturday, the second of January. I tried to focus in the darkness of my London bedroom, searching my mind for the reason I needed to be up at this time of the morning, as my body urged me to drift back to happy sleep. Then it came to me like a kick in the guts. Falconry. I had received an invitation to join the British Hawking Association for a game hunt on their corner of the Derbyshire Dales. What on earth had I been thinking to accept?

My phone started to beep again. It was a friend from my university days wishing me a happy new year. He was on the way back from a party and wanted to know if I was still up. Yes, I was awake, I replied. But I was on my way to work. The windows were fuzzy with frost and I could see my breath in the pale blue light of the phone, which I used to illuminate the stairs. I switched on the TV in the kitchen – anything to get my brain in gear. India was playing Australia at cricket in the sun-drenched city of Sydney. The visitors' Sachin Tendulkar, one of the greatest batsmen to have played the game, had just reached his double hundred and the crowd were going potty, basking in the summer heat. I nearly choked on my toast with envy.

South London was covered in a glaze that would have looked pretty in that sunshine, but under the struggling street lamps it was just cold and slippery. Yet no matter the conditions or the time of night, there is always traffic in London. Where are all these people off to? Possibly stealing back from an illicit affair or a high stakes poker game? I'm sure none of them were going for a day's falconry in Derbyshire. Sadly, my car started first time. But, there was only a fraction of the usual number of cars, so I could speed through Victoria and Hyde Park Corner with comparative ease, carefree of the sleeping cameras that spy out Mayor Ken Livingstone's congestion charge. Soon, I was roaring up an empty M1, wide awake and scornful of those slugheads who were fast asleep in their warm beds. I had never seen falcons and hawks in action, save for the odd reluctant raptor at a game fair, and I was assured it is one of the most exhilarating field sports there is. Besides, my middle name is Peregrine, so I feel I have some affinity with them.

We were to meet at a service station at five thirty for breakfast. No description, save that they 'would be easy to spot'. Sure enough, they were the group of lads in moleskin trousers, checked shirts and baseball caps emblazoned with the words British Hawking Association. They were also the only grown men in this grey, soulless restaurant to be giddy as six-year-olds on a Christmas morning. They were excited about hunting their beloved birds, but they also seemed excited about inviting a journalist, a complete stranger, into their inner circle, so I could learn about the lifestyle they hold so dear. It is something I must never take for granted.

There was an added excitement this morning in that many of the members were trying out a new patch of ground in the Derbyshire Dales where the BHA had acquired the sporting rights. It was a culmination of long-term planning, hard work and financial investment, which allows the falconers to stay for a weekend and hunt their precious birds on live quarry. The farm had facilities to keep raptors, dogs and ferrets in warmth and security, while the owners could let their hair down in the local pub with their pals. I sensed that for a falconer, this is about as close as you can get to paradise.

If only the weather would play ball. The temperature continued to drop as we climbed into the Dales and the unsalted roads sparkled menacingly in the headlamps. As we rose, we entered freezing fog like a thick curtain lowered by a troupe of brass monkeys. Radio 2's *Sounds of the Sixties* was playing a cover version of a famous Beatles song by a Japanese tribute band called the Mendips. 'I wanna hold yer ha-a-a-and,' they crooned. 'I wanna hold yer hand.' It seemed rather apt for what lay ahead.

The hunting party looked like a throw-back to ye olde England, though the jerkins and tights had been replaced by neoprene and Gore-Tex. In total there were seven falconers, two peregrines, two Harris hawks, a goshawk, a red-tailed hawk, an English pointer, a Hungarian vizsla, a German wirehaired pointer, a gamekeeper, a journalist, a photographer and a ferret in a box.

On a group hunt like this, two birds will operate at the same time, although they take it in turns to fly. Any attempt to catch prey, whether successful or not, means your turn is over and your team-mate's bird takes up the baton. First off was the red-tail, a surly looking bruiser called Tara. Her owner explained that red-tails, which are members of the buzzard family with a striking red-brick tail, are built to be robust and are capable of crashing through thick undergrowth with their strong talons outstretched, unafraid for personal safety. This was quickly demonstrated as the dogs flushed a bunny from a hedge. Tara surged from her master's leather glove and gained on the fleeing rabbit with deep wing beats. Bugs made it to a pile of logs, but it was still in grave danger as Tara smashed into the logs with a force that splintered kindling. This time, the rabbit had escaped.

It never ceases to amaze me how passionate sportsmen become when there are animals involved. Whether it is a young lad with his ferret, a huntsman with his hounds or practically anybody who owns a gundog, there is an increase in intensity and enjoyment when pets are involved. Falconry epitomises this extra dimension to the hunting experience provided by a dependent that has been raised, trained and worked by the owner. There is a profound bond between handler and bird, developed from the thousands of hours spent nurturing these complex creatures, which borders on the fanatical. You don't have to be a little unhinged to be a falconer, but I'm sure it helps! 'This is not a hobby,' explained a large man called Ray, who was now on point with his majestic goshawk Mia. 'It is a way of life. You have got to put the work in 365 days a year – indeed it is something we insist on from all our members. It is all about watching the birds fly – you never lose that surge of exhilaration when you see it go for prey.' Goshawks, with their short wings for daring aero-acrobatics, are the middleweight prize-fighters of the raptor family and lethal against fur or feather. A few years later, on a hawking trip in Lincolnshire, I was fortunate to witness a goshawk flying down a hen pheasant that tried to escape through woodland. It was like watching a Renault Espace racing an Aston Martin. The power, pace and agility of this ultimate killer was breathtaking.

For now, it was about rabbits. Gizmo, the German wirehaired pointer, stiffened to the spot as though the icy ground had seeped through his paws and frozen him still. The dog was pointing at a hole under a tree, so it was time for the cavalry, which was released from its wooden box. The ferret needed no second invitation and disappeared underground. 'It's uncanny how the birds immediately know that the ferret is there as a team-mate,' explained Ray, as Mia kept both eyes on the burrow. 'A hawk will never go after a ferret as you might think.'

Three rabbits erupted from the earth and took off for a nearby copse. Mia was way ahead of them and picked her target, launching herself off Ray's glove. Five seconds later it was all over for the hindmost rabbit, as Mia's crushing talons closed on its skull. Human, dog, ferret and goshawk had pooled their resources to outsmart a rabbit in its own backyard.

The conditions rendered the peregrines redundant, as their owners were nervous about losing them in the fog. It was not thick enough, however, to cloak a large dog fox that skulked about a strip of maize, before bounding off into the gloom.

'That was a magnificent beast, the sod,' said Peter Bertorelli, who keepers the farm for the falconers. Peter is one of the receding number of old-school countrymen who has at least one story to tell about every facet of rural life, each told with affection. His face is a criss-cross of lines borne from a cheery smile and too many hours spent laughing in the wind and rain. That fox would be safe from Peter's rifle for now. 'It's always a treat to see a healthy fox. I tend to leave them alone until the lambing starts, but then I'll hammer them. Even so, when you see them in the cross-hairs, you can't help feeling that it's a terrible shame.'

There was no doubting whose side Peter was on that day. While the falconers grow to love their birds, so too does the keeper and he wills his pheasants to escape every time the chase is on. 'If I was going to be a pheasant,' he whispered so the falconers could not hear, 'I would come and live on this farm. They get away far more often than they get caught. But if they do get one, I hope it's a cock. I don't like them getting at my girls.'

In the afternoon, we entered a snug wood that was ideal cover for cold pheasants. But the low-hanging branches and stubby bushes also provided perfect hunting ground for the pair of Harris hawks, named Mac and Taz. In their native America, these chocolate-coloured hawks will work as a family, chasing and ambushing rodents and lizards in the desert. This social background makes them biddable pets and they are often called a beginner's hawk, although Harris devotees may disagree!

The pair hopped forward from branch to branch, scouring the floor for signs of life, ready to swoop down in a pincer movement. A flash of grey from within a bush gave the hen pheasant away. Mac darted down, knocking Peter's girl off her stride before Taz did the rest. The keeper raised his eyes skywards. The Harris' handler Jose was straight onto the birds to allow the senior Taz to feed first, so avoiding a scuffle that can end in disaster. 'We wouldn't usually let them eat so much at the scene of the kill,' Jose said, breathless with excitement. 'But on a cold day like this, it is important to let them drink some of the blood, if only to warm up. If you think we're cold, you can double it for a bird of prey.' In that case, they must have been near frozen to death. It was one of those days when your bones chill and nothing will lift it. In Canada, I once witnessed minus thirty degrees but that was a dry cold and it felt nothing like the seeping, grasping, wet cold you get in this country. I had booked myself into the local pub and, once the birds had been packed away for the night, I raced there lusting for steamy baths and thick fluffy towels. I would have gladly showered at Bates' Motel, as long as the water was hot.

It was a disappointment. Indeed, it was the bathroom from hell. Lukewarm water spluttered into a pea-green plastic bath with brown stains and a crack down the middle. The towels, carpet and walls were damp and smelled of mould. I won't tell you about the loo, except to say that the pub evidently hoped it would clean itself. At least my bed was dry, if a little lop-sided.

The hospitality of the falconers in the bar soon warmed me though and it was a lively evening, as they told story after story, of which the basic tenet was that they loved their birds. One chap received respectful intakes of breath when he recalled how the rats he bred to feed his raptor had given him Weil's disease. 'My whole body had seized up and I couldn't tell the doctor what had happened,' he crowed. 'It was lucky for me he guessed what it was!' Another chap hawked a story about his wife, who would listen to him talking to his beloved bird in the conservatory. The punchline, of course, was: 'I wish you would talk like that to me sometimes!' At 1 a.m., I managed to steal away and leave them to it. My twenty-one-hour day was over, but at least I had a big tick in the falconry box.

2.
Snipe

The attributes of the pretty little snipe contribute to its downfall. I imagine that if it flew slowly in a straight line and tasted of the worms that it eats, it would not be such an attractive proposition to shooters. As it is, this jinking Houdini is a challenging adversary and it boasts about the most delicious flesh in the game arena. And for that, it must be on its guard throughout the winter months.

From a journalistic point of view, snipe are a great deal of fun too. For one, they tend to congregate on the coastline, so the potential for striking photography is limitless. Its favoured bogs and marshes provide drama and action; it is canine heaven, especially for spaniels; while the walked-up nature of a snipe shoot provides a more relaxed atmosphere than, say, a formal driven day. Besides, the snipe seem to attract those laid back genial characters who freely accept that they may not see, let alone hit, a single bird all day.

They reckon that once you have aimed at a snipe you have already missed it. It is all about instinct: you sense the movement in the reeds, raise your gun and fire at the fleeting shadow. The Guns tend to line out across a stretch of likely bog, often with a dog spaced between them that will (ideally) quarter from side to side within range of the Guns. There will be a flash of white as the wings flick the bird forward on its mazy escape bid, dinking like a Welsh three-quarter and gaining height, until it is but a speck in the distance. By that stage, the novice will have raised his butt to his shoulder.

The first time I covered a snipe shoot was in Devon, a traditional haven for snipe and woodcock. With an early frost, the migrating birds will move south to warmer climes, and that is where the snipe shooter is waiting for him. It was classic wetland near the northern coast with stout stone dykes and streams that spilled out into soggy fields: lovely soft ground for a hungry wader in search of tasty arthropods.

This particular group of Guns try to make it to Devon every year to ambush the snipe and let off some steam at the local pub: all very good for the local economy, if not their heads. They had invited me to join them for a glass or two of strong red wine that one of their team had liberated from Greece, but happily I was unable to make it west before midnight. The next morning, it seemed a wise decision, although it did nothing to impinge on their ability to lock onto snipe. 'I always need to hear that first shot of the morning to wake me up and get the adrenaline flowing,' said their shoot captain, a thick-set man called Trevor. 'In a wisp of snipe there's going to be one good bird for you and you have to get on it as soon as possible. I always think that if you can see a snipe, then it's in range. There's nothing quite like it to stir the blood as when you hear a snipe alarm call as it gets up. This is my favourite shooting – snipe are so wild and make such a sporting quarry. And no matter how long you've shot at them for, they can still make a fool out of you!'

By the end of the day, there were eighteen snipe casualties. To see them all lined up in a row was a terrible shame. Yet, hypocrite that I am, I gladly accepted the offer of a brace to take home.

At the other end of the British Isles sits Scrabster, a tiny fishing port to the left of John o'Groats that is a ferry dock for the passenger boat to the Orkneys. A lot of folk do not realise just how much of Scotland there is north of Inverness. If you have not been to the very tip of the mainland, then put it on your list of things to do, especially if you can get some stalking or fishing along the way. We were guests of thirty-five-year-old wildfowl freak Tim Bonner, head of public affairs at the Countryside Alliance. It is his hideaway from the rigours of political life in London and a place where he can remind himself of the freedoms and scenery for which his organisation campaigns. Tim's Scrabster retreat could hardly be further removed from his daily suit-and-tie London life. Just a quick glance round the cottage itself explains what goes on up here. Widgeon and mallard hang

Tim Bonner walks the marshes near Scrabster with his dear spaniel Otto

from the wooden fence that skirts the building, while incomers must climb over a small mountain of wellies and waders to reach the kitchen. The sitting room has been taken over by fishing rods and the kitchen table is a sporting still life, littered with spent cartridges, boxes of nylon and spare line, a fly-tying loom and this morning's breakfast plates. There is not a diary or press release in sight.

'They call this bit of Caithness the Lowlands above the Highlands and it's easy to see why,' explained Tim, as we walked along the sheer cliff tops that look over the treacherous Pentland Firth, arguably the most dangerous stretch of water in the British Isles. Those with a fear of heights are best to stay at home. Tim's old springer spaniel Otto bounded about at his feet, shaking off any stiffness in the expectation of hunting. 'The flat boggy fields are just perfect for snipe, especially if there is a frost. Our farmland on the coast is the last part of the country to freeze so they will gather here in their droves. You'll always get half a dozen shots if you take your gun for a walk. But, whether you hit them or not is a different matter!'

The plan was very simple: Tim would walk through a reedy damp spot, while Otto would hunt about and put up any snipe that were feeding therein. If there was a mallard, widgeon or golden plover that happened to pass over head, then that was an added bonus. Both man and dog were kitted fore and aft in camouflage neoprene, a uniform that keeps them concealed, warm and, if needs be, afloat when they go wildfowling on the foreshore. Tim was decked out in nipple-high waders, while his 'hot dog' was wrapped in a tight-fitting neoprene tunic.

Fifty yards ahead of us snipe were getting up and moving forward. Tim would flinch each time, but the sensitive birds were never in range for a shot. Less talking, more stalking. Larks would also flit up from the cover, causing the press officer to lurch forward, before settling back with a wry grin. Within minutes, however, Otto stopped again, as though bumping his nose against an electric fence. This time the scent was fresh snipe and a white blur shot up from the reeds in front. Tim was entirely in tune with his dog's movements and was on the snipe in a flash, bringing it down with a single barrel. The little wader fell ten yards ahead of Otto, who padded forward triumphantly.

Not that he was ever going to retrieve it. 'He is a hunter, not a retriever,' said Tim proudly, who was forced to fetch the bird himself. 'His father Oscar was just the same. I've never seen a dog as good at flushing game as Oscar. He would go through anything. Otto is almost as fearless and he's paying for it in his later life, as he gets incredibly stiff. He'll find a dead bird easily enough, but as soon as he knows I've seen it, he'll just stand there with his paw on it, until I come and take it. He's saying, I've done my bit, now you can bloody well walk over here and pick it up, you lazy sod. Which is fair enough, really.'

Otto is likely to be Tim's last spaniel for a while, as work and family will curtail the number of hours he can spend with his dog. 'Labs are much less high maintenance than a spaniel,' he conceded, pushing the snipe into the poacher pocket of his camouflage jacket. There was a touch of regret in his voice. 'You need to be out every day with your spaniel to keep the bond going, while a Lab is an ideal family dog.'

The idea was to ambush some ducks on a reservoir further inland, but there would be more snipe en route. Indeed, in the corner of one field, three birds got up in quick succession. They were all to Tim's right and his semi-automatic rang out five times in under a minute. One snipe was shot as it dodged over a dyke and a second, a superb shot at over thirty yards, fell into some thick grass. The third squirmed through a volley of shots and flew off to safety. In Tim's excitement, he could not be one hundred per cent sure where the second bird had fallen. Indeed, for we sensory deficient humans, it would have likely taken us the best part of an hour to find it. Otto was far better equipped for the job, although even he did not make easy work of it. Tim set him off a good twenty yards further from where the rest of us thought the bird had fallen.

'We've got plenty of time,' he said, by way of justification. 'By starting him off there, he can work back this way, into the wind, and he will find it. All too often, dog handlers will send their dog to where they think the bird has fallen. Either they are wrong or the bird has moved, and the dog is looking in the wrong place. They start blaming the dog for not finding their bird, when it is never the dog's fault. I think a dog should be allowed to hunt in its own time. It will always find the bird eventually.'

Sure enough, after all of five minutes, Otto pounced forward in the long grass and reappeared with the snipe. He then took five paces towards Tim with it in his mouth and his owner showered him with vocal praise. Otto spat the bird out, placed his paw on its breast, and waited for Tim to scramble over the wall that separated them. 'I think I'm going to have to get myself another spaniel after all,' the press man said, beaming. 'I can't live without one of these!'

3.

Red deer hinds

A good lesson I've learned in this job is how to escape from a hotel bar without attracting attention. Shooting folk tend to be extremely generous and determined to show their captive journalist a damned good time, so it is important to steal away without causing offence. Here's what you do. First of all, you ask your two neighbours what they are having. Go to the bar; buy them their drinks and return. 'I'll just go back to grab mine,' you say with a cheery smile. Then walk straight to your room and lock the door. It has never failed yet.

I once put this into action at the Glen Clova Hotel near Kirriemuir towards the end of a season. The hotel itself is no more than forty-five minutes from Edinburgh, but you feel you are in splendid isolation. Alongside it runs the Brandy Burn. They say it is the only place in Scotland where you put brandy in your whisky! Boom boom.

We had come north to cover a pheasant shoot on the Friday, stay the night and then go stalking for my first red hind the following day. The shoot party was made up of Angus farmers who insisted that anybody who shot had to stay the night and enjoy themselves. Wives were left at home. You can guess how the evening went!

The decision to turn in first seemed all the more sensible the next morning when I woke with a clear head. I had been warned that the stalker Sandy Mearns, who has walked these hills all his life, sets a rare pace for the Rifle and given this was my maiden run, I was glad I wouldn't be lagging behind in a post-party stupor. However, the weather was not on our side. Scenic hilltops were shrouded in mist and cloud, and rain was spitting on the Land Rover windscreen. I could only imagine how beautiful it would have looked on a clear day. But one of the benefits of having a stalker with forty-plus years experience on the same patch is that he has a fair idea of what the deer will be doing in any given conditions. 'You don't always get it right,' Sandy explained, quickly scanning the rocks for signs of deer before his binoculars steamed up. 'You can get careless from time to time, and the deer will surprise you by being in the wrong place. But as a rule, you tend to know where they'll be sheltering up. Getting to them is another matter, mind.'

Sandy has a kindly face with glinting eyes and a ready smile. He exudes a calmness, as though nothing I could do would surprise him, which was exactly the reassurance I was hoping for. If half the hill had slipped down

In the freezing fog with Sandy Mearns.

into the South Esk below, I am sure he would have done nothing but nod with acceptance.

The strategy was to take the vehicle as high as we could up the forest at the far end of the glen, before tracking back to the hotel along the top of the hill. The Glen is of the straight-up-straight-down variety, so there is no avoiding the breakfast-churning climb before you can think about stalking. It must have been so much more gruelling before the days of four-wheel drive. As we hiked up the forestry track, a proud cock pheasant tailed us, trotting in our footsteps with his chest puffed out, as he has done for the last few times Sandy has come this way. It was hot work in the insulation of the conifers, and the barrier of cold air at the top was a chilly reminder that this was a dreich day in the January Highlands. I opened my mouth to make some unnecessary reference to it, but Sandy's raised hand caught my tongue. The hunt was on and the stalker edged forward to where the wood ended and the moor began, pausing to glass whatever was on the other side.

'It's worth a go,' Sandy hissed.

He nodded my way, as if to say 'follow me, keep up, keep your mouth shut and you'll do just fine'. The stalker was over twice my age, but I was no match for his speed across the rough terrain as he led me a merry dance up a burn that was carrying snowmelt to the South Esk below. Sandy had explained earlier that he will often creep along the water side as the movement of the flow can hide our own. 'If you're careful, you can fool their ears and their eyes. But we'll never fool their noses.'

We pressed ourselves through a gap in the hill fence that crossed the burn; Sandy like a mink over a weir gate; me like a ballerina hippo, praying I would not slip on the polished rocks and splash the game away. I followed Sandy up the bank on the other side, keeping my head down. It nearly bashed against the soles of his boots, as he stopped suddenly. I raised my eyes slowly and followed the stalker's gaze over eighty yards of heather to a hind that was gently grazing, unaware that she was under surveillance. Sandy beckoned me forward, positioning the .270 rifle in such a way that I could slip in behind it. Silently, he slid the 130g bullet into place. It was only the second time in all these years that he had taken a 'cack-hander' on the hill, so the novelty factor was not all my own.

As I made myself comfortable and looked at the deer for the first time down the 'scope, my heart going at least twice that of hers, she shifted her position from a helpful broadside to stand facing our way. The ideal shot would pass through the heart or lungs, without damaging the edible bits and without entering the stomach, which would in turn tarnish the meat. We would have to wait. Sandy quickly closed the scope covers so they would neither reflect nor steam up. But instead of bending her neck to the grass, the hind extended it sharply and looked our way. Had she seen us? Were we rumbled?

All three of us remained frozen in time for a good fifteen seconds, as though the party music had just stopped. She was the first to blink, her ears coming off tenterhooks as she relaxed to take another mouthful of chow. She was still stood at the wrong angle, so there was nothing to do but lie and watch. This hiatus allowed me time to gather my thoughts. The first was a realisation that I had hardly breathed for the last minute, so I re-engaged my lungs.

It is funny what goes through your mind at certain crunch times, but at that moment I started to think about cricket. I remembered a TV interview I had once seen with the sensational West Indian cricketer Sir Vivian Richards. The snowy peaks of Glen Clova could not have been further removed from the Antiguan beach where the 'master blaster' had been explaining the secret to his success, yet the advice he had given to novice cricketers was no less relevant to my own predicament. 'If ever I was nervous before going out to bat,' he had growled in his deep Caribbean treacle, 'and there is nothing wrong with being nervous. Then I would simply take five deep breaths and I'd be ready.' It evidently worked for Sir Viv and I can faithfully say it worked for me too. As I pulled in the fifth drag of air through my nose, I could feel my heart rate slowing.

The hind shifted back into her original side-on position. 'She's good to shoot,' Sandy encouraged in a whisper, clicking back the lens caps again. It was a straightforward shot, but I was delighted and relieved all the same when Sandy turned back from his binoculars and held out his hand for me to shake. We moved forward to check the kill was clean. She was dead as she lay. But there was no time to feel pleased or guilty, as Sandy had spied another two deer not seventy yards away.

The pair was circling the hill above us, trotting forward twenty yards, before stopping to scan for danger. Of course, each time they did, they were putting themselves in more of it. But when I positioned myself for a shot, they moved away in time, as if toying with me. Before long they were behind a hillock and out of range. Not that I was complaining. I was elated.

Closer examination revealed the entry point was fractionally behind and had touched her liver. 'The net result was the same,' Sandy said, expertly removing the beast's working parts, a graphic reminder if needed that this is not just target practice. 'It's why I always prefer the lung shot, because if you miss you'll likely hit the liver. The heart shot can end up in the stomach and the beast can run for miles. Or it may smash a foreleg. I've never seen any need for a head shot. The worst thing you could do to a deer is damage its jaw, so why take the risk? If needs be, you could go for a neck shot, as that is a hit or a clean miss.'

Sandy had one last job to complete. He artistically smeared a heady mixture of blood and stomach contents on both my flushed cheeks as the mist descended on us. The facial cocktail smelled acrid and metallic, combined with a lingering aftertaste of chewed grass and urea. Certain people are against the tradition of blooding, saying it is barbaric, anachronistic, even disrespectful. I could not disagree more. For one, Sandy saw it as a rite of passage that he took pleasure in administering, which in itself was justification enough. It was also a poignant statement that I had just taken a life, which must not be done lightly. Like a puppy having their nose rubbed in it, I would not forget.

It started to sleet. At my feet a tiny frog was hopping its way along a sheet of snow, seemingly oblivious of the hostile conditions, while a dart of snow buntings passed overhead. Sheer slopes rose to our left that were streaked with mini avalanches – no go areas for a high-powered rifle. Back in the Fifties, forty deer were killed in one such avalanche, so we dared not follow the hinds over a certain height. With the strong wind at the top of the hill doing its best to blow us off, photography was a futile concern, so we decided to call it a day. By the time we made it back to the hotel, I felt like I had just been through the wash cycle in the laundrette, but all the better for it. While an ideal day may have resulted in a few more stalks and kills, I was thrilled.

Sandy seemed contented too. 'If I never shot another deer in my life,' he said, as he sipped his dram in the hotel bar afterwards, 'I would not worry at all. But I would hate to never be able to take someone else stalking. And taking people up on the hill who are new to stalking or new to Glen Clova, that is what I love most of all.'

May I also take this opportunity to thank Dick Hardy, owner of Hardy's gun shop in Forfar, who organised the day. A Derbyshire man originally, Dick was once a fine cricketer, and having read my tangent about Viv Richards, he sent me a tie he had been given by another West Indian legend, Sir Garfield Sobers. It is that sort of generosity, so typical of shooting folk in this country, which makes my job such a delight.

4. Ferreting

Charlie Gibson watched the Guns loose off both barrels at the bolting rabbits and shook his head. 'Pair of muppets,' he growled, both thumbs pointing to the ground. 'Their heads are scrambled, these two. If we'd brought our nets along we'd have been home by now.'

For the cost of shooting a brace of pheasants on Home Counties' parkland, a sportsman can get a full day's rabbit shooting on the hills above Kelso with Charlie and his old mate Barry Moore. The tariff includes breathtaking views of the Borders, your lunch and five hours of merciless leg-pulling from two rabbiters who know what they are talking about. Those of a sensitive disposition need not apply.

Dressed in matching army surplus jackets, hard-wearing boots and skin-tight gloves, Charlie Gibson and Barry Moore were well equipped to deal with the worst Scotland in January could throw at them. Their waterproof trousers had an extra layer of insulating mud and a cocktail of grime that would take weeks for a forensics team to identify. Charlie's grey hair hid under a fleecy bonnet in the compulsory green camouflage, while Barry bared his smooth scalp to the elements. From the contours of their faces, neither cared much for moisturiser, preferring the rugged, natural look. Yet today only a few rippling clouds broke up the expanse of pale blue and it was almost warm.

'That's Cumbria you can see in the distance,' said Charlie in his warm Geordie accent, scooping an albino ferret from the vacated hole. 'Those rabbits are probably halfway there by now. But you're not the first two to miss rabbits on this hill, as they can take some hitting,' the ferreter continued, pushing the reluctant pink-eye into a homemade wooden carrier. 'Going that quickly down the slope you've got to lift the gun as you shoot to give them some lead. It has to be instinct. As soon as you aim at them, you've missed.'

'Aye, they say you should go for a head shot,' added Barry, with the same colloquial lilt. 'But that's not easy. You'll notice that most of them, to start off with at least, will be shot up the bum.' We worked our way slowly up the incline, traversing to each set of burrows that showed signs of occupancy. 'You always move up the slope,' said Charlie, pointing out a well-worn rabbit run, linking two sets. 'The last thing you want to do is go chasing after rabbits that have already been bolted higher up the hill. They won't come out and neither will your ferret once she gets hold of one. You'll spend your whole day digging.'

On reaching each set, Charlie would select one or two of his ferrets from the eight in the box, drop it by a likely hole, before retreating at speed like Wily Coyote to see what would happen. Often the ferret would disappear immediately and a rabbit would scoot out of another hole. Like two opening batsmen who had played and missed a few times, the Guns soon began reading the speed of the pitch and each would earn a thumbs-up from Charlie when they bowled over a bunny cleanly. But sometimes, despite the best laid plans, nothing would happen. At certain sets, where Charlie swore blind there would be a good showing, the ferret would reappear immediately from the hole, lope about in a disinterested manner, blinking at the sunshine, before wandering away from the site altogether.

'Well, I suppose they know better than we do,' Charlie would grumble. At one point the ferret scampered right back to her wooden box, unimpressed by her handler's choice of warren. 'I think she's trying to tell you something,' Barry smirked, putting her back in the box. 'But that's what you want from a ferret,' snorted Charlie. 'If there's nothing there she comes out immediately and it's on to the next set. There's no shame in having a blank.'

Every warren had a story to tell, with Charlie and Barry reading signs that would have gone unnoticed to the untrained eye. A piece of fluff told of a courtship tussle between a buck and doe. 'At the bottom of the hill, they'll already be breeding,' the master rabbiter said, 'but the colonies at the top won't come into season for a few weeks yet, until the vegetation has grown up some more.'

Barry showed us the small piles of grass and moss, neatly spread out beneath a hole that the inhabitants were drying out for a warm nest. 'And do you see this black ground around the mouth of the holes?' asked Charlie. 'That's why the farmers don't like rabbits. Eventually the ground goes sour with all the built-up excrement and it's no use to anyone. That keeps us in business. And here's a tip for free,' he added, tapping his nose and dropping to a whisper, 'if a farmer ever asks you to clear a field of rabbits, make sure the first one you get is the one he sees from his Land Rover every day. He then thinks you're doing a good job. But you're not going to print that, are you...?'

Charlie and Barry are well into their sixties, yet both retain the same boyish enthusiasm for the sport that attracted them so many years ago. But while the spirit is as keen as ever, neither can sprint up and down the inclines like they once did. Indeed, only last year, Charlie received a gentle reminder that time marcheth on. He was out on the hill alone after rabbits, when he tripped on a hole, went over an ankle and ripped his calf muscle.

'I was truly crocked and totally deserted. I could have fired as many distress shots as I wanted, but no-one would have come. They'd just think I was having a good day. I knew also that there'd be no stockmen in the area – there are so few of them nowadays as it is – so I had to crawl down the hill to the nearest road. From that day I've carried a mobile phone – switched off, mind – just in case. My wife, bless her, doesn't like me going out on my own anymore, though I'd like to think I'm a bit wiser than I once was. Experience teaches you when to chicken out.'

29

More often than not Barry will be with him, as he nearly always has been for the last thirty-five years. They worked together at Nestlé and Charlie taught his colleague the dark arts of ferreting, taking off to the hills at the weekends to hunt rabbits. But despite Barry's wealth of experience, he is still the junior partner in a master/apprentice relationship, filled with non-stop bickering and goading. 'I used to batter Barry's lugs at work and I batter them still,' said Charlie, unable to hide the affection in his voice. 'Thirty-five years he's been rabbiting and he still doesn't have the first clue what he's doing. All he does is talk. I swear he was vaccinated with a gramophone needle as a baby.'

Barry quickly came back at his old chum. 'He's the one like a scratched record. Always was at Nestlé and now that we're retired, he's even worse. But I tell you, there's only one thing I miss about work and that's the holidays.'

'What's that, pet? You yabbering on again?'

'I'll "pet" you!'

'You don't say that when we're alone!'

'Oh… Shut your cake hole!'

It needed one of the Guns to intervene or they would have been at it all day. 'For goodness sake, ladies, will you stop your squabbling. I thought we were here to shoot some rabbits!'

The ferrets were the true stars of the show, although they were not in it for the glory. They wanted a rabbit so they could gorge on its blood and sometimes they got what they wanted. A faint squeaking noise would reverberate around the subterranean maze telling fellow rabbits, and those above, that a ferret had chased a bunny down a one-way alley. Like the thirsty vampire, a ferret cares not a jot whether its victim lives or perishes, just so long as it gets its fill of claret. Likewise, he is an expert sleeper, capable of dozing in a cosy earth for the rest of the day when his belly is full, so Charlie and Barry needed to act swiftly if they were to keep their charges hungry for work. Each scamp wore a transmitter round its neck that would emit a signal to a hand-held locator. Charlie barked orders and Barry began to pace about the set, swinging the locator above the grass like an orang utan with a Geiger counter. The gizmo pipped louder and faster as it approached the transmitter below and Barry soon had his mark. Once content that the ferret was stationary – most likely feeding – a seasoned spade removed the top layer of turf before a long metal graft excavated deep into the web of tunnels below. All the while Charlie offered advice as though Barry was digging out a ferret for the first time. 'Slowly Barry, you're about on him, pet. Careful of my ferret, now, do ye hear!'

Once the hole yawned wide enough, Barry turned from ape to ostrich, pushing his head under the surface to return with a grubby, bloody-nosed, disgruntled ferret, which he stowed away in the wooden box. Charlie then reached into the hole to retrieve and dispatch the unfortunate coney. 'You always want to grab the rabbit by its back legs if you can,' Charlie advised, holding the rabbit aloft for examination like a midwife with a new born baby. 'Rabbits can give you a nasty nip otherwise.' After the soil and turf had been replaced, the old rabbiter took out his trusty pocket knife and sliced the ends off the creature's soft ears for later identification. 'No shot in this one, you see, so I'll keep it for my supper. When I was a kid, if you didn't catch a rabbit, you didn't eat meat. This youngster will be beautiful!'

Charlie's preferred recipe for rabbit involves pressure cooking the jointed back legs and saddle for an hour, before casseroling the meat in gravy with tins of potatoes and vegetables. 'And the only thing better than that, is to eat the leftovers cold in a sandwich.'

'I'm also quite traditional,' added Barry, pleased to get a word in. 'I'm not keen on those curries or kebabs or what not. My wife makes the best rabbit hot-pot with black pudding, sliced potatoes and thick crusty pastry. When I eventually snuff it and go upstairs, I hope He is not a rabbit!'

Three hours later, with the shadows lengthening, Charlie put two of his angels into the last set at the top of the slope. The excitement had stayed with the party throughout the day and fifty rabbits were now in the bunny bag with the Guns out-killing the ferrets at a ratio of four to one. Seconds after the two polecat fitches were dropped into the warren, a pair of rabbits bundled out of an adjacent hole. We all rocked forward in anticipation, only for them to disappear into another orifice. Yet still they were not safe and the chase continued, with the noise echoing up to the surface. Suddenly, two bunnies erupted from the underworld and bolted across the field towards the safety of a hedge. Both Guns fired a single barrel and the two fugitives somersaulted to a standstill. The ferrets quickly emerged to see what the fuss was about, before trotting back to Barry.

'That's good shooting!' cried Charlie, his hands held high in celebration. 'And here's the ferrets to tell us the warren is empty. Now, I do like that!'

31

5.
Beagles

The first full-length feature I ever wrote on country sports was for the *Country Life* website, who asked me to follow a pack of beagles in the New Forest for a day, so those particular hounds will always retain a special place in my memory. At the time, there was non-stop speculation about how the Government was going to legislate against foxhunting and the hare-hunting beagles looked likely to be caught in the crossfire. I was not long gone twenty-five years old and I did a fair amount of running, including a couple of marathons, as well as weekly rugby matches; so I reckoned on being fairly fit. A day out chasing cute little dogs over some flat fields held no fear. Not for the last time, I was proved wrong.

It all started off very sedately, as the huntsman worked his hounds through a turnip field. Twenty-nine beagles, fourteen and a half couple to be accurate, spread out across the field, noses to the ground. A beagle looks like a mini-foxhound, standing between fourteen and sixteen inches at the shoulder.

'Their faces are so pretty and expressive,' said Jean, a fellow beagling-virgin, who had brought her daughter Fizz along for the day. 'They look like they're always having fun.' The hounds were directed by the huntsman Adam and two whippers-in who wore matching green jackets, white plus-twos, riding hats and Adidas cross-trainers: a happy combination of the traditional and practical. Adam controlled the pack with his voice and horn, and is (nearly always) instantly obeyed. Between the three huntsmen, the hounds are accounted for at all times.

It was a warm sunny afternoon, a godsend given the heavy showers throughout the morning, but it meant a hare's scent would be quickly burned off by the sun and hard to trace. The beagles drew the field, zig-zagging back and forth in formation. After ten minutes of fruitless searching, Adam gave a short blast on his horn to signal the field has 'drawn blank' and it was time to move on.

There was nothing to this, I thought, watching two eighteen-month-old novice beagles called Sixpence and Snowball (like cars, each beagle litter has a registration letter) wander away from the pack towards a group of hunt-followers. The huntsman will not train pups, but they soon learn the form from established members of the pack, similar to a pack of wild dogs. But they still had short concentration spans and the lure of a cuddle from friendly humans was too attractive. They were petted by a range of members of the local community, aged from five to eighty-five, who relied on the hunt during the season as a social outlet on a Saturday morning.

Having reached the next field, Sixpence and Snowball were called to heel by the huntsman and they eagerly complied, glad of the attention. Sixpence ran straight over a hare. A hare lying in its form (a shallow depression scraped in the earth), with its ears pinned on its back, is virtually invisible, but a beagle's sensitive nose will sniff it out. The hare bolted and the two pups instinctively spoke to the rest of the pack, alerting them to their triumph. The chase was now on. All the hounds spoke together and tore after the hare, followed as closely as possible by Adam. In a flash, all three parties were out of the turnip field and gathering pace. Followers have the choice of joining the chase or staying put until the hounds and huntsman return. Hares are territorial animals and will often lead the hounds in a loop back to the starting blocks, so the more canny followers can limit their exertions by pre-empting the course of the chase and walking to the start of the next draw.

Being a bullish newcomer to the sport, I was not canny, and gave chase. After three minutes running flat out, I began to wish I had not. It must have looked like something from the Benny Hill show, with the weaving procession of hare, hounds, huntsman and gasping journalist. All that was lacking was the music. I came a very distant fourth.

The ground was a sodden mixture of mud and clay, interspersed with puddles, ditches and turnips. Every field was enclosed with a barbed wire fence (just the wrong height to go over or under) or a single electrified wire. Jumping from furrow to furrow in a ploughed field, my lungs burning and face turning a shade of beetroot, I kept telling myself the hare would double back soon. My boots caught a rut and I was sent prostrate into the mud. By the time I looked up, the pack had disappeared over the top of a hill.

I eventually caught up with the huntsman twenty minutes later. Both he and his charges looked pretty fresh. The beagles were milling about as Adam called out their names one by one to make sure they were present and correct. Beagles never stand still, so they can be difficult to count. Garter, Hawthorn, Jasper, Minnow, Poppy and Robin all took their turn to come forward on cue. Sixpence and Snowball completed the roster up to fourteen and a half couple.

The hare had escaped. Indeed, only five per cent of hares chased are caught. Out of those that are, most are either old or infirm. This hare was a 'travelling jack'; a young male hare without his own territory, who had no reason to return to the turnip field. Hence he could streak off in a straight line and out of sight or scent. It was becoming increasingly obvious that the odds are heavily stacked in favour of the hare and it was no great surprise when darkness fell and the bag was empty. Nor was it a disappointment. For a £5 cap (the standard cost of a day's following), it was an excellent day out and more than enough fresh air and exercise for my London lungs.

Beagling is a sport for all ages, as you can be as involved and energetic as you like. We must have covered over five miles in the day, but the group had not moved out of the same few acres of land. Above all, it is an opportunity for those who cannot or do not want to ride a horse to see what hunting is all about. Throughout the afternoon, the topic of conservation repeatedly returned to Westminster and whether this would be the last year for the New Forest Beagles.

'I wish the MPs would come out of London and see what it's really like,' said Frank, a silver-haired ship builder, who had been crawling through hedges and ditches all afternoon. 'They would love it! It is probably not too late for pups like Sixpence and Snowball to adapt to life outside the pack. But for the other hounds, which are not house-trained and have grown up in the pack environment, there could be no conversion to domesticity. Most of them would have to be put down,' concluded Frank gravely. 'And that would be a crying shame.'

JANUARY

FEBRUARY

MARCH

APRIL

MAY

JUNE

JULY

AUGUST

SEPTEMBER

OCTOBER

NOVEMBER

DECEMBER

6. Wildfowling

As mentioned earlier, I was wet behind the ears when I arrived at *Shooting Times*, but I didn't know just how sopping wet until I went wildfowling. Wildfowlers are a breed apart from other shooters and I suspect many would enjoy being described as such. Not for them the steady stream of driven pheasants. Not for them the warmth of a pigeon hide or the chatter on a friendly partridge afternoon. No, your wildfowler prefers the solitude of the coastline, watching alone with his beloved dog as the sun rises or falls. He revels in the unpredictability of his quarry and the physical challenges they make him surmount. He cares not a jot that the terrain is slick with treacherous mud; that the tide snaps at his heels to drag him under; that the cold would kill him before anyone else was awake. They are the hard men of shooting and they earn that title willingly.

As much as I admire them, you won't find me at the front of the queue to join them on the foreshore. I'm quite sure it would be a different proposition if I had grown up on the coast, held the gun and ate the ducks; and had trained the dog by my side. If I was taking photos, that would help too. But for the scribbler who loves a warm bed, then sitting in silence on a mud bank at 5 a.m. when the temperature is touching zero offers little in the way of incentive. It is also extremely difficult to get information for an article. Many wildfowlers are men of few words, especially with strangers; while it is impossible to note those words down in environments where dictaphones or white notepads are useless. And it is hard enough walking through a foot of mud in the dark as it is without trying to remember what the sky looks like or whether the shooter prefers bismuth to heavy shot. It is certainly a test of an ability to multi-task.

The worst example of this brain freeze happened to me on a wildfowling morning in Morecambe Bay, close to where the thirty Chinese cockle pickers were caught in its icy waters in February 2004. Back then, the country took a collective shudder as terrifying stories emerged about the workers stuck out on the shifting sands as the strong and unpredictable tide rushed in about them. Many of the shellfish pickers stripped off their inadequate clothes in the dark to help speed their escape as they swam for their lives. Others did not know how to swim. Twenty-one bodies were later retrieved from the treacherous mudflats, while it is believed two more were never found. These were not the best thoughts to be carrying as we edged off the sea wall onto the marsh at the start of February three years later. There was a certain comfort to be taken, however, that our guide for the morning was Tom Fell, vice-president of the Grange and District Wildfowlers Club and a 'fowler with over forty years' experience on the foreshore.

'This is why I never come out here without a stick,' he whispered, charting a path through the ditches, gutters and pools of quicksand. 'Fall into the wrong one of these and you could drown.' After you please, Tom. No, no, I insist.

Melodrama aside, the weather could have been so much worse. It was the mildest morning for a good few days, with no frost on the ground, and there was not a single ripple of wind on the splashes of water that remained from the low tide. Hardly ideal 'fowling conditions, but at least we were warm enough. For now.

'We could have done with a bit of a breeze to give them something to duck under,' Tom rued, 'but we should see something.'

That's the thing about wildfowlers. They're at their happiest when it's cold and miserable. Tom was searching for the ideal nook to pitch camp and wait for the sun to rise. It needed a deep mud gutter to hide in; a good splash of water to one side for duck decoys; and a stretch of grassy marsh on the other to place his home made goose deeks. Carved from wood and skilfully painted, they soon looked like a small flock of geese at their breakfast.

Once in position, we made ourselves as comfortable as possible in our muddy ditch, Tom's thick-set black Labrador Pepper tucked down at his side. Built like a pride lion, Pepper is an old-school Lab that would dwarf many of the modern finer-boned retrievers. He is a cult figure at Tom's local pheasant shoot where he enjoys a reputation for independent thought. Indeed, his owner was once presented with a doctored photo of his dog, in which a penguin had been superimposed over a pheasant. 'Where have you been?' read the caption below.

For now though, Pepper was in place and all eyes were on the horizon. Small plumps of protected shelduck took turns to keep our interest alive and the odd pair flew overhead in curiosity, the white bars on their wings a sign of diplomatic immunity. The challenge for a wilfowler in this part of the world is ever-changing, as the topography of the inter-tidal bay shifts and groans like a rheumatic giant. In fifty-year periods – roughly the wildfowler's career – the sands will be churned from one side of the bay to the other, and the birds will change their habits accordingly. 'This year on the west plain, for example, hundreds of thousands of tons of sand moved to reveal ancient fish traps, once used by monks many centuries ago. Nobody had any idea they were there,' Tom explained later. 'Twenty years ago our stretch of foreshore didn't have the thick grass it has now. It was just sand. For local sheep farmers it has been a boon too, as they can now market salt marsh lamb, which is all the rage.' For many years there was a rich harvest of tasty samphire, otherwise known as sea fennel, which attracts expensive restaurateurs and wildfowl alike.

'We used to get plenty of the grazers – especially geese, widgeon and pintail – but that seems to have gone now.'

From nowhere a gang of ten teal crept up behind us and flared over the decoys in the half-light, but they were gone before I realised what they were. The temperature was falling steadily, or was it just the inactivity of sitting still? Either way, the frigid water in my trench was quickly sucking the heat from my toes. Again, my thoughts returned to the cockle pickers.

'There is no getting away from the potential hostility of the Bay,' Tom had told me earlier. 'With an ever-shifting landscape, the perils change too. In more settled foreshores you know that if you keep that tree lined up with that house lined up with that tower, then there is a safe route back, but that is not the case out here. You can soon be up to your neck in it.'

Newcomers to the Grange wildfowlers are greeted with a kangaroo court in which the longstanding members will put the fear of God into the applicant, lest he or she be in any doubt what they are getting into. 'I would not say we put new members on probation as such, but we do want to see that they will do all right. Some of the old codgers will recount horror stories of times we didn't think we would survive, but then I suppose we are all still here to tell the tale. Again, we don't insist that all members have a dog, but we will ask why not. They can have mine, if they like!'

The wind still refused to pick up and the only movement in the sky was that of the passing shelduck. It was difficult to keep my senses alive with cold seeping in to numb the joints and it was in one such lapse in concentration that the inevitable happened. A pair of mallard arrived unannounced, swooping down not twenty yards from my face. An experienced 'fowler would likely have spotted them earlier and been on them before they flared away, but my reactions were too slow.

PQ was snugly wedged in with Tom in their gutter, chatting away like fishwives, talking about bass fishing probably, while I was sent to sit by myself. The cold began to spread up from my toes, eating its way up my legs like a python slowly devouring a cow that is scared frozen to the spot. I ought really to have jumped up, stamped my feet and made light of the moment – it was not as if I was going to shoot anything anyway – but that was poor form. Besides, the other two sounded as if they were having a hoot.

Eventually Tom took pity and sounded a retreat. On another day, there could have been at least one teal and one mallard on the deck, but I hadn't even raised my gun.

'These things happen all too often,' Tom said flexing his fingers to get the circulation going again. 'Could you manage some hot tea and a cooked breakfast?' I nearly hugged him.

It has not always been as miserable as that. Tom is just one of the remarkable people I have met by wildfowling and I thank them for showing me their little world, which they ordinarily keep for themselves. There were two friends from Northumberland who took me out in the early morning in front of the Holy Island of Lindisfarne. We watched the sun peer over the North Sea horizon, spreading a warm glow over the cold stones of Lindisfarne Castle. Up above, the banks of clouds soaked in the rays of the sun, transforming the sky into a canvas of flashing orange, amber, pink and gold, as the calm water below shimmered back like a pool of mercury. 'It's as if the sky's on fire,' said one of my hosts, who goes by the nickname of 'Killer' because he's so good at it. We were huddled in a World War II observation trench that looked out over the causeway to Holy Island where the monks would lead pilgrims across the deadly sands at low tide. 'There's nothing quite like watching the world wake up in the morning,' sighed Killer.

On another sortie, we were out early with members of the Bridgwater wildfowling club in Somerset, who wanted to highlight their struggle to retain shooting ground on the Levels. As the sun started to rise, we walked out along a path towards a splash of water on reclaimed marsh land. It was the same path that soldiers in the ill-fated Monmouth Rebellion of 1685 once used to creep up on the King's forces. In pitch darkness, the troops were following a cattle boy, Richard Godfrey, but he lost his way along the myriad of ditches and bogs. The hours passed as they searched for a bridge that would allow them to surprise the enemy, but Godfrey had blown it. As the sun rose, they heard the sound of the drums beating an alarm. Their advantage in the dark made them sitting ducks in daylight and over four hundred rebels were cut down at Sedgemoor, the final land battle on English soil. Our guide that morning was a gentle giant, who sported a shaggy beard down to his chest and an ill-fitting eye patch that would flap open to reveal the empty socket behind. If you bumped into this gun-carrying pirate in the early hours you might jump with fright, but he was our host and very kind with it.

Wildfowlers are a weird and wonderful crowd, fiercely territorial, often troublesome, but always intriguing company. No doubt many sneer at the driven pheasant shooter who never ventures further than his peg or Range Rover. Theirs is a tough, rugged existence filled with moments of great satisfaction and personal fulfilment. Yet I doubt I will ever count myself among their number. Perhaps I lack the heart to slog out early in poor weather with limited chance of success. But then, your wildfowler will be glad I haven't caught his bug. It is one less soul disturbing his muddy peace.

7.
Herm
rabbits

Whenever I arrive at a shoot, I am rarely met with suspicion or coolness, but it has been known to happen. After all, we journalists weave plenty of rope to hang ourselves, so it comes as no surprise when a shooter, beater or picker-up opts not to open up to a complete stranger. Almost everyone I meet is happy to talk, indeed getting them to shut up can be a problem, but you do still get the odd clam. A question about foxes, wild boar, their dog or big cats will often get them started, but failing that, I move on to the banker: do you find shooting has changed a lot since you were a kid?

It can be like whipping a bull's nose with a wet towel. The chest puffs out, the nostrils flare and the chin juts forward. 'When I was a boy,' it begins, 'we had freedom. We could go wherever we wanted, because the farmers were glad to see us shooting rabbits, pigeons or crows, or digging up rats. We would spend all our holidays in the woods setting traps or down by the river with jars and rods. As long as we were home by dark, our parents were glad to have us out of their hair. We got into trouble from time to time, and you might cut yourself or even break a leg, but it was all part of growing up.' After the nostalgia comes the indictment of these modern times. 'Nowadays, children are wrapped in cotton wool,' they say, with a shake of the head. 'Computer games and TV stifle their imagination. All of them have these mobile phones, so they are never truly independent. Health, safety and the threat of litigation have turned kids into a liability that landowners won't risk.'

At this stage, having unhinged the jaw, I usually try to turn the conversation before we bite into the prickly pear that is firearm legislation. But all too often they have already booked into the moan zone and my attempts are futile. 'When I was a boy,' their cheeks now in full bloom, 'I was given a catapult at the age of six; an air rifle at eight and a .410 single-barrel shotgun on my tenth birthday. There were never any accidents because we were well disciplined. If my father had learned that I'd been playing silly buggers with a gun, he would have taken it off me for weeks. He'd have skelped me good and proper, mind, but that would have been nothing against having the gun taken away.'

These comments are either insightful or unhelpful, depending on your point of view: there are plenty of arguments in favour of mobile phones, health and safety, and gun law. Perhaps it is simply a natural assertion that 'things were better when I was a lad', as it was a time of mystery and adventure, before hormones, work and mortgages took control. Either way, it is probably not such a terrible society nowadays as the doom-mongers would have us believe. They need only visit the Channel island of Guernsey and they will see that our freedoms on the mainland are comparatively intact.

I have been to Guernsey a couple of times and I would jump at any opportunity to go back. It seems to be a happy hybrid of Devon crossed with Brittany, combined with the small island independence of the Scottish Hebrides. The welcoming capital St Peter's Port and the rolling countryside with its rabbit warren of roads and hedges retain their old-fashioned charm despite the big banks and accountancy firms that take advantage of off-shore tax relief. Indeed, the ancient and modern survive very well side by side. But one tradition that has suffered in recent years is shooting, once a very common sight on Guernsey and the nearby island of Herm. Every Saturday during the winter months, the countryside would jive to the sound of gunfire as members of the Guernsey Association for Shooting and Conservation (GASC) would hunt for rabbits along the steep coastline. Nowadays, the Saturday shoots have all but stopped.

A few of the old hands remain to keep the traditions alive. My guides on the island were Rex Trott and David Wilson, both life-long members of GASC, who took me across to Herm on a Saturday morning ferry. Although both in their mid-sixties, they look a good ten years younger. Rex still has his original thick ginger hair, while David sports a fine pair of sideburns that would grace a Victorian sergeant-major's cheek. Trips to the island of Herm are still cherished and they are both well known on the ferry. 'Guernsey is that small an island, we all know each other anyway,' explained Rex, his spaniel Ginny taking her seat under the benches. A low sun had risen above Jersey and it paved a golden runway over the flat calm of the Channel. 'Twenty years ago we would sleep out all night at the harbour just to be at the front of the queue to get on the boat, as there were that many rabbiters going to Herm on a Saturday. But now there are just a few of us left.'

In those days the boat would be jostling with Guns, dogs, ferret boxes and empty rabbit bags; everyone at the edge of their seats for the twenty-minute crossing. As the ferry pulled in to the little harbour, the rabbiters would pour onto dry land and disperse across the island like bees to find the best pollen spots. 'It was first come, first served – you took your patch and stayed on it all day, until the last ferry home,' David said. 'Often that would mean running as fast as you could along the cliff paths with all your kit to the other end of the island. But everyone would come back with rabbits. There were always plenty.'

High adrenaline sport it was too. Herm is built like a giant hovercraft with a long plateau on top and steep sides that plunge into the sea. It takes a quick eye to hit a rabbit as it bolts down the sheer slopes. 'Those bunnies are pretty nimble,' David continued, as we looked out across the water towards the islands of Jethou, Sark and Brecquou. 'We've been here with clay shooters and they couldn't hit a thing. I swear some of those rabbits can change direction in mid-air!'

'Oh, they're crafty too,' Rex added. 'How many times have we chased a black rabbit down a hole, put down a ferret, and seen a grey one come instead?'

When I visited, however, there are very few rabbits on Herm or Guernsey, as the cyclical Myxi has taken its toll. 'They'll be back next year though,' Rex assured. 'There are a few healthy ones still about, but we've left them to get the numbers back up. Guernsey is a very seasonal place, whether it is woodcock, mackerel, spider crabs or rabbits. I remember one year we had a plague of mackerel – there were so many that you could fish them out of the water with pierced buckets.' Herm, especially in the last century, has a rich and varied history. Prince Blucher von Wahlstatt, grandson of the famous Prussian Field Marshal Gebhard Blucher who fought with Wellington at Waterloo, bought the island lease in 1889 and during his twenty-six-year stay he tidied up the island, transforming it into his own private kingdom, including a herd of wild wallabies. He was evicted during the First World War and was replaced by the *Whisky Galore!* novelist Compton Mackenzie, who is thought to have taken inspiration for the best-seller from his time on Herm. Mackenzie sold the lease to Sir Percival Perry, chairman of the Ford Motor Company, who in turn introduced the first motor car to the island and painted the lampposts and cottage fronts in blue or orange: the colours of Ford.

This rather grand era came to an end with the second World War, when the Channel Islands, including Herm, were occupied by German troops. The Nazi propaganda film *The Invasion of the Isle of Wight* showed German troops sweeping ashore on Herm. During the Nazi invasion, David's father drowned whilst diving for the shellfish ormers, a great delicacy on the island. His boat capsized when surprised by a German vessel that was enforcing a nighttime curfew. David was too young at the time for the occupation to be a clear memory, although he does remember the sound of jackboots clicking along the roads. Rex, along with the younger members of his family, was sent to spend the war years in Huddersfield.

As kids, the pair would later play in the air-raid shelters and the intricate series of shoreline trenches that the Germans had skilfully constructed to repel invasion. They were given the run of the island, with most of the farming smallholdings only too happy for their land to be rid of rabbits. 'Back then, there were small farms with just eight or ten Guernsey cows each and they used to watch us as we worked,' Rex explained, removing a large thorn from Ginny's paw pad, as we walked along the cliff top paths. The dog yelped before rushing back into the thick brambles. 'Gunfire was just something you expected to hear in the countryside. Now the old farmers have sold up and the newcomers have horses instead. A lot of them won't give you access to their land because they think that we will shoot their livestock. We are actively looking to buy the rights to as many places that we can so that the sport as we know it will continue.'

For two sportsmen who take such pride in their island and pleasure in their simple pastimes, the steady erosion of their right to live their lives as they always have has been a bitter pill to swallow. The temptation is there to see GASC's struggle to keep its traditions going as a microcosm of what is happening here on the mainland. But that would be trite. We have it easy in comparison.

Already in Guernsey you need two permits – one to own a gun and one to hunt – although the code of conduct for the latter was drawn up by GASC for the local police. Wildfowl is protected throughout the island, despite there being huge numbers of wildfowl! For Rex it is maddening. 'It all happened back in 1969 when some scientists decided there was too much pressure from hunting. They did allow us snipe and woodcock, however, because the chap in charge believed they were "too fast to shoot anyway". It shows the ignorance we were up against. The conservationists now have to cull many of the nests because there are too many ducks.'

'We are very fortunate for all the wonderful experiences we have enjoyed down the years,' David added. 'But it is difficult to be optimistic for the next generation of shooters. They will not have the same opportunities that we did.'

8. French drag hunting

According to Noel Coward, only mad dogs and Englishmen go out in the midday sun. On a swelteringly hot day in the middle of February, unseasonably hot even for the south of France, the local members and hounds of the Pau Hunt Club were true to their English heritage. I felt overdressed in short-sleeves and shorts, but it was nothing on the locals. Although all of the riders and followers of the only mounted foxhunt in France were as French as D'Artagnan, you could be forgiven for thinking you had been transported to rural Gloucestershire. The tailored pinks and blue jackets of the riders, the polished leather boots catching the sun, horses immaculately turned out and schooled, would have delighted a hunting purist. Children with large grins on nimble ponies, dressed every bit as smartly as their parents, would guarantee a future to a cherished tradition that had endured since 1840.

Pau and the verdant Bearn region have long attracted British immigrants since soldiers from the Duke of Wellington's army made it their home at the start of the nineteenth century. Winston Churchill and King Edward VII both rode out with the Pau hounds, while eminent American visitors to the local equestrian scene included President Franklin D. Roosevelt and James Gordon Bennett, founder of the *International Herald Tribune* newspaper, who was Master of Hounds in the 1880s.

Nestled in the foothills of the picturesque Pyrenees, which provide a snow-capped backdrop throughout the hunting season (1 November to 31 March), Pau's pleasant climate is still a lure to hordes of incomers filled with the promise of Channel 4 property makeover programmes and low-fare Ryanair flights from Stansted airport. When I went out there to investigate this slice of merry old England, it was just weeks after the hunting ban had been enforced in 2005. Nobody quite knew what effect the ban would have and disgruntled hunters were looking at alternatives such as keeping their horses and hounds in France.

Tradition is taken very seriously in France. If you can prove that an activity has its roots in the past, then it will gain support from officialdom, almost as fiercely as our own Government seems intent on dismantling pageantry. In the village where the hunt met, the local mayor provided champagne and foie gras to show his support, while the mayor of Pau recently signed a grant to refurbish the charming hunt clubhouse, stables and hound kennels that have provided a social base for generations of French, English and American members. The mayor is determined to preserve the town's 'Englishness' and with the French anti-bloodsports movement ailing compared with its hyperactive colleagues across the Channel, the going is good for foxhunting in the region.

With an area of one hundred kilometres in length and thirty kilometres in width, full of interesting gallops, banks and ditches, there would be plenty to set the heart racing. But there was no chance we were going to kill a fox today, unless one ran into the path of the vehicle that laid the scent for the hounds to follow. For years the Pau Hunt has been purely a drag hunt, with a set course that allows the huntsman to lead the riders and hounds over the best obstacles and flattest fields. As it stands at the moment, there is no thrill of the chase or notion of vermin control: the hunt is simply a riding club with an excellent social life that culminated in a feast at a local restaurant.

PQ and I were there by invitation of Jeffrey Quirk, a retired accountant who lives at the magnificent Chateau de Sombrun nearby. Jeffrey has hunted all his life and now runs a riding school and hostel at the chateau with his wife. He has become a joint master and can bring guests along to ride out with the Pau Hunt, and believes firmly that the area has plenty to offer disaffected hunters in Britain. 'There is no reason why the region could not hold a live fox hunt,' he said, as we drove round to follow the drag hunt in operation. 'Everybody has been very supportive and there is a genuine fox problem that we could assist with. The terrain is ideal for riding – somewhere between Leicestershire and Tipperary.'

The present master of hounds, Monsieur Georges Moutet, was also excited that the hunt could offer a safe haven for British huntsmen, whilst giving

A hound named Tony Blair pokes his head out the keyhole.

Tony released!

a much-needed shot to the arm of the Pau Hunt, whose numbers have dwindled to just over twenty regulars. 'We would be delighted to help out the English in their hour of need, as we owe our existence to them,' he said. Georges was having a day off from leading the pack, as it was Ladies' Day and one of the female members took the horn. 'Our hunt would certainly improve with their guidance.'

However, at the meal afterwards, opinion seemed divided among other members, as to whether an invasion of les Anglais would bear fruit or upset the apple cart. There was no doubting the hunger to learn more about the traditional methods of hunting that could be fed by English emigrants, as well as a genuine desire to increase the excitement levels by chasing live quarry. However, this was tempered by a kindly old gentleman who explained that he had been attracted to the Pau Hunt because it was a drag hunt and he was guaranteed a decent ride out for his horse every time. 'I have been to live fox hunts and there is just too much hanging about woods, waiting for the hounds to catch a fox,' he said. 'After all, foxes rarely follow the best riding routes.'

The local mayor gave one last caveat. 'Of course it would be good if there was an influx of English to the area, especially for local businesses.

Up in the Palombiers hide out.

But they must remember that this is a French hunt and they must respect the way we do things here. The last thing we want is a hundred mounted Englishmen charging about as though they owned the place.'

We stayed for another couple of days in the region to soak up as much of the local country sports flavour as we could. Our greatest problem was how to overcome the local hospitality. Wherever we went it was 'time for a pastis' or 'cognac o'clock' or 'you must try my new firewater'. The culmination of this bacchanal was an evening feast held by Jeffrey's local shooting club in the town hall. This club shoots boar, deer, foxes and even badgers for one month in the year. It was Oscar Wilde who described hunting as the 'unspeakable in pursuit of the inedible', and testing Wilde's observations against a French setting is a neat way of highlighting how hunting differs from its English counterpart. While, rightly or wrongly, an English foxhunt is seen as the quintessentially aristocratic sport, up there with polo and croquet, the French do not have the same class-ist hang-ups. A hunting association in France will attract all members of the local society with no pressure to dress up smart. The concept of horns, horses and hounds is ultimately the same, but it is much less formal than the hackneyed image of the exclusive English hunt. As for the 'inedible', only the most desperate hunter would ever eat a fox! For the French, however, hunting is all about eating. Central to the hunt is the desire to sit down with friends and eat whatever quarry they have caught, be it wild boar, deer or hare. This *fête de la chasse* could not be any further removed from the lampooned hunt ball in this country, with all its pearls, silver service and red-faced Jorrocks. Out there it is trestle tables, paper plates, mountains of freshly cooked game, flagons of wine and sing-a-longs. Which one would you prefer?

After six courses accompanied by a plastic wine cup that was never allowed to be less than half full, PQ and I were invited onto the middle of the floor to join in the party games, including French versions of the Grand Old Duke of York, the Conga and a race which involved teams 'rowing' across the floor on their bums. There was no chance of sneaking off to bed, as my bed was four miles away. With escape impossible, there was nothing for it but to do as the locals did. That evening, we also met a couple of gents who insisted on showing us their pigeon hide the next morning. It seemed like a good idea at the time. But when the alarm went off at half seven, it didn't seem so clever, especially as I feared it would be nothing I hadn't seen before. After all, how complicated can a pigeon hide be?

In truth, it was astonishing. In a small wood on top of a hill, three friends had built a tree house in the canopy, some fifty feet from the ground. Not the sort of ascent you want with a foggy head! Up there, they had furnished the hut with tables, chairs, a gas cooker and a wine rack. From this central hub, the shooters could sit and wait for the birds to arrive, which they do in their hundreds. Often, their wives will not see them for a whole month. They assured me this was half the attraction!

The *palombe* pigeons migrate across the south-west of France in November and the *palombiers* are waiting for them. When the clouds of pigeon arrive, the trick is to draw them to their branches around the tree hut for a rest. Much like the pigeon decoyers in this country who use whirligigs, flappers and bouncers (more of this in a later chapter) to give the illusion that there are live pigeons in range of their guns, so the French do the same. But here's where the Gallic interpretation of animal rights is different from our own: their decoys are alive! When the *palombes* appear in the distance, these armed tree-huggers will pull a set of levers to activate an intricate system of cogs, pulleys and wires that cause metal grilles in the canopy to move back and forward. Attached by its feet to these grilles are the unfortunate live pigeons that naturally flap for all their worth.

To the unsuspecting migratory *palombes*, it looks as if the decoy pigeons are taking up residence in the treetops (why would they think otherwise?) and they fly over to join them. The shooters sit still in their turret until the last moment, before opening gun slits and letting rip. It certainly takes pigeon shooting to a new level!

9.
Ratting

The growing fast food culture in the UK has been blamed for the rise in many of society's recent shortfalls. Obesity, heart disease and social malaise have all been attributed at some time or other to the increase in burgers, chips, doughnuts, takeaways, ready meals and high-fat sandwiches in the nation's diet. The breakdown in family values is also pinned on the advent of fast food eaten on the hoof, as television suppers and couch potato lifestyles have eclipsed the old-fashioned sit-down meal.

There is another growing social problem, which does fall in the remit of a country journalist, that has also been laid at the podgy feet of the fast food industry. Rats! But this is not an isolated problem with a few thousand more rats in the dirtiest, most litter-filled cities of the UK. No, sir. This is a countrywide problem and the numbers of brown rats are swelling in their millions. According to surveys by the National Pest Technicians Association (the vermin controllers' union), the population of rats in this country has risen by over a third in the last decade. There used to be one rat per human, about sixty million, but now they outnumber us three to two with nearly ninety million at large and little sign of stopping there. In ideal conditions, rats can mate twenty times a day. The female can produce 120 litters a year, each with twenty baby rats that will quickly mature into parents themselves. A single pair of rats has the potential to create a colony of 15,000 descendants in a calendar year. And the reason: wasted food. Yet, how does this affect we clean-living rural folk? Sadly, rats like to take their summer holidays too and the countryside with its natural food and cover from predators is the preferred choice.

I like to think I am as plucky as the next man when it comes to creepy crawlies. But with rats, I start to struggle. Maybe it is just the thought of their sharp teeth gnawing at my toes or their filthy tail spreading disease across the kitchen floor that fills me with dread. Maybe I'm just a wimp. But I do know I am not alone. A rat can reduce PQ to jelly in seconds!

The first time I got up close and personal with rats was at Weston Park in Shropshire, where I was reporting on a ratting trip with inner city kids from Liverpool. We were profiling the Merseyside Terrier & Lurcher Club, which acted as a social club for underprivileged boys and a vermin busting service for farms and businesses. The plan was to track the ditches and fields where the keeper had seen signs of rat infestation. It was not long before the action began. As the first rat burst from the riddle of holes that pocked a hedgerow, grown men leapt high in the air and squealed like small girls, clutching at invisible petticoats. While we adults looked to our trouser legs, in case the creatures mistook them for drainpipes, the teenage boys held their nerve and their ground, blocking the furry grey varmint from returning to the safety of their burrows. Despite leaving downtown Liverpool in the early hours of the morning, they were chocked full of energy and throwing themselves into the chase.

PQ initially held fast to take an action shot, but his courage soon failed when a rat grew in his viewfinder, heading right for him. The intrepid photographer performed a starjump with twist, worthy of a 9.5 in the Olympic gymnastics, as the speeding rodent was intercepted by a two-terrier pincer movement. A few shakes of their crushing jaws and the ratbag had its first inmate. It was the lads who were running the show. Each in their early teens, they divided themselves between the various tasks that would add weight to the ratbag. Be it slipping a terrier when a rat bolted or digging a hole if it disappeared again, the boys were furiously committed. One lad, a thirteen-year-old bruiser called Conker, was already making a name for himself in Liverpool as a boxer. Although smaller than his mates, Conker looked as hard as polished marble, with a square jaw and broken nose. A black bother jacket and woollen beanie pulled over his shaved head completed the 'tough Scouser' look. In the rat field, Conker channelled his competitive instinct into a custom-built smoker made from a defunct strimmer and a length of garden pipe. By adding a couple of capfuls of engine oil into the fuel mix, it produced clouds of smoke that was pumped underground. It would either drop the rats in their hole or send them scuttling out into fresh air and the jaws of death.

Once the hedgerow had been cleared, the band moved to a strip of clapped-out maize, a relic of the previous pheasant and partridge season. It was clear that the rats had long claimed this food store as their own and the dogs all strained at their leash, rushing from hole to hole, as though the rats and not just their scent were above ground. One huge rat, about the size of a wine bottle, was caught unawares as it returned from a foraging trip. It never saw what hit it. Another made a dash for freedom, startled by the soil caving in around it as sharp spades sliced through the topsoil. It did not get far.

As far as stately homes go, few can rival the splendour of Weston Park, home to the Earls of Bradford and the Midland Game Fair. For the young ratters, all of whom were raised in the poorer suburbs of Liverpool, it must have been like arriving in a foreign land. The endless, open parkland decked with copses, spinneys and ancient trees must make a stark contrast to high-rise flats and shopping precincts, were green is paved with concrete grey. Hedgerows, quiet lanes, clear cool streams, varied bird song: the peace and quiet must seem a world apart from a city where fumes, congestion, constant noise and the blare of sirens elicit no reaction.

'We set up the club to get the lads into places exactly like this,' said the organiser Kevin proudly. It would be easy to underestimate the sacrifices and risks that he took to set a plan like this in motion. Many of the parents mistrusted what the club was trying to achieve and would be reluctant to give their kids permission to participate. Some could not afford the £2 annual subscription and Kevin would beg or borrow to pay their way. But still, he had got his lads a full day out of the inner city in the fresh air, and for that he deserved a medal.

'I was given the chance to get involved in country sports when I was younger and it teaches you so much, not just about the countryside, but all of the discipline, hard work, teamwork and respect that are part of the day out.' Besides acting as a top grade ratting unit (they would never want to be seen as a charity case), the club also provides a place for members to come for advice if there are problems at home or school.

'It is really about giving the lads a chance to see another way of life and we have been very fortunate with the support we've received from the likes of Weston Park. The Countryside Alliance has also been very supportive and we made sure we were active at the March. We all have to stick together, because we are categorised as "hunting with dogs" too. Seems crazy, but there it is.'

Conker's smoke pipe struck oil as six fat rats scurried from the same hole and dashed off in different directions. Terriers of all shapes and colours dashed after them, while the kids tried to herd the rats into their lethal jaws using sticks or boots. The field was transformed into a giant game of Twister as the players lurched and lunged to block the escape holes. All the while, the pint-sized boxer filled the underground tunnels with smoke that drove the vermin to the battleground above. Wisps of smoke emerged some twenty feet away from the pipe, testament to the extent of the rats' intricate lair. As each hole was covered, a new white plume would emerge from another vent in the catacombs.

One lad called Steve whooped with delight as his mate Robbie was 'nut-megged' by a fleeing rodent that ran through his legs, before running after the fugitive with his black-and-tan Lakeland cross. But Robbie had the last laugh as Steve tripped on a maize root and fell on his front. 'I though that rat was going to bite me!' he shouted, regaining his feet. The terrier presented the still-twitching rat to its master. 'Urgh, that's enormous! That must be the granddaddy!'

Please don't think I am trying to glamorise what was going on: it was barbaric, basic stuff. I remember vividly two terriers grabbing a rat at either end and ripping it asunder. As both left with their share, all that remained was the rat's heart, stubbornly beating in the dirt. As I gawped and squirmed, one of the older lads stomped over and crushed the heart with his boot and a satisfied grin. It was a grotesque act and wholly unnecessary, but somehow it was acceptable in the circumstances. If beating merry hell out of a bunch of rats was their only ticket into scenery like this, then it was fine by me. Psychologists and sociologists, discuss!

The only pacifist at the party was a midget Jack Russell called Jess, who looked on with wide-eyed amazement. She could have been no bigger herself than some of the rats, but she slowly located her backbone and decided that the best form of attack was to bark. Incessantly. Indeed, her shrill yapping soon reached glass breaking pitch. A lap dog by trade, used to a life in the Great Indoors, this sudden need to act like a dog was getting all too much. Her canine comrades were learning new tricks too, waiting for the smoke or spade to reveal the rat, rather than digging themselves.

Finally, Jess was given her chance to shine. The centuries of ratting heritage that had lain dormant in her DNA kicked into gear, as her lips rose to reveal angry fangs. Pouncing upon a monster rat (that was struggling from smoke inhalation); the mini-terrier grabbed it by the head and shook it like an old pro. Her previous notion of hunting would have been stealing a chip from the kitchen table, yet here she was doing what terriers do best.

By the end of the day, seventeen corn-fed rodents had been added to the ratbag. The lads were full of it. 'That was wicked, man!' said Robbie. 'I'm going to get me a terrier next year!'

Everyone wanted to do what they could to make sure the Merseyside Working Terrier and Lurcher Club kept taking them to places like Weston Park.

The final word goes to Conker. 'Some of my mates couldn't make it today, but when I tell them about this, they'll be well gutted.' Just like that rat.

JANUARY
FEBRUARY
MARCH
APRIL
MAY
JUNE
JULY
AUGUST
SEPTEMBER
OCTOBER
NOVEMBER
DECEMBER

10. Greyhound racing

Greyhound racing is a sport on the rise in Ireland, so it was only right that on a visit to Cork we should have a night at the dogs in nearby Youghal (pronounced Yawl) on the south coast of Ireland. The track opens its gates to the public on a Tuesday and Friday evening, running ten races with six dogs chasing the hare round the oval.

I'd been to the dogs before in Nottingham and Wimbledon in England and it is a relaxed night out. While I don't gamble a great deal on sport, I will have the odd flutter on horses or dogs, simply because there is very little fun to watching them otherwise. Indeed, without the excitement of a bet, the whole affair would be largely tedious. Gambling on dogs seemed to be a simple proposition. You read the form of each dog in the programme and then bet accordingly. The longer races are 480 metres, one and a half times round the track; while the sprints are just under three hundred metres, with the dogs reaching top speeds of forty-five mph. Everybody tends to have their own theories on picking the right dog. Some will say that one track is faster than another; others look at the condition of the dogs; while one theory is to bet on the dog that, shall we say, 'offloads excess weight' on the way to the traps. Perhaps the best method is to bet on the one with the name you like.

But not for the last time, I had misjudged the situation. After all, if it really was as simple as that, there would be more rich gamblers than broke ones. My eyes were opened by a local greyhound owner and trainer called Tom, who has won races before at Youghal. Lean and drawn, he had the nervous look of a greyhound before a race, his eyes darting from side to side, scanning the scene for something to chase. Rather than the hare, Tom's quarry was information that would give him the edge over the bookies. 'You are really betting on a dog's potential,' he explained, running his eye over the entrants for the next race. 'Anything can happen in the race itself, so luck does play a part. But you want to look at the split times. If the dog is consistently fast to the first turn, then it can get out in front of the traffic. Once ahead, it will stick on the inside and be difficult to beat. To get round it the other dogs will need to run outside, which takes so much more energy. Read the section times, is my advice.'

A little knowledge can be a dangerous thing, especially as the first two dogs I picked were bundled over on the first corner. For the next race, I tried a reverse forecast, in which you pick two dogs to finish in either first or second place in any order. My pair of misfits limped home in fifth and sixth position. I'll admit though that I was hardly betting big bucks: just a couple of euros per race. For bigger stakes, there are the bookies with their sheepskin jackets and blackboards, while those betting shrapnel like me take their chances with the Tote booths, which accept a minimum one euro stake. Children are typically given ten euros to bet across the ten races.

Now running at a six euro loss, my next bet reverted to picking a dog on its name alone. It was a fast race too, with the winner Society Assassin racing round in nearly twenty-nine seconds flat. As it passed the winning line, there was a mighty cheer from a large section of the crowd, who had clearly backed it heavily, while streams of excitable children sprinted down the concourse to collect their winnings from the Tote kiosks. My dog, Redhot Missy, trailed home in fifth. I was now eight euros down and getting tetchy. Tom, however, was animated. 'That's a savage time,' he enthused, scribbling the split times on his programme. 'That dog is now worth about twenty thousand euros. Oh, with a time like that, his phone will be ringing in the morning. It may well be ringing before he gets out of here. That's a savage time.'

The dogs have grown in popularity in Ireland due to a marketing strategy of benefit nights, which have attracted new punters to the tracks. Under the terms of a benefit meet, an organisation will fund the prize money by selling sponsorship packages for each of the ten races at three hundred euros each. Once that is covered, the charity or club is then in the black. Any extra money made through individual dog sponsorship (thirty euros per dog) and ticket sales (ten euros for an adult) is pure profit. It is not uncommon for a benefit night to raise over twenty thousand euros for the organisers. Standing on a ledge behind the bookies' boards and feeling like a tourist with the street map upside down, I looked at the programme for the next race. Tom tugged at my jumper. 'Have a look at those boys down there. The young lads by the toilets.' There were three of them, in their early twenties, all dressed in denim jackets, stone-washed jeans and cowboy boots. To the uninitiated, they just looked like three lads having a smoke. One then passed a thick white envelope to his mate, who put it in the inside pocket of his jacket with an air of exaggerated nonchalance as though it contained nothing more than raffle tickets for a charity fundraiser. Perhaps it did, but Tom thought otherwise. 'Now, watch him. Let's see where he's going with that cash.'

My heart picked up a beat. We weren't doing anything wrong and neither were the Envelope Boys for that matter, but I started to feel like I was on the inside of a sting operation. The lad with the dough walked slowly over to a group of punters, who were milling about in front of the bookies' boards. The next race was due to start in four minutes, but they all stood still, watching for a change on the boards that would make a bet worthwhile. The courier, if that's what he was, sidled in next to a tall man with a cricket ball face and a spiky grey moustache below a flat-topped buzz-cut. I felt like he was staring right at me, but he was simply eye-balling the boards between us.

'Did you see that? He's given the money to that big lad,' whispered Tom, drawing me further into the subterfuge. I hadn't seen the drop, but rather than show my novice frailties, I nodded knowingly. The dog handlers were removing the runners' coats and leading them down the paddock to the traps, but still Buzz Cut didn't move. 'Get your money ready,' hissed Tom. 'When he goes to a bookie, you go too. If he stays put, keep your money in your pocket.' We were not the only ones watching him. Like a scene from a Cold War spy film, there were four others glancing up at Buzz Cut from behind their programmes. Some would throw looks at one another or the bookies. Were these punters or the book-keepers' spotters? I had no idea. And there was another question that remained unanswered. 'Tom,' I breathed, doing my best to sound cool. 'Which dog do I put it on?'

My tipster didn't take his eyes off Buzz Cut. 'Dog number five.'

My tongue was as dry as a stick of chewing gum, so I gulped to moisten it. 'Why number five?'

'Because it's his fecking dog!'

When the first of the runners was loaded into the trap, Buzz Cut made his move. Tom slapped me on the shoulder and I skipped down the steps to the nearest bookie to place ten euros on dog number five. The dog came second. I tore up my slip in mock anger, shaking my head at Tom. 'You did put it both ways, didn't you?' he replied with a grin. 'You can't blame me then! Not my fault!'

Indeed, it wasn't. I had been caught up in the moment. It was probably lucky the first note I grabbed was a ten and not a fifty. Besides, for the adrenaline rush, it was well worth ten euros. I didn't see Buzz Cut again, so whether he collected any winnings by hedging his bets, I couldn't tell you.

I asked Tom if greyhound racing was a fair sport. It has a reputation for skulduggery, but is that just the moanings of upset punters?

'In the old days, there was all sorts that went on, from switching dogs at the last moment, to a grand cocktail of drugs,' he said. 'But now, it has all changed. Only an eejit would start injecting them with banned substances, as you'll only get caught and banned yourself. The standard is that much higher too. In the old days, you might have four or five eejits in a race, so you had a good chance of winning most times if you had a good dog.'

By the tenth race, I was eighteen euros down. 'It's all or nothing on the last race,' I told Tom, pulling out a crisp five euro note from my wallet. 'Seven euros on the nose. Don't let me down, now.'

For the final time, Tom scanned the race card. 'Cracked Fairy,' he said eventually. 'Track two. There's no such thing as a sure thing in a dog race but I'll be mighty surprised if Cracked Fairy doesn't win.'

I ran to the kiosk and laid the bet just as the dogs were being led to the start. The hare was soon on the move, curving round the outside of the track until it passed the traps, which sprung open to release the hounds. Cracked Fairy got a quick start in track two and was half a length on from Rebel Brave and Dark Gossip by the first turn.

'You'll win from here,' said Tom confidently.

On the outside, Ashville Nikita and Transtown Jack in tracks five and six collided with one another and struggled to keep their footing in the wet sand. Cracked Fairy was a full length ahead now, extending up the back straight, with only Dark Gossip staying in touch. Tom grinned at me. 'They'll not catch him now!'

Charging round the final bend, I half expected the dog to trip and fall, given my fortune to date, but Cracked Fairy ran through a comfortable winner by three lengths. I collected my winnings: a whopping twenty-one euros. I was one euro up for the evening. So, it's not just the Irish who are lucky!

11.
Las Vegas

Las Vegas takes the prize for the most bizarre place I have visited under the influence of *Shooting Times*. This may sound a bit spoilt, given I was there on a freebie and there are plenty of readers who would have gladly taken my place, but I didn't like the place. Perhaps it is a sign of my descent into middle age, but if I had a choice of that cottage above Scrabster or the four-star Mirage

Hotel on the Vegas Strip, it would be the Scottish fishing port every time.

As you fly across the desert towards the airport, Vegas twinkles back at you like a fairground in a car park. It is an oasis of glut: a physical embodiment of the lure of gambling. It is a city built on the promise of wealth, where you are expected to feel special and glamorous and successful. Everything is done to excess, from the twenty-four-hour lobby daylight to the all-you-can-eat buffets, where as much is wasted as eaten. Everybody wants to be your friend and everybody wants to get rich quick. I don't want to sound like a prude (I even lost fifteen bucks in the slot machines), but I could not buy into the culture of over-indulgence. Maybe I'm too tight-fisted to risk having nothing to show for it.

For all that, it is the perfect setting for the Shot Show, the largest trade fair for hunting, fishing, shooting in the world. There are literally miles of aisles to walk down of all the latest guns and gadgets in the American sporting business and nearly every one is manned by an over-excited salesman who genuinely believes their product is the answer to your hunting prayers. Given the size of the place, it was difficult to know where to start, but there seemed no better place than the biggest noise in American gun culture: the National Rifle Association. Although nobody knew it at that time, Vice-President Dick Cheney, one of the NRA's highest profile members, had only just shot an old friend by accident whilst hunting quail. Sadly, the story broke the day after the Show ended. So it was not on NRA spokesman Ryan Irsik's mind when I asked him about the pressures that currently face hunting in the USA.

'One of the greatest threats we have at the moment is complacency,' he explained. 'There is no current problem with legislation and there won't be with George W. Bush in the White House. As a result, our membership is lower than it has been for years. Campaign organisations need plausible threats to survive, so I think some of the smaller organisations are struggling for resources. But if Hillary (Clinton) goes for it in 2008, then we'll see a rise in membership.'

The NRA is currently getting itself watertight, should any future storm start brewing. 'I'm sorry to say that we use you guys in the UK as an example of what can happen if you let Government impose their will,' continued Ryan. 'But in the meantime we are trying to boost the number of young men and especially women who hunt. If you look at a shooting field or hunting party you always see too many white-haired men.'

One of the clearest messages from the show is that if you're not yet into realtree camouflage, then you will be soon. Everything can be bought in realtree. From sensible items that help you hide in the undergrowth such as jackets, hats and trousers; to the eccentric such as vehicles, sofas and neck ties; to the downright bizarre like toilet seats, baby-grows and silk lingerie: it's all coming this way. Just don't lean your camouflaged gun against a tree unless you can remember which tree it was.

As with so many things in the US, shooting can be a world apart from our own fair shores. Some of these differences are inevitable – for example we have no turkeys, raccoons, coyotes or Fourth Amendments. Unlike the Americans, we may not own pistols, combat rifles, nor shoot an arrow from a bow at a wild animal. Apart from anything else, there is territorially much less of the UK, so we don't have the same 'hunting for all' mentality. But then there are the subtle differences. Millions of dollars are spent each year over there developing the most lifelike quarry calls and scent markers, which might be deemed unnecessary over here or perhaps even unsporting. Scents, and in particular urine, are a hot topic. One product called 'Rite in the Rain', offers natural whitetail doe urine with oestrous secretions. It also contains a 'touch of secret musk that really increases the drawing power. It's the smell your trophy buck has been waiting for.'

Part of the entertainment at the Shot show.

One stall from Quebec called Buck Expert had everything that would satisfy your urine needs, including skunk, moose, wolf and boar. You wonder what the turnover of staff at their factory must be. There was even a spray to cover up your own scent if caught short. Their bear incense sticks are also very popular and come in various flavours including honey, bacon, rotten fish and doughnuts. And boar urine.

Blasting off
rounds with
Winchester in
the Nevada
Desert.

The US is often teased for having no history or heritage, but walking through the weapons section of the show, it is clear that this is at least one area where the Americans have a distinguished past. Winchester, Remington, Springfield, Colt, Weatherby, Smith & Wesson, Ruger are all household names alongside John Wayne, Clint Eastwood and Charles Bronson. Add to them the great European names of Browning, Glock, Heckler & Koch, Walther, Franchi, Benelli, Beretta and Merkel, and you soon have a who's who of sporting hardware. Interestingly, Smith & Wesson are now sinking a lot of dollars into recreational ware such as BBQs, meat smokers, safes, watches, footwear and even bicycles. Everything Dirty Harry would need for his retirement.

The highlight of the weekend was a sojourn to a rifle range in the Nevada desert, courtesy of Browning and Winchester, to test out their new and well-established products. Within just half an hour of leaving the hotel, the bright lights and twenty-four-hour casinos were behind us, replaced by miles of arid moonscape. For three hours, the journalist rank and file were left to test every imaginable shotgun, rifle and handgun over distances up to four hundred yards. I realise guns cause huge problems throughout the world, but in the right environment they are hellish good fun! It did strike me just how difficult it is to be accurate with a pistol,

'Would Sir like to buy this gun?'

even at ranges as short as ten yards. So many cowboy or cop movies show the hero picking off baddies at fifty yards, usually on the run. With my accuracy, I wouldn't make it past the opening credits.

As an aside, the Winchester family was involved in one of the ghostliest stories in the US. When the gun magnate William Wilt Winchester died in the 1880s, his wife Sarah inherited his fortune. Suffering from grief, the widow was said to have sought solace in a spiritual medium, who told her she was being haunted by the vengeful souls of all the many victims of Winchester rifles. The solution, apparently, was to build a house with no corners so the ghosts would have nowhere to lie in wait. And the house should be extended every day or Sarah would die of fright. For the next thirty-eight years, Sarah oversaw the construction of a new house in St Jose, California, hiring builders twenty-four-seven. The mad old goat slept in a different room every night to keep the spirits away. On 5 September 1922, after spending $5.5 million, the house was finished and Sarah sent the builders away. That night, she died of heart failure.

There are a good many products on sale that are unlikely to take off in this country, but they do at least give an insight into the American market, such as specialist body armour for hand to hand combat, or a patented wall vault that allows easy access to your house pistol. Happily you can also get child guards for guns to stop your kids playing with them. Anything you want in the way of night vision is there at the Shot Show. There are hats, knives, ear defenders, binoculars, all with special night lights attached. Battery-powered heated vests and socks; scopes with a handy cam on top to film as you fire; a golf club that will launch your dog's favourite ball; a gun oil called Gunzilla; 'extra spicy' pepper spray; fire lighters that work on water; laser-sighted sling shots and clothing that makes you smell invisible. If you see what I mean. So be warned, Britain, the future is coming. And the chances are, it's available in realtree.

12.

Trapping

On a driven shoot day, I always feel the odd butterfly on arrival in the morning, as it is not a guarantee that as journalists we'll get a warm reception. That's not to say that anybody is ever overtly rude, but there are people who don't want a reporter or photographer poking their nose or lens in. Which is fair enough. It only becomes a problem, however, when that person showing indifference is the headkeeper. Again, this happens rarely. Most will come striding over, bear paw outstretched (they always have big hands), offering the keys to the kingdom. 'Anything you want, just ask!' he'll boom, pumping my arm like a pneumatic drill. 'Come ride in my Land Rover, son. I'll show what you need to know!'

But there is the odd headkeeper who doesn't want to know. He scowls at you, surrounded by his lieutenants, as you kick a stone about in the middle of the yard, hoping for the ground to swallow you up. More than likely, his boss has only just told him the press are coming. Or the wind is from the North with hail forecast. Either way, the last thing he wants to deal with is an inquisitive journalist.

Again, I have every sympathy, as being a headkeeper in season is a stressful occupation, much more so than in years gone by. Even as recently as a few decades ago, his primary function was to make sure the birds flew straight. Back then he was a vermin controller, bird rearer, loader, bailiff

Keeper Jeff Handy assembles a tunnel trap.

and leader of the beating line. Nowadays, he has to be so much more. He is an accountant, totting up figures and margins on the estate computer at night. He is a health and safety officer, with diplomas and certificates in hygiene, machinery operation and bio-security. He is a full-time recruitment agent, competing with other shoots for stops, beaters and pickers-up. Many are also politicians, clocking up hours for the excellent National Gamekeepers Organisation. There is no free time or work–home balance for these guys between April and February. No long weekends away or summer holidays. It is perhaps little wonder that so many keepers smoke and that their marriages creak under the strain.

But there are days when even the headkeeper can let down what little hair he has left. These are the jeans-and-holey-jumper days between the end of one season and the beginning of the next when there are no guests to be polite to, no bosses to impress. The work goes on, but they are old-fashioned keepering jobs: messing about in rearing pens, shooting crows, lamping foxes or deer control. On those days, you see a headkeeper at his best. They are the assignments I enjoy the most.

One such trip took me to Kent and the three thousand acres of Torry Hill Estate, a wild bird shoot run by headkeeper Jeff Handy. Every day from February to mid-May, he will cover up to forty miles on his quad bike, checking the 185 tunnel traps on the estate for weasels, stoats, rats and squirrels. Nearly a decade ago, the owner decided to convert the shoot from reared to wild birds, shifting the emphasis of Jeff's work from incubators and release pens to full time predator control. Although plenty of eyebrows were raised at the time – not least Jeff's – the calculated gamble appears to have paid off.

'Managing a wild-bird shoot without full-time predator control is like running a bath with the plug out,' said Jeff, as we admired a tunnel he had adapted to trap vermin underneath a water trough. 'As fast as the water comes in, it will leave through the bottom, and though you will always have a level of water in the bath, you will never fill it.'

Jeff is clearly proud of his homemade traps that have taken many hours of trial and error to site and fashion in a way that works best for that location. The tunnels are camouflaged with all manner of organic and artificial materials which blend in with the local scenery in a way that is alluring to an over-curious beastie. 'Stoats and weasels, especially, are inquisitive animals and they will investigate an intriguing tunnel or aroma. It is the same with us – if you have the choice of snooping round a modern semi-detached or a rambling Elizabethan home with all sorts of nooks and crannies, which do you go for?'

Jeff demonstrated his Blue Peter skills, replacing a rotting tunnel with one he had made earlier. It was then covered with turf and the old wood of the last tunnel to create a welcoming refuge for rodents and mustelids. Situated at the edge of a gap in the fence line, Jeff had high hopes for its efficiency. 'Gateways and openings in the hedge are ideal places to site a tunnel,' advised Jeff as he nonchalantly placed a primed Fenn trap in one. Safety catch off, he showed me its gaping metal jaws that would spring shut with bone crunching force. 'A prey species such as the weasel will dash across the gap looking for cover from avian predators such as owls or kestrels, and dive straight in.' Out of the frying pan….

It is a labour intensive business sitting and building effective tunnels, so Jeff can manage no more than ten a day if starting from scratch. 'If you were to convert an estate like this into a comprehensive trapping strategy from cold, it would take you the best part of four years to get it right.'

The keeper places his traps two hundred to two hundred and fifty metres apart as that seems to be the average territory of a bitch stoat or weasel. The dogs move about these territories and Jeff will usually catch seven males for one female. November and early December also prove a worthwhile time to trap travelling dog stoats. Squirrels are a major target this year for Jeff, as their population has exploded in recent years. And by selling the lead-free carcases to a regular customer, the beaters' wagon was treated to a new waterproof cover. Weasels and stoats are also kept and frozen down, although Jeff makes a point of donating them to taxidermists who are sympathetic to shooting.

Jeff arrived at Torry Hill in 1987, the same year that much of the county was devastated by Michael Fish's hurricane. That night Jeff sat transfixed in his new home, deafened by the noise outside, watching an old oak tree twisted up from its roots by the wind. 'The weirdest thing was that you couldn't hear the tree being torn up,' he said, gesticulating with his big hands how the trunk was wrenched up as though picking a lettuce.

The first four years of his tenure were spent clearing the thousands of tons of timber. Much of the landscape still looks like a malevolent giant has gone on a an axe-wielding spree. 'We did some work back then. Nobody's had the heart to chop down a mature tree ever since.' At the foot of one survivor, a one hundred and fifty year-old beech tree, Jeff has built an intricate trap that accounts for the vermin foraging round its gnarled roots. 'I tried setting it up through the roots of the tree itself,' he recalled, 'but it didn't work very well. So I placed the tunnels next to the roots and it's proved very effective. I have no idea why.'

Jeff removed the V-shaped excluder that acts as a gate at the front of the tunnel to stop bigger animals such as cats or pheasants from making a silly mistake. Taking his trusty short-handled hoe, he cleaned away leaves from inside the tunnel and then used the tool to rough up the soil outside to give the impression that a rabbit had disturbed the ground. 'If you scratch the soil, a stoat will come along thinking, *what's been going on here then?'*

The trap had not provided a kill, but further down the boundary line a weasel had only just entered the wrong tunnel, possibly startled by the sound of the vehicle. The Fenn trap had served its purpose, catching the hapless mustelid in the classic body lock, administering an instant death. Its eyes were bulging from the force of the trap's grip. It was a dog weasel and gave off a pungent musk. 'Often the strong smell of a dog weasel or stoat will attract another one wanting to check out the competition,' said Jeff. 'Also, if there is a squirrel in a trap with bite marks around its neck, I will soon catch a stoat that has associated the tunnel with a free meal.'

By the middle of May, Jeff may only be finding six or seven occupied Fenn traps and, with the round costing £5 in petrol a day, it is no longer the most efficient use of his time. So the traps are removed until the next year.

Jeff still gets a thrill every time he sees one of his traps has worked. 'Even after all these years, I find it very exciting and challenging. More enjoyable that any other discipline in shooting I've been involved in over the years. It is the satisfaction of catching a wild animal with a trap I have made from my own hands.'

13.
Decoying crows

'Every crow in the county is watching me right now,' said Chris Green as he removed decoys from a plastic bin-liner. 'They've got amazing eyesight – I swear they can see you blink sometimes – and they will spot a human's face or especially his hands from miles away.' Chris is one of those country folk who really does know it all. His life has been spent crawling about fields, streams and woods learning about the flora and fauna, usually with the intention of pot-hunting or vermin control. If necessity is the mother of invention, then Chris is one of her offspring. Stand close enough to this Cornishman and you will hear the cogs and pulleys whirring and jacking in his mind as he works out angles and blueprints for his next gadget. Since he was a lad, Chris has shot, fished and investigated his patch of Cornwall to the extent that every bird, beast or bush we pass has an entry in his memory bank. They say that the old-fashioned countryman, who is steeped in local wildlife, agriculture, folktales and beauty, is a dying breed that looks certain to be wiped out by a modern tsunami of second homes, stifling legislation and microwave TV meals; yet with Chris a little of that tradition remains.

Wiry is the word that springs to mind, whether describing Chris' slim physique or his ginger hair that is usually hidden beneath a wide range of hats to fit the purpose. Ruddy cheeks and tanned arms reveal a lifetime spent outside in the elements, whether fishing for mullet and bass off the quayside; lying in wait for pinkfeet on the mudflats; or decoying crows. 'I was brought up in the Sixties. In those days nobody had much money, so you couldn't just go out and buy something you needed. You had to make it. I suppose I've always had that mentality – I'm always trying to work out how I can solve problems with my own mind and hands, rather than buy ready-made solutions.'

In full show of the opposition, Chris laid out the plastic imitation carrion crows and jackdaws, as well as a couple of pigeons and doves bobbing on a string. We were at the top of a sloping field with views across the rolling sunlit valley. At the base of the slope, sixty crows laughed at us from a huge oak tree, wondering why three humans were placing lifeless dummies on their dinner table. They were like a rabble of barbarians watching a Roman general manoeuvre his troops round a battlefield. 'You don't fool us,' they seemed to be saying. Chris paid them no heed and converted the empty stretch of grassland into a bird convention. 'A bobbing woodpigeon always instils a bit of confidence that it's ok to land, while my trusty dove is highly visible and adds a bit of light.'

It was a perfect day for feasting on juicy leatherjackets and crunchy bugs exposed by the farmer who had cut silage the day before. Without a breath of wind, Chris decided to face the birds in random directions. 'If there was a strong wind, I might have them facing into it,' he said, placing the final plastic crow. 'There. A bare field is now alive!'

On a nearby fence post, the crowman also perched a decoy peregrine falcon, complete with dangling crow's wing in its talons. Even from ten yards, there was no mistaking the guilty pose of speculative raptor, just asking to be mobbed by angry crows.

'It's worth a go, but I don't hold great hopes for it. I did once watch a young peregrine attack my decoys. He couldn't work out why the other crows didn't fly away. The poor chap wandered about attacking each one before flying off bemused.'

Ever the perfectionist, Chris had chosen his ambush position in order to benefit shooting with both gun and camera. If he couldn't find a place to hide not only himself but also two onlookers and a high powered lens, there would be no article. He had driven round the fields to gauge the angle of the hedges, trees and other bits of cover in relation to where he needed to be and good light for photography. Of course, the spot X would also have to appeal to the crows. Chris is something of a cameraman himself and now that his blood lust has mellowed down the years, he uses his fieldcraft to creep close enough for a click rather than a shot. But today, PQ had the camera and Chris was out to do the local farmer a favour.

Using two rolls of camouflage netting painstakingly woven with straw and reeds, our host fashioned a press enclosure behind a nearby metal gate leaning on a hedge, including a roof to keep us out of sight from aerial surveillance. 'You're going to have to keep perfectly still. These crows are extremely suspicious and pick up on any movement.'

Yet one question still lingered. How on earth was Chris going to get sixty intelligent crows that all knew he was there to fly within thirty yards of his twelve bore shotgun in broad daylight? It was a similar head-scratcher that the Greeks faced some three thousand years ago outside the walls of Troy. There are not many occasions when the worlds of Homeric poetry and vermin control collide, but here was one! Chris knowingly pulled his 'Trojan horse' from the Land Rover. His creation, fashioned to his own design in a workshop that he rents for two pints of bitter a month, was made of a large plastic canister about five foot in length and cut in half lengthways. The top half was then sliced into flaps that were hinged to the bottom to create a trap-door, through which Chris can spring when the target is in range. The whole

Chris Green shoots a crow from his Trojan Horse.

vessel is then wrapped with camo netting, straw and reeds. Moving from the classical to the biblical, it almost looked like the thatched basket that Moses used to float down the Nile and away from the bloodthirsty Pharaoh.

Space is cramp in the crib. He must curl himself in on his back, leaving a ninety degree field of vision and a blind spot behind his head. The traditional swing through method of shooting is impossible, so he has developed a type of snap shooting that relies on hand–eye coordination and practice. Chris first used his contraption on mudflats chasing wildfowl (he has a tented annex for his dog) and so the natural progression was to adapt it for crows. 'It is not comfortable, but it is snug, even on the foreshore. You and your dog will never get cold. It also floats!'

Yet, surely this would not work! Every sharp-eyed corvid with a vantage point could see what was going on. I'd read about how crows can solve puzzles, make tools and show evidence of learning, which implies memory use. But Chris was not so sure. 'They are in a different league to other birds, but they are not rocket scientists. I am very interested in their memory powers. The old farmers' saying is that crows can't count higher than the number of eggs they lay.' PQ also has a theory that crows can't count at all. For example, if three hunters enter a forest, wait a little, then one hides and the other two leave the forest, the non-counting crows will think that all the hunters have left.

'Get on,' replied Chris in his Cornish brogue. 'Well, we're about to put that theory to the test.' The press retired to the enclosure, while the crowman donned facemask, hat and gloves like a sniper and disappeared into his casket, entirely hidden save for the barrel of his Beretta twelve bore. What followed was a fascinating study of man's ability to outfox the most wild and wily of creatures. It took just minutes for the action to start, calling further into question just how long the memory span of a crow really is. Indeed, the first crow clearly had poor eyes, or nothing between them, as it landed right next to the peregrine decoy. It grubbed about for a minute before flying back to its pals. If it was a scout then it did a bad job!

A jackdaw arrived to survey the scene, a seemingly tranquil picnic around a mound of straw. It had no reason to think otherwise. Chris is also a master bird caller and the two chatted for a couple of moments as it circled overhead in ever decreasing circles. Soon it was in the kill zone and Chris twitched the barrel of his semi-automatic, dropping the jackdaw to the ground. No sooner had the bird landed and the shooter was up and out of his shell, turning the dead jackdaw on its front so it no longer looked like a corpse. Crows may not be the bird brain of Britain, but they will smell a rat if one of their cousins is belly up.

Again, Chris had shown his hand to the crows by climbing in and out of his hide. Yet, it was not long before the crows had forgotten. Within just five minutes, hunger had gotten the better of caution, sending two crows on a mission over the decoys. They circled the stage, crawing to each other, possibly discussing the merits and dangers of landing for a snack. Chris butted in to their conversation with a few blasts on his call, a reassuring 'come hither' that said there was place at the top table. It worked and the two crows dropped down into range. The upside-down turtle belched forth fire and lead, and the crows nose-dived to the grass.

Within an hour, there were ten additional crows propped up like decoys next to the plastic imitations. No matter how many of their brethren flew to the death trap, they were soon forgotten and replaced. Throughout, PQ snapped away from his enclosure, taking some excellent photos of the shooting in action. Indeed, it was a wonder that none of the crows could see us as they flew overhead.

Afterwards, Chris was delighted with the afternoon's work. 'There are times, whether it is pigeons, geese, ducks or crows, when they are in the mood for it. Whatever you do, they will be determined to fly over you. There are enough times where they refuse to play ball; but on those lucky, golden days you have to cash in.'

They say that you make your own luck. I suspected that Chris had more golden days than most.

JANUARY
FEBRUARY
MARCH
APRIL
MAY
JUNE
JULY
AUGUST
SEPTEMBER
OCTOBER
NOVEMBER
DECEMBER

14.
Deerhounds

The British countryside has no end of curios linked to the rich history of fieldsports. It is strewn with follies and towers that were constructed so that the landed gentry could enjoy shelter or a glass of something warming when out shooting, fishing or hunting. Add to that the number of hedges, copses, woods and river banks that were managed with sporting pursuits in mind, not to mention the pubs that bear the name of those pursuits, and you begin to see how much this green and pleasant land owes to its sporting heritage.

When I managed to escape London, the first place I lived was near Burford in the Cotswolds. The kennel conversion (upgraded to The Stables) was right on the boundary of the Sherborne Estates and very pretty it was too. Nearby was Lodge Park, an enchanting seventeenth-century grandstand, lovingly restored by the National Trust and a fine example of architecture born out of a passion for hunting.

For the thousands of visitors that look round the lodge itself and walk the old deer park, Lodge Park is a reminder of the quaint traditions of ye olde England. It was built in the 1630s by John 'Crump' Dutton, a wily politician renowned for his hunch-back and quick temper. Owner of the vast Sherborne Manor and MP for Gloucestershire, Crump was once noted as 'a learned and prudent man, and as one of the richest, so one of the meekest men in England'. However, different sources remember him as a determined gambler and drinker who was reckless with the family fortune. One story goes that on an extended binge in the local inn, having lost heavily, he suddenly offered to stake Sherborne Estate itself. But when his faithful butler heard the wager, he grabbed his master and carried him back home, kicking and screaming.

This darker side of Crump's character seems more applicable when looking at the motives behind Lodge Park. It was built entirely for the ancient sport of deer coursing, and while there would be some satisfaction drawn from the hunting abilities of the hounds, the primary purpose was for betting. The park was as self-sufficient as any greyhound dog track nowadays, with a corral for the deer and a mile-long walled enclosure erected for the chase. Visitors and gamblers were able to view the courses from a specially constructed grandstand that survives to this day. But it was a far grander affair than the pies, Bovril and sheepskin jackets of today's greyhound racing. Crump's guests would ride out in splendour across the four thousand acre parkland from Sherborne House to the lodge, where roaring log fires would await. They were then able to watch the races from the roof of the grandstand, before joining in fine dinners in the Great Room. Wagers could be considerable sums of money too, with one sizeable bet recorded at £4,000, a huge amount of money back then.

The course was funnel-shaped, measuring about two hundred metres wide at the start and ninety metres at the grandstand end, with two-metre high walls. It is thought that the deer, usually a fallow, was pushed forward by a terrier or 'teazer' (likely to be a sort of lurcher) before the deerhounds were slipped by the slipper. In a 'breathing course' the deer would have a long enough head start to reach and jump a ditch that was too wide for the hounds to follow. They would then be led back to the corral. In a 'fleshing course', usually for the higher stakes and fees, the deer would be caught and killed by the leading hound. It is also thought that the grandstand seats allowed the gentlemen to practise their crossbow archery at the deer below, no doubt to impress the wives and girlfriends.

Crump Dutton died in 1657, but deer coursing is thought to have continued at Lodge Park for another century, before falling out of fashion with the advent of foxhunting. How times have changed!

Nowadays, at the end of September each year, visitors are able to see the lodge used for its original purpose: deerhound racing. Of course, there are no live deer courses, but races are held throughout the afternoon with over sixty deerhounds chasing down the old track once used three hundred years ago. For any hound lovers it is a wonderful celebration of this special breed with many of the top pedigree owners and Crufts competitors on show. Some arrive dressed in period costume to recreate the seventeenth-century social occasion that was as much about dining and revelry as it was about deer coursing.

There are few more stately looking dogs than the deerhound with their serene, almost arrogant gaze and learned whiskers. But once loosed after the lure, the turn of pace is astonishing as their powerful shoulders and haunches bound up the course. Once a foot follower of St Hubert, these sprinters have over twelve hundred years of hunting genes in their blood and to see them in full flight is an exhilarating sight. As with the original competitions, today's hounds are slipped by a trained slipper, although

Lined out for inspection, these hunting hounds have lost their natural instincts to chase. Will greyhounds and lurchers go the same way?

instead of a live deer, they are encouraged to chase a fake rabbit on a string, which is reeled in from three hundred metres away. Think terrier racing, but without the brawling. Two hounds go head to head in each knock-out bout, with the winner continuing to the next round. All too often though, the winner was the hound that did not run immediately back to its owner.

Licensed slipper Wayne Drew, who was tasked with getting the hounds to run in the right direction, was often at his wits' end to coax any hunting instinct at all from the competitors. Indeed, one wonders what the original owners of Lodge Park would have made of the fancy doggy jackets, grooming lotions and reversible 'poo-bags' that are important pieces of kit in the modern deerhound owner's locker.

'The problem is that so many of these hounds are just show dogs,' he explained. 'Back in the old hunting days in Scotland, before the rifle, a hound like this would travel at thirty mph with great stamina, bounding over three feet of heather, able to bring down a twenty stone stag. A good hound would hit the stag behind the ear at full tilt. And there were either good hounds or dead hounds, because if a hound went for the stag anywhere else, it was likely to be its one and only chase.'

For Wayne the inability of many of these deerhounds to hunt quarry is a sombre sign of the future that awaits the greyhound and lurcher breeds following the coursing ban. 'The great benefit of coursing is the physical test of a breed's confirmation, bravery and ability to hunt live quarry. You can see with these hounds that they have lost the hunting instinct they once had. I fear that with the limitations on greyhound and lurcher coursing, we have lost a way to test their speed and agility.'

I left with mixed feelings. On the one hand, Lodge Park is a stirring example of this country's sporting heritage. Yet, on the other, it is a demonstration of how society is moving away from that heritage. How long before greyhounds, beagles, bassets and foxhounds are no more than fireside pets? What future for Labradors, spaniels and terriers? Some would call it progress, but I am not so sure. The more we put distance between ourselves and our wild, hunting instincts, the wider the gap between society and nature. When you have no connection or interaction with wildlife, you don't notice when it's gone.

15.
Mole
catching

The country sports media is spoilt when it comes to cartoonists who can represent its many characters and quaint customs. They often deal in stereotypes and exaggeration, but they are no less funny for that. Such is their expertise and popularity, you will find at least one of Thelwell, Loon, Bryn Parry or Annie Tempest's Tottering-by-Gently in most country loos throughout the land. My brother is a talented draughtsman, but somehow the artistic gene passed me by, as I struggle to draw a set of curtains. My favourite shooting 'toonist is the *Shooting Times* man Keith Reynolds, who has saved several of my more lightweight articles with a clever illustration that perfectly captures a scene my words could not.

If I were to ring him (usually in a panic the day before going to press) and ask that he draw a mole catcher, I can be sure it would be a very humorous picture. The mole man would probably have sloping shoulders, a pointed face, small piggy eyes with spectacles, black hair sprouting from his cheeks and ears, hands like spades and maybe a worm or two sticking out of his pocket. In short, he might look similar to the pest he was chasing.

Historically, he would not have been far off the mark. The local mole man would often have been a retired keeper, terrier man or gardener with a bent back and fading eyesight who would shuffle from hedge to field with a bag full of worms laced with lethal poison. 'Do your homework or Arthur Mole will come for you,' parents would have warned their kids.

But, as with so much of country life, most of these old stereotypes have been blown apart. When I travelled up to Grantown-on-Spey to interview George Byers, Scotland's youngest professional mole catcher, I did not expect to meet someone who looked like his victims. Tall, lean, straight-backed and blond haired, George is part of the new breed of pest controllers who are leaving the old days of strychnine behind. At twenty-four years old and riding a quad bike, he would leave the cartoonists searching for a different angle.

Born and raised in the Borders, George moved north to work as an underkeeper on a Highland estate when he left school. But competition for good long term jobs is tight in this part of the world and the young keeper spotted a gap in the market that would allow him to work for himself. 'It was not what I had always set out to do,' he explained, as we made our way across a client farmer's field outside Grantown-on-Spey. His red van and quad trailer are now a common sight in these parts. 'But when the idea came it grew quickly as there is plenty of opportunity around here. There was not the turf war that I might have expected in other areas where there are more pest controllers than pests.'

A mole catching business is not something that can be started overnight. There are plenty of hoops to jump to become a registered pest controller and member of the British Pest Control Association (BPCA). When George started out in 2005, the Department of Agriculture still allocated licences for buying strychnine, but the poison was banned in 2006 following legislation from the European Commission.

Strychnine is one of the most bitter compounds on earth. While I'm not willing to test this, you can apparently taste it in water at one part per million. It comes from the fruit seeds of the strychnine tree, also known as *Nux vomica*, an evergreen tree in southeast Asia. If you swallow a spoonful, there is no known antidote, so this is what you can expect to happen. Fifteen minutes after exposure, your muscles will begin to spasm, starting with the head and neck. The spasms then spread to every muscle in the body, increasing in intensity and frequency until the backbone arches continually. Death comes from asphyxiation caused by paralysis of the neural pathways that control breathing or by exhaustion from the convulsions. This would be within two to three hours after exposure. At the point of death, the body 'freezes' immediately, even in the middle of a convulsion, resulting in instantaneous *rigor mortis*. When put like that, it is probably no surprise that the anti-strychnine lobby got their way!

Now that poisoning is outlawed, trapping is deemed a humane alternative and there are plenty of local farmers who need the services of an effective mole catcher. 'When people think of moles, they tend to imagine that people dislike them for aesthetic reasons – digging up their lawn or golf course,' he said, vaulting over a fence with ease. George plays full-back for the local Strathspey Rugby Club based in Kingussie and takes some keeping up with. 'But the greatest threat from moles is agricultural, because when a mole hill is scooped up into a baling machine, there will be a small reservoir of soil inside wrapped silage where grass will germinate and grow. This soil can contain bacteria such as listeria which can contaminate livestock. The damage caused to farm machinery from mole hills is also extensive.' Famously, the mole was blamed for the death of King William III in 1702 after he was thrown from a horse that had stumbled on a mole hill at Hampton Court. The king broke his collar bone and having insisted on returning to Kensington Palace rather than rest, he aggravated the condition. He soon developed a pulmonary fever (which may or may not have been related to the fall) and died in due course. In England, the mole became vilified as a regicide, while in Scotland the Jacobites toasted the 'little gentleman in black velvet', for bumping off their enemy! George does not show the same generosity when striving to rid a field of a mole infestation, but he does hold his chosen adversary in high regard.

'They are remarkable creatures,' he said, prodding a fresh tunnel with a sawn-off ski pole. 'All these mole hills you can see here are produced by the same mole. They hate each other and are extremely territorial, except when they have to breed, of course. It just goes to show the power they have in their paws that they can cover such distances.'

This mole catcher will often be paid by the hour to catch the pests and the pressure is on to produce results. 'Most farmers are happy to let me come and go as I please, so I have to be on top of my time management skills. They do like it too if you present them with the moles that had been digging up their fields. You have to prove your worth! But there is an exploding population of moles in Scotland at the moment. Their numbers swelled after foot and mouth, while the strychnine ban has hampered mole catchers. But also, I think the milder weather has meant reproductive success, like with so many other creatures.' In the last six months alone, George had caught one thousand of them.

Looking like a modern-day vampire slayer, George stakes out the route of a fresh tunnel. Gently teasing back the turf to reveal the hole just a few inches beneath the surface, he can then slowly lower in a coiled Duffus trap, trying to ensure the deadly spring does not catch his finger. A blue plaster hints that this is not always successful.

'You quickly learn the patterns of moles and where their tunnels lead,' he said, replacing soil over his trap and making a mark on his map. It can be easy to forget where you laid them. 'Mole hills can be misleading as there will be an intricate pattern of holes and shafts between them. I will tend to catch a mole quickly enough, but there is always the odd one that gets away. It is very difficult to begrudge them that if they are clever enough. They are extremely complex and although their eyes are practically useless, they can 'see' with their noses and whiskers or *vibrissae*. Indeed, they are able to pump more blood when needed to their noses to make these *vibrissae* more sensitive. They also have *vibrissae* on their tails and they move about like dodgem cars with their tails in the air. Their teeth are razor sharp for biting into worms and insects and they will eat their body weight in earthworms a day. Moles are also one of the few animals that will create a larder in times of plenty, as they will bite the heads off worms, but not eat them. This keeps the worm in the same place and by the time its head has grown back, the hungry mole comes back to eat it again!'

Moles will go where the worms are, hence the reason they tend to be found in good soil which abounds in worms. During times of flood, they will find drier or higher ground, likewise following the worms to warmer soil depths in winter.

'People believe that moles hibernate, but they are just busy deeper underground or under a hedge where it is warmer. But in truth, nobody is all that certain where moles go.' Over and above moles, George will also rid clients of other infestations such as wasps, cockroaches, rats and mice, while he also helps out with deer stalking, heather burning and picking-up during the season. But his bread and butter is the humble mole. 'I am lucky that there is not a huge amount of competition in my patch, so I have been able to define my territory.' Maybe George is not that unlike his adversary after all.

16.
Lurchers

Of all the hunting dogs, lurchers probably get the worst press for all their connections with illegal hare coursing, syndicate gambling and the fact they are very often tied on a piece of string to someone who you would not trust with your house keys. Of course, this is not the lurcher's fault and the countryside is full of wonderful examples that are adored in many respectable households – indeed, I can see one outside as I write this. But the fact remains that plenty of these good-natured dogs live a life of crime. Which was what truly incensed the hare coursers after the Hunting Bill banned their sport. The legal, responsible, hare-loving coursers who didn't trespass, break gates and rob farms were made outlaws like the rougher element who did. Of course, being law-abiding citizens, the do-gooders stopped all coursing; while the criminals carried on as before.

A lurcher is a dog cross bred from a gazehound – such as a greyhound, whippet, deerhound or Afghan that uses sight rather than smell – with another breed such as a terrier that will bring other attributes such as strength, muzzle power or intelligence. You may lose a little of the speed, but the right cross will give you plenty more in the tank. Lurchers have long been a favoured companion of travelling gypsies – indeed the word is widely believed to come from the Romany word 'lur' meaning 'thief' – who would use the dog to catch rabbits and hares, with or without the permission of the landowner. In recent history, these fleet-footed coursers have grown in value more for their gambling potential than any need for fresh meat.

Sgt Mark looks out over the stubbles in Suffolk for illegal hare coursers.

A few years ago, I went down to Suffolk to meet a bobby who had identified illegal hare coursing as a means of building links with the rural community. The flat arable fields of East Anglia are perfect for the lurcher boys who would drive out from the East End of London, run their dogs, kill as many hares as possible, have a fight with the farmer and maybe steal some diesel. A couple of wheel spins and it's back home to London. The farmers were left threatened and helpless, as there was little they could do legally to stop the coursers. The police would always arrive an hour or so after the event, if at all. Indeed, if the farmer showed any sign of retaliation, he ran the risk of having his firearms confiscated. Tony Martin, the farmer who was jailed for taking the law into his own hands and shooting a burglar, was still fresh in the memory. Throughout the countryside, there was a growing feeling that the police were all too keen to book you for speeding or to bar a firearms ticket, but slow when it came to tackling crime. Sergeant Mark saw the opportunity to strengthen an ailing link with the community. He had to stop the coursers.

The first step was some good old-fashioned police work: Mark went tea-drinking. By making himself a regular friendly face with the farmers, he was able to gain their trust and convince them he was on their side. The sergeant persuaded them not to get involved when a band of coursers came on their land, but to let him handle it. Mark also knew the law, so booking the trespassers for illegal hare coursing under the Wildlife and Countryside Act 1981 was going to achieve nothing, save for a small fine that would probably never be paid. So the copper started impounding and squashing their cars, which soon put the message across. The problem has not entirely disappeared in East Anglia, but a precedent was set for any forces trying to find a way round an ineffectual law.

Following the Hunting Act, all coursing for hares is illegal, but running your lurcher on rabbits is still allowed. I went up to the Yorkshire Dales to catch up with a lurcherman called Malcolm, who has owned the dogs all his life. We joined him on a night patrol for rabbits with his greyhound-cross-strong terrier Buck. It was a cool, clear moonlit night, just days before the full moon, and the drizzle and mist that threatened to make it a dank, dark affair had lifted to reveal the undulating slopes of the Dales. Buck knew exactly what was about to happen, and strained at the leash. There was no mistaking his thick, strong terrier jaws and square shoulders on his mottled brown torso, pointing at both power and pace. Although only a year old, he had developed quickly and was already a lethal force against bunnies.

Malcolm was excited too, although a little miffed that the valley was now basking in moonlight. 'If the drizzle had stayed we'd have been guaranteed a few rabbits, as they'd sit tight on the fields, allowing us to sneak up on them,' he says, as Buck jumped effortlessly into the back of the Land Rover. 'A bit of wind would have helped too. But tonight they'll see and hear us coming from a mile away.' Good news for rabbits and photographers alike.

Being a gazehound, Buck has to rely entirely on the accuracy of Malcolm's lamp if he is to lock on to the target. As a result, the dog will also learn to follow his master's lead, rather than searching for himself, so the two have to be on the same wavelength to succeed. Lurchers are treasured as not only rapid and rugged runners, but also loyal, intelligent and affectionate pets. It seems this relationship was no different.

'Every so often you come across the odd bit of human nocturnal action, if you get what I mean,' says Malcolm, with a knowing grin. 'I once flashed the lamp through the car window, but they didn't seem to care.'

Buck chases a rabbit into the netting of a goal.
Excellent night photography by PQ.

The first couple of fields proved fruitless, although Buck did get a short run at a rabbit that bolted for the safety of the woods. Perhaps a fox had already scared the others into hiding. As we reached the top of the brae, close to a chapel, we stopped for a break to take in the view. 'I love this spot on a clear night,' said the lurcherman. 'There's nobody else making a racket and you feel on top of the world. See – that's York Minster in the distance, all lit up, Leeds is that orange glow over there, and, well, that's the local prison,' he demonstrated, pointing. A fitting reminder of the freedom were now enjoying. 'I think every sportsman has that special place, where they are at their most content.'

In the next field the action started. The ground seemed bare, but Malcolm spotted a lone bunny tucked in against the sticky mud and shone his full wattage in its direction. The rabbit slinked even deeper into its rut, as though hoping against hopes it would not be seen. Buck reacted to the lamp and tore off along its beam when Malcolm slipped his collar. As the coney ducked further into its scrape, surely sealing its fate by refusing to run, Buck gained to within a few metres and we awaited the crunch as it he grabbed it in his lethal jaws.

But Buck did not see the rabbit and ran straight on by. Malcolm kept the beam trained on our plucky rabbit and Buck reacted, turning tail to follow his master's direction. Again, he failed to see the rabbit, this time jumping right over it, as though he were vaulting a stone. As Buck circled, the rabbit recognised he had pushed his luck, and set off as fast as its legs would carry it towards the sanctuary of the hedge, some fifty yards away. Malcolm charted its progress, with Buck gaining at breakneck speed. At the last moment, as though blessed with rear-view mirrors, our rabbit side-stepped out of the grasp of the chasing hound, which crashed forward and skidded on the mud. The triumphant rabbit dived into the undergrowth, with an extraordinary tale to tell. 'I can't believe that!' said Malcolm, as a panting Buck returns to his side. 'Just goes to show how well a rabbit can hide itself in an open field though. They're pretty strong runners round about here too.'

By now it was past midnight, so Malcolm decided on one last throw of the dice, at a nearby school where he has permission to reduce numbers of rabbits on the sports fields. Being an assortment of cricket, football and rugby pitches, they are also good training grounds for lurchers. Within moments, we were back on a bunny. The rabbit bolted immediately the lamp found it, realising it was a sitting duck on the tight-cut lawn. Buck soon accelerated into a striking position. But the fugitive managed to dodge at the final moment, like a scrum-half outmanoeuvring a lumbering second row. As with the modern lock-forward, our tackler had a rare turn of pace and was soon back snapping at the heels of the hapless rabbit. Escape seemed impossible. Then, by luck or judgement, the rabbit's next movement saved its neck. It jumped through a hole in the netting of a football goal, daring its pursuer to follow. Buck, either bullish or foolish, took up the challenge and folded into the netting before clanging into the metal post. The rabbit, sensing half a gap, doubled back and dived for the sanctuary of a hole under a tree.

'I'll admit I am a bit disappointed,' Malcolm said later, as Buck sucked in a good litre of water in the Land Rover, with a generous handful of sugar-rich biscuits to replenish lost energy from a punishing work-out. 'But if you were successful every time you wouldn't get the thrill that comes with a success. Besides,' he added with a grin. 'I blame you guys. Only *Shooting Times* would organise this on a full-moon!'

17.
Roe bucks

Roe bucks have caused me more grief than any other species in the last four years, but they have also afforded me some of the best experiences. I put roe stalking in the same bracket mentally as wildfowling, as there are the same early starts and a similar rate of success. At least with wildfowling, both sexes are fair game and it matters not if the duck or goose is old or young, handsome or ugly. Roe deer are altogether more complicated.

As a result, roe stalking for a feature in the magazine is a stressful assignment. For a start, it is hard to write a decent action piece on deer if you don't see any. This may not be the stalker's fault – weather, wind or simple luck may be against him. You may see plenty of deer, but invariably they are off limits by virtue of their sex. On other occasions, it may be the right sex, but far too good an animal for a non-paying journalist. When the estate can get over a thousand pounds for a trophy buck, it is understandable that they won't let me shoot it for nothing. This doesn't pass any muster with the editor, however, who has planned in four pages of seasonal roe stalking for the next week, so you quickly hone an ability to waffle.

This was the case at my first attempts at roe stalking on ground belonging to Sparsholt College in Hampshire, where the head tutor Martin Edwards manages the deer across a few hundred acres of fields and woodland. Belgian clients pay top dollar for big bucks, so I was invited to bag a youngster or runt that would add little to the gene pool. We were out at dawn that first morning and saw plenty of deer in the half light. At least two were browsing within range, but the rifle remained slung on my shoulder throughout. 'That's a tinkler, not a sprinkler,' Martin would say, as one doe after another appeared in front of us. The females were out of season and they seemed to know it well. In the three hours it took for the sun to rise, we saw not one buck.

'I'm afraid that's roe stalking for you, lad,' my guide said. 'You'll learn soon enough that one shot in three outings is a good ratio. The rest of the time you can simply enjoy a mug of tea and watch the world wake up or shut down. You'll always see something, whether it's a fox or stoat, owl or bat. If you don't like that, then you're better off elsewhere.'

I decided I did like that, so a month later I returned, brimming with optimism. Bucks were sparring for supremacy at the height of the rut, so

Scouting for deer in the late sunshine.

there stood every chance that Martin would call a yearling close. 'They've only one thing on their mind at the moment,' he said dryly, 'and it isn't self-preservation.' This time we climbed a high seat and waited in silence as the shadows shortened with the rising sun to reveal a roe buck on his morning forage. Martin squeaked twice like a fawn to grab his attention. The buck was grazing over two hundred yards away across a clearing and I watched him react to each squeak like he was leaning on an electric fence. His ears pricked and nose twitched as he entered sensory overdrive. This suitor was in the mood for love! The high seat Siren squeaked twice more and our bewitched buck trotted around the wood-lined field, stopping every thirty yards to check his bearings. One seventy yards…one forty…one ten… I took a deep breath and then exhaled, settling myself for the shot. 'No no, not this chap,' the stalker hissed. 'He's far too good for you.' The buck eventually approached to the foot of the high seat, his broad chest heaving in anticipation. His deep hazel coat beamed summer's vitality, while the loveliest of heads exuded a class and condition that I did not merit. I could only watch in fascination as Martin interacted with this wild creature in its natural environment.

Over the next months I went out time and again, searching in vain for a cull buck or doe. We saw deer every visit, but rarely the right one at the right time of year. When we hunted does, there were bucks; when bucks came back on, we could hardly move for barking does. There had been close shaves, like the evening we crawled over a dung heap for seventy yards to get within shot of a small buck. But just as I set up for the shot, he chose to move behind a hedge. Throughout these near misses, I would watch and learn about roe stalking. We had seen bucks chase each other across fields and surveyed countless deer from the vehicle like safari tourists. Often, we would find the perfect spot, only for the wind to change. Once, for a wonderful half hour, we studied a doe fussing over her two tiny fawns. It may have been the same family that we spied from a high seat as the sun rose the following April: a mature doe with two yearlings. Bucks were back in season again and a pair of short spikes pricked from the nearest deer's brow. I was in business. For what seemed an eternity, the cull buck mucked about, either pestering his mother or standing adjacent to his sister. Eventually Lady Luck granted me a reprieve as the buck advanced towards us along the hedgerow. At 140 yards, he turned to stand broadside on. His mother and sister were no longer in the line of fire. 'Take your time, now,' came the calm voice over my shoulder.

PFFFFTTT went the bullet through the sound moderator. A brief pause and then three perfectly healthy roe deer disappeared across the clearing. 'Ah well,' Martin said with genuine sympathy. 'You're not the first and you won't be the last. At least it was a clean miss.'

Three weeks later and I had recovered enough pride to face my demons, this time with my father in Perthshire. My roe troubles had at least given me a valuable insight into a sport that my father has enjoyed all his life and it would be a neat ending to my tale if I could bag my first roe with my old man's .243. He orchestrated a text book stalk, approaching a young beast from beneath the brow of a hill, marching in line to minimise our silhouette, before creeping forward on hands and knees under the cover of a dyke to within a hundred yards. He set the rifle up and I crawled in behind it. Again, I missed a sitter. 'Ah well,' sighed my father, as the buck scampered off into the woods unharmed, 'there's a lot of Scotland around a deer.'

It was all very confusing. I knew I could hit the centre of a paper target at 150 yards and further, whether lying prone, sitting or standing with sticks. I had shot other species of deer. The unavoidable truth was that on both occasions I came down with a heavy dose of nerves, jitters, hoodoo, buck fever, call it what you will. In the heat of the moment, I had lost my bottle.

Each time I had been out, I updated the sorry saga in the magazine. There must have been the best part of twenty pages with no result. However, the benefit of having a sounding board for my troubles was that one reader felt sorry for me and offered to help break my duck. John Gosden is a stalker over a sizeable stretch of Hampshire and was confident he could find me a makeable shot. Indeed, there was one-horned buck, 'a killer' as he called it, which needed extracting, so we set off for the spot where he had often seen it.

Creeping out through the wood to the high seat, we soon shimmied up a ladder and onto the thin wooden platform that looked out across an open field towards a copse which lay some hundred yards away. It was one of those still, balmy May evenings when the sky, which has been a heavy blue all day, becomes a pale shadow of its former self, as though someone up there has watered down the paint in his palette. The first two deer appeared almost as soon as we had sat down. A buck and a doe, both out for a sun-downer and disinterested in each other. The doe strutted forward from the cover of the trees to the lush grass of the field, stopping only occasionally from her forage to listen, look and smell for danger. The buck was more cautious, as though aware that its head was a prized one. It loitered a good 150 yards away, staying close to the trees.

John scanned it with his binoculars and was impressed with what he saw. 'He's too good for you, I'm afraid,' he said with an apologetic grin. 'He's a beauty.' Beneath us, ten wild peahens, second generation fugitives from a nearby stately home, were pottering about in the grass, each one a mini alarm system if we made too much noise. There was still plenty of time for my luck to change, however, and within a mere ten minutes, it looked like it had. There, no more than one hundred yards right in front of us, was a young buck that had emerged from the wood. It had a couple of points, so it was not our 'killer', but it didn't have a head to make a Belgian twitch. Better still, it was small. Surely, this was finally going to happen.

I watched it move back and forward along the edge of the copse through John's telescopic sights, getting myself comfortable and relaxed, while my host decided whether the shot was on. 'I think it's about time you got your first roebuck,' he whispered. 'Take your time, now.' Quietly as I could, I flicked the safety catch. The deer was standing perfectly square, its slender neck raised to nibble a drooping branch. I brought the cross-hairs down its torso, took a breath, exhaled gently, extended my finger onto the trigger and told myself to squeeze.

I could have squeezed with all my might and it would have made no difference. With no bullet in the chamber, I'd have been better off throwing stones. John chuckled, shaking his head as I pulled the bolt back and forward. By the time I re-focused on the buck, it had wisely turned its head into the trees, shoving its bum in my direction in salute. With that, it was gone, another in a long line of mishaps.

Rather than wait in hope for another beast to appear, John decided we were better off taking destiny into our own hands. He had spotted a pair of bucks to our right, five hundred yards up the edge of the wood. The

I finally get my first roe buck.

wind was on our side and there was a slope that would hide our approach. As long as the shot was safe we might be in business. At this stage, I presumed that I had blown my chances yet again. John was having none of it. 'I've never failed to get someone a deer on this estate and you're not going to ruin my one hundred per cent record, are you?'

We scurried off through the trees and reappeared along a ride that would lead us out along the edge of the wood to where the deer would be. When we got there, however, the coast was clear. John looked about for Plan C and it presented itself to our left, rising up from the grass where it had been lying. There was a doe with it, which was no more than eighty yards away. By now we were out in the open. Surely they had seen or heard us?

Indeed, the doe trotted on thirty yards in alarm, before stopping to stare in our direction. We froze to the spot, waiting for her to give the game away or convince herself that she was seeing ghosts. The buck stood where he was, calmly chewing on grass as though bored of the doe's amateur dramatics. There were a few branches of a tree between myself and the buck, so we eased further out into the open. John passed me his shooting sticks and I gathered myself into position as soon as I could. Far from the calm deliberation of the high seat, my ticker was buzzing as buck fever set in.

'Take your time,' John repeated, although this time he added, 'but not too much of it!' as it was only a matter of moments before we would be rumbled.

I took the shot and the beast careered off to the right in the long grass. My immediate reaction as I saw it run off is unprintable, but suffice to say I thought I'd missed again. John had been watching through the binoculars, however, and held out his hand in congratulations, before walking off to get the vehicle.

How did I feel, now that my quest was over? Triumphant certainly, but a little bit dazed, perhaps a post-adrenaline dip. It proved the benefits of having an experienced stalker by my side, and a good dog, as try as I might, I couldn't find the animal. I was a good forty yards away from where it had actually fallen and it took a fine track by John's multi-purpose yellow Labrador Jess to locate the buck.

And did the end product justify the effort put in over the last year? Oh yes, and plenty more besides. I may never shoot another roe buck, but at least I would have one tale to tell.

18.
Woodpigeons

On the numerous occasions when I have been sent off pigeon shooting, I've always enjoyed it. Pigeon shooters tend to be down-to-earth souls who are just as happy having a cup of tea and chat as they are when the skies are grey with woodpigeons. I've been lucky too that the days have been action-packed, which always makes it easier to reach the word count back in the office. But if I'm honest, I feel a bit of a fraud writing about pigeons, to the extent that I almost dread that phone call in spring and late summer, when my editor asks me to organise a piece for the magazine. I don't have these insecurities when it comes to writing about other subject matters I know little about – it is a journalist's challenge to sound knowledgeable when you haven't the first clue – but when I re-read my pigeon pieces before submission, I am always left with a hollow feeling that I have fallen short. (Indeed, I kept on putting off this chapter in the book, because I couldn't face it!)

Self-diagnosis has led me to the conclusion that I am afraid of failing to hit the high standards of previous pigeon specialists. Now, before I get accused of insinuating that the wildfowling, dog-handling, ferreting and deer stalking correspondents are somehow inferior; please accept that this is the workings of a febrile mind. But pigeon writers like Major Archie Coats (the godfather of pigeon shooting), John Humphries, John Batley and Will Garfit set such high standards that any attempt to compete seems inappropriate. Frederick Forsyth too writes in fine style about pigeons. Finding a new angle is almost impossible, while describing the flight of a pigeon or the technique of a shooter is like trying to reinvent the wheel.

The basics of pigeon shooting have remained the same since these old pigeon tyros were first reading about them as young pigeon tyros. You find a crop field where the pigeons are likely to be feeding – be it oilseed rape, beans, peas, brassicas or stubbles – and set up camp on the edge, preferably on a likely flight path. To be successful you need to convince the pigeons that a) you are not there; and b) it is a safe place to eat. So you must build a hide against a hedge, tree or ditch. And you must set up a convivial scene of decoy pigeons to dupe passers-by that this is a popular feeding ground. Birds of a feather and all that. Indeed, it is similar to wildfowling, but without the mud, cold, dark, inactivity and early starts.

John Jeffrey ready for action in his hide.

The sole chink of light for the modern sporting journalist has been that pigeon shooting has changed a certain amount in the last ten years, not least since Archie Coats passed away. He was loved by readers for his ability to get within range of pigeons using homemade kit and crafty fieldwork, which he would describe with vivid language that demonstrated his deep understanding of the countryside. Using women's tights, sheets and plastic drain pipes, he could create a hide and decoy pattern that brought the pigeons flocking to his gun. Certain readers still get dewy eyed when they hear his name.

My articles have all dealt with the 'modern' methods of pigeon control that claim to benefit from advancements in technology. Nowadays, it is possible to buy all manner of gizmos and mechanised kit that will draw the birds in close. Everything from synthetic hide netting to the lifelike decoys can be imported cheaply from China. The greatest revolution, if you'll pardon the pun, has been the introduction of the so-called pigeon magnets. These whirligigs act like helicopter blades with decoy pigeons cradled on the end, mimicking the swoop of a landing woodie.

As with any invention that improves the chances of success, they have been accused of being cheats or unfair. This could be dismissed as a nonsensical, nostalgic argument given the primary objective of pigeon control is for crop protection. It is like saying that lumberjacks should use axes and not chain saws. But, with the increase in the number of commercial pigeon shooters, there is perhaps a case to say that too many pigeons are being drawn to these magnets and that the flocks are too heavily hit. On the other hand, the number of pigeons in the UK has doubled in the last twenty-five years, while many other farmland species have declined, so it isn't a strong case. The cost to farmers from pigeon crop damage runs into millions of pounds each year, largely due to the expansion of oilseed rape, which seems set to increase further with the need for biofuels.

On one crisp Spring morning, I joined a joiner called John Jeffrey who controls the pigeons on a stretch of arable farmland in Berkshire. As a boy, my hero was the Scottish flank forward John 'the White Shark' Jeffrey, so I'm afraid this one was always going to be a disappointment, but we shared four very enjoyable hours nonetheless. Working on auto-pilot developed from twenty-five years' practice, John quickly set up camp, reaching in the back of his truck for his Hessian bag of tricks. The first task was to lay out the decoys. 'I like these new rubber pigeons because they are non-glare and they are also a bit heavier than the ones I have used for the last twenty-five years,' he said.

Under each one are the letters JJ written with a number, like the identification number on the top of a police squad car. 'I'm not saying that my fellow pigeon shooters do it deliberately, but sometimes you go home with fewer decoys than you arrive with,' John added with a knowing grin.

Then, connecting it to a car battery, he rigged up the magnet. Each decoy was set 'feeding' in an arc around the whirligig, facing into the strong breeze. 'It's simply because that's the way pigeons feed at this time of year. Their feathers fall out very easily, so they wouldn't let them be blown out by a strong wind like this.'

John is a convert to the new pigeon gizmos, although he is not as rapturous in his praise as some. 'It is all about movement and the pigeons will home in on that. If anything, the magnet serves to bring the birds in close enough for a shot,' he said, screwing the support pole deep into the soft ground.

'But we used to have great days at the pigeons before all the gadgets. The idea for bobbers, for example, I learned as a boy from the great old pigeon shooter Archie Coats. We would take a whippy length of hazel stick, sharpen one end and push it through the pigeon's gearbox, and that would bob all day!' Archie Coats again. I could feel my self-confidence ebbing away.

This pigeon shooter picks up most of his tips from the four or five game fairs that he visits in the summer, a time of year he especially enjoys. When he was a lad, his local Chertsey show used to hold pigeon plucking competitions. 'We would shoot clays in the morning then retire to the beer tent. In the afternoon, some old boy would arrive with a big sack of pigeons and we'd all sit in a long line. The first person to remove every feather, save for the head of course, would be the winner. It was a right good *craic*. You'd think you were nearly done, but those little feathers on the arms were really fiddly, especially if you'd had a pint or two! I don't suppose they could allow it nowadays.'

A red kite came over to inspect, before soaring off into the blue skies with a flick of its forked tail. 'It's astonishing how many of them you see in this part of the world,' said John, securing the wings of two defrosted pigeons with crocodile clips onto the magnet spokes. 'I must have counted twenty in less than five minutes on the M40, riding the currents from the cars below, searching for carrion. I've a keeper friend who puts out rabbits for them, so they stay away from his poults. He sites it within range of a high seat, so he can have a safe shot at an opportunistic fox if there is one. Two birds with one stone.'

Having set out the smoke and mirrors, John set to work on concealment. The site for this deceit was in the corner of a mouldy maize field that was waiting to be ploughed into next season's cover crop. A leafless hedgerow ran along the side of the field, which John hoped would provide a flight line for passing woodies. He chose an ancient hawthorn bush as a natural backstop and pegged out netting that attached to brambles on either side. Behind us were two fields of rape, a supermarket for hungry pigeons.

Ordinarily, when you have a shooter, photographer and writer, things can get a little cramp; but not chez Jeffries! We were in five star luxury complete with comfy camp chairs and more leg room than a first class jumbo. 'I don't like to struggle,' said John, producing yet more pegs and nets. 'I've done all that before. Comfort is important.' I wish he'd have a word with the wildfowlers.

While movement in the field is important to bring in the birds, we were under strict instructions to keep still in the hide. 'They are just like geese,' whispered John, who has enjoyed many a morning and evening flight with the Fenland Wildfowlers among others. 'They get easily spooked by movement. But as long as you are not doing a song and dance in the middle of the field, they should come in.' Within minutes of settling in to our marquee, two pigeons flew in close to have a look. John simply shook his head and smiled. 'They're rock pigeons. It's always the case round here: the rockies are perfect decoyers. I wish they'd teach their mates in those trees over there! But sometimes, if you get a few rockies or feral pigeons jinking about among your decoys, then it can tempt in the woodies.'

We had been chatting too much, so it was time to start filling the breathable Hessian potato sack that John uses to cool any fallen birds. A solitary woodpigeon flared up in front of the decoys and, although it was a good fifty yards away, John let off a hopeful volley that sent the pigeon off with its ears ringing. However, this was more than blind optimism. The bang had the desired effect of rousing a band of thirty pigeons sat gawping from a tree across the next door field. Another flock, hitherto hidden behind a wood to our left, also took to the air, this time one hundred-strong. Soon the air was filled with the flap of grey wings as though John had just flicked a switch on at a fairground.

Two woodies came in from in front of us in classic squadron formation, hitching their wings and diving in over the magnet like Stuka bombers. John waited until he could see the whites of their eyes before bringing down the bird to his right. The other banked up quickly and made good its escape over the hedgerow, but John was quickly on to another bird that was crossing over his head. For ten minutes, the shooter was ducking and swinging as pigeons flew at him from all sides. Each time a bird tumbled to the ground, one of us would scurry out to retrieve, as pigeons, just like the crows, do not like seeing one of their own belly up.

And then as quickly as it started, it stopped. 'There's no sport quite like it,' beamed John, breaking his smoking Winchester to show it was clear. 'I never could understand why people can pay so much for driven pheasants, when this is so much more fun!'

JANUARY
FEBRUARY
MARCH
APRIL
MAY
JUNE
JULY
AUGUST
SEPTEMBER
OCTOBER
NOVEMBER
DECEMBER

19.
Muntjac

I had never seen nor heard of the Reeves muntjac deer before getting involved in shooting. It was only red, roe and fallow deer that I knew roamed wild in the UK – sika and Chinese water deer were also new discoveries. But in defence of my ignorance, it has only been in the last few years that the muntjac population has truly taken off to the extent that it is now a regular sight in certain parts of the countryside, while there are still few if any in Scotland.

When *Shooting Times* was drawing together a list of species for a four-month extravaganza on pest control, we deliberated on whether to include the muntjac. It is a deer, after all, protected by the same firearms restrictions as the biggest red stag on the highest hill in Scotland. But it does not have a close season like a roe deer, nor is it protected like the badger, so it can be shot at any time of the year like a rabbit, hare or fox.

Depending on personal situations and beliefs, some readers may have been surprised or even disappointed to see the muntjac termed as a pest. But it was a question worth asking: at what point is a deer species reduced from an edible quarry that adds value to an estate to a nuisance that causes more harm than good? While all creatures – pests or otherwise – should be treated with respect, the distinction is relevant.

Of course, this is not a question that is peculiar to muntjac. There are many areas where the red, roe, sika and fallow deer would be termed a pest by farmers, grouse moor owners, golf courses, airports and gardeners. One man's sport is another man's menace. For estates over-run with muntjac, the voracious nibblers are a curse. But for those landowners with manageable numbers that can lease the odd stalk or supplement their income and larder with venison, then the muntjac is a welcome immigrant.

What seems beyond discussion, however, is that muntjac numbers are on the increase. Every year I see more dead muntjac on the road than the year before. I agree that is an inexact science: coincidence, location, seasonality may have played a part. But as a keeper in Somerset once told me, you see more muntjac dead on the roads nowadays than badgers, and that's saying something! Pest or not, the muntjac still makes for an exciting stalk and an excellent meal. So when I was invited to join Tom Norman, a beat keeper at an estate near Woodstock in

Oxfordshire, to bag one of the many feral muntjacs that inhabit this arable countryside, I jumped at the opportunity. It was early May and the first batch of Tom's pheasant and partridge eggs was due to hatch. After the obligatory cup of coffee, we set off for the woods, passing 'Stalag 17', a small village of pens and huts where his hens peck, strut and lay their eggs for him to gather. Sometimes he'll have to pick five hundred eggs a day for the incubator. Why is it that keepers get bad backs? Tom drove his Land Rover across the wet fields towards a block of forestry where we were guaranteed to see a few 'munties' on an evening forage. Young bunnies scattered in front of the 4x4 as though playing chicken with the wheels and we stopped to watch a guilty stoat dragging a juvenile rabbit into the undergrowth.

It started to rain, so we sought refuge under the wide canopy of the sycamore, cherry tree, Scot's pine and others that joined to form mature mixed woodland. The plan was simple, but solid. Tom would creep forward along a likely looking ride where he had often seen muntjac at around 7 p.m. If he could take a shot, he would.

'We would have got in one of the high seats,' he whispered, pulling his flat cap over his bleach blond hair, 'but the next door estate is borrowing them. I'm afraid I don't go in for much of this crawling through mud on my belly, but we should be ok. They tend to be a bit dopey at this time of day – too interested in feeding. If needs be, we could wait in under a fallen branch for a half hour if this doesn't work. For now, could you two wait here by the old water wagon?'

Within seconds of leaving us, Tom was down on one knee, adopting the classic stalking pose, his bum secure on the heel of his boot. He had spotted something in the trees, and peered down the scope of his rifle to find out what it was. Like a fox stalking a rabbit in long grass, Tom crept forward, lifting his legs high to avoid excess noise. He was like a pantomime burglar, exaggerating his movements as he tiptoed down the garden path with a bag of swag. Occasionally, the stalker paused to wait and watch, leaning against a tree or folding back down onto one knee. Perhaps the deer had its head up, looking for signs of danger? This game of Grandmother's Footsteps continued in the silence of the evening forest for ten minutes, until the tension was cut by the flash of fleeing deer through the trees.

'It was a lovely big fallow buck,' Tom said with a smile, having whistled for us to come join him at the other end of the ride. He instinctively rolled a cigarette, as so many woodland stalkers like to do. 'Lucky for him that he's out of season. I could have shot him six or seven times!'

It had rained steadily for the last few days and the woodland grass could not have been more sweet and lush for hungry ungulates. It was just a case of being where they were. 'This is so typical,' Tom grumbled, slinging his Brno .243 back over his shoulder and firing a dirty look at a grey squirrel that ran a tightrope of branches above our heads. 'If we had come here to get squirrels, say, then I bet we would be walking into munties left, right and centre.' Tom stubbed out his cigarette on his boot. 'That said, if I see a fox, then I'm afraid your muntjac will have to wait!'

Like the munties, Tom is a newcomer to these parts, although his native Norfolk is a good deal closer than south-east Asia. Since hearing stories about gamekeeping from his best mate at primary school, he set his heart on joining the profession. Hard work learning the trade in the holidays eventually resulted in a job at the famous Broadlands estate in Hampshire, before moving north to Oxfordshire. On his first tour of the new estate, he met the groom Lucy, out exercising a horse. 'When I saw her come over the brow of the hill: that was that. Happily she seemed to think the same!' The pair are now engaged and at twenty-seven years old, Tom believes he has found his niche in life.

The stalker led us down the hill to the ride below and edged forward along the meadow, sticking close to the overhanging branches. He stooped forward to avoid catching the barrel on the leaves above, halting regularly to glass the ride with his scope. There was movement ahead. Tom had seen it, already kneeling down, his palm stretched out to his side like a native Indian before John Wayne's campfire, instructing us to do the same. It was a fallow, probably the same one. I began to raise my eyebrows in frustration, but they never reached their full arc. A new shape had emerged in the open of the ride, some 150 yards ahead of Tom.

Again, the stalker had already clocked the newcomer and edged forward on his haunches at glacier pace, pausing when the pale creature leant forward to crop the grass. There was a leafy branch between Tom and a sure shot, so he needed to widen the angle to find a clear path for the bullet. Every movement brought him further into the open and more likely to lose what could be our only opportunity.

The final movement was too much and the vigilant deer scampered for the other side of the ride. But all was not lost! For a second muntjac darted out into the open. She hesitated, staring back down the meadow towards the kneeling figure that fixed her in his rifle scope. It was an unfair contest. That split second was all Tom needed to take aim and fire. He reloaded just in case, but there was no need. Once more the ride was silent.

'You can't hang around with a muntie,' Tom said, wiping his hands on the grass after removing the yearling doe's working parts. 'They are forever on the move and if you wait to get in the perfect position, then the moment has gone. We were just very lucky that there were two of them together.' Muntjac does will be pregnant for most of their adult life after reaching maturity at eight months old, but this doe did not have a noticeable foetus. Their successful reproduction rate – a doe will often come back into season just days after producing young – has allowed this plucky deer to spread so quickly, with predictions that it is only a matter of time before it colonises urban Britain too.

I carried her carcase up the hill by the back of the head, no heavier than a fistful of pheasants, and Tom quickly skinned the beast when we made it back to the yard. 'People will tell you that a muntie is difficult to skin, but that is only if you leave it to hang for a week. If you skin it immediately, then you should have no problem.' There is not a huge amount of meat on a muntjac, but you can get a fine meal from each of the two forelegs, haunches and delicate fillets. PQ had saved the liver and heart for his breakfast in a plastic bag, but when his back was turned, the resident Alsatian guard dog swallowed them both, including the bag!

The stalk a success, I asked Tom his thoughts on whether the muntjac is a pest or not. 'If you had come here ten years ago, then yes. The place was alive with munties, but their numbers seem to have settled down now. Perhaps they have set out their territories. Yet for me, they are a pest. After all, they are not meant to be here, are they? I don't have any time for any non-indigenous species like grey squirrels or American mink. They can only upset the local ecosystem. If we want to shoot a muntie, there is always one available. The price from the gamedealer is hardly worth the bother, so we'll get them bagged up at the local butcher and give them away as presents to estate workers or eat them ourselves. I believe it is about the best venison there is. There is no way we could ever get rid of them, so I suppose we have just learnt to live with them.'

20. Rabbits

The keeper navigated the all-terrain Ranger buggy along the side of the silage field with one hand, while his other held the .22 rifle like it was an extension of his arm. Chipped and battered from regular use and abuse, this tool is still as reliable as the day Mike Appleby bought it fifteen years ago; an old and trusted friend.

There were eight sets of rabbit ears further up the field, all enjoying a nibble on green shoots between the downpours that had soaked this part of Dorset. It was a boon time for bunnies, many just two months old, with fresh growth to feast on. But there were dangers too, and not just from tooth and claw. Green grass was not the only food on the menu tonight.

Some of the rabbits, perhaps the older and wiser among them, bolted back to the thick weeds and shrubs on the field edge as the vehicle approached. However, two were not so fearful. The furthest out, a young buck, unwise to the threat posed by the growling machine, sat back on his haunches and tested the wind with his twitching nose, straining his long ears for sounds of imminent peril. Satisfied, the doomed creature went back to his supper.

Mike, on the other hand, had not been dithering. Bringing the buggy to a halt, he slipped a bullet into the chamber of the rifle in a fluid motion. Sliding the bolt forward and clicking the safety catch in the same direction, he raised the barrel to rest between his finger and the edge of the Ranger's windscreen. On cue, the rabbit sat up again and it was done. The only sound to come from the silencer and Winchester forty grain sub-sonic bullet was a gentle thwack.

To the buck-toothed spectator sitting just ten feet away, it must have looked as if its buddy had been fatally stung by a bee. Quick as a flash, Mike had reloaded the rifle and was in the process of moving the sights onto this gormless bystander, when survival instinct kicked in. Just as the keeper brought his finger towards the trigger, our bunny flinched forward and leapt into the safety of the hedge.

As mentioned earlier, these are the assignments I like most of all. While gamekeepers on a driven shoot can be cantankerous, taciturn grouches, understandable given the pressure they are under, on evenings like this they are relaxed and forthcoming. Indeed, vermin control seems to bring out the best in everyone. That may sound like a callous comment, but I have met a great many country folk who would prefer a day out with a couple of friends after rabbits and pigeons, rats and rooks, rather than stand alone at a peg and look to the skies for pheasants.

Mike is built for gamekeeping: square shoulders like the proverbial outhouse, hands like saucepans and a pair of boots that would launch a poacher into the next door valley. But the headkeeper of the Sherborne Estates was smiling tonight, even though the rabbit got away. Was he not tempted to take the shot anyway, aiming just in front of the fugitive?

'I would never take a moving shot on a rabbit with a rifle,' he replied emphatically, glancing up towards the beautiful village of Sherborne across the valley. 'If you start swinging with a rifle, you forget what your background is and the bullet could end up where you least want it to. For the sake of a rabbit, it's not worth it.'

Tonight was about pest control. While Mike can see the attraction of dressing up in camo to creep up on a sporting rabbit for the pot, his laying sheds take up too much time at this time of year. 'We will certainly eat whatever we shoot, but the main reason is to save our cover crops,' he explained, as we entered another field on the rolling hills that form this most scenic of districts. 'If a rabbit takes the head off a maize plant in the next few weeks, then it will not grow. The maize will survive only if it is allowed to grow for another month, so we must give it a helping hand.' Bad news for the bunnies.

But that evening when we arrived at the strip of maize plantation at the top of the hill, it was not the grey fur of rabbits that we saw scrambling over the wet brown soil. The place was crawling in rats! Big ones, too, that braved the daylight with brazen contempt for their own safety to eat the decaying cobs from last year. Some were barely smaller than the earlier rabbit. I saw PQ's cheeks grow pale, but they took on colour when the keeper started knocking them over with his .22. Mike's predatory eyesight was quick to spot the scurrying rodents, waiting for them to stop and dig at the earth, before arrowing in. Soon there were three fat rats lying belly up on the clods, an easy meal for whichever buzzard got there first.

Buzzards will get many a Dorset keeper reaching for the gin bottle, but Mike seems very phlegmatic about their recent rise in numbers. Indeed, he seemed to be pleased that the rats would provide them a snack if they got there before the other opportunists, least of all the other rats. We watched as a pair duelled on the airflows, attacking each other playfully with talons

Keeper Mike Appleby with grass-fed rabbits, held belly back to avoid flashing their white stomachs.

outstretched. The game was eventually interrupted by a bossy crow that mobbed and harried until they moved to the other side of the wood.

Still the rats came though, possibly driven into the open through hunger, and we could have sat in that field for hours, plinking at the kamikaze scramblers that thought they were invisible against the dirty background. They were ideally camouflaged, but their movement gave them away. 'We ought to come back here with a lamp at night, then we'd see how many there are,' Mike thought out loud, keen to put his boot into the large numbers of rodents that would be preying on any eggs and chicks in the hedgerows, be they game or song birds. 'Better still, I could put up a high seat and lease this out – it is fantastic sport!'

Before we spent the whole evening there, the decision was taken to 'shoot something we could eat'. Mike therefore gave us a guided tour of the newly planted cover crops that would later provide a launching pad for pheasants and partridge to fly these undulating fields. Every so often he would stop at a favoured rabbit haunt to search for signs of life.

We saw very little. Ordinarily, this would be good news for a keeper, a sign that his crops were free of pests. But Mike was more confused than happy. 'They are out there, I guarantee you,' he said, scratching his head. 'They say that rabbits don't like wind, so that might be why they are all tucked away tonight, but truly I am at a loss. We would usually have seen many more by now.' If the Flopsies were playing hide and seek, then they were not letting the rest of local wildlife join in. Round every turn, we were greeted by yet another species out revelling in the break between showers. A brooding partridge hen trotted haughtily in front of the buggy, miffed that we had interrupted her meal of clover. A pair of mallard, perhaps reared on this estate and a potential right and left for a visitor later this year, lifted from some muddy puddles beside a barn, before searing off over the trees in tandem formation.

Rooks and jackdaws squabbled in the trees like Italian washerwomen before a mayoral election: each determined to put their case, no matter how often they repeated it. Large confident crows stalked the fields and lifted weightily onto roofs, hedges and machinery, always keeping a shiny black eye on the keeper and his rifle. They suspected that the buggy meant danger and they were not about to put their hunch to the test.

The local beagle pack had hunted these fields earlier in the year, but the resident hares were too quick for them, much to Mike's pleasure. We watched one of the mysterious creatures as it loped across the grass, before sitting back on its powerful haunches as high as it could, as though to remind us, 'I bein't no bunny'. Grey squirrels would not be shown the same sympathy, but the only one we saw ran up a tree next to a main road.

A handsome roe buck ran out in front of us, smarting at the invasion of his territory. His rich summer coat and exquisite head may well be worth a few hundred pounds to the estate from a gentleman later in the season. From just fifty yards away, he looked us up and down in our overalls, no doubt sneering at the underpowered rifle that was fit only for vermin. But reason is always the better part of valour and he was not going to push his luck. We waited silently as he made his leave into a neighbouring field on his own terms. Prettier still, in a nearby copse, legs deep in bluebells, stood a shy doe, with a coat every bit as shiny as the resident male. She was far less bullish, however, skipping away under the branches as though bouncing on a purple trampoline.

All these diversions were an added bonus, but they were not filling the bunny bag, which currently numbered just one. We had suffered a few near misses, with rabbits honing their sixth sense to bolt at just the wrong moment. Luck was a bunny tonight.

Enough time had passed for the cluster of rabbits in the first field to reappear in the open, so Mike gambled on a second helping. Sure enough, the earlier fall of their comrade was long forgotten and all the mini-lawnmowers were back out to strim the farmer's silage grass. Again, the more wary and experienced hot-footed it to cover, but still two remained, perhaps frozen to the spot in panic, or hoping that sitting tight would render them invisible.

Either way, it was the wrong course of action. The first unfortunate was hit on the neck, bowling over in a somersault to its left like a tumbling wicketkeeper after a thick edge. The remaining rabbit did not react to the death of its neighbour, choosing instead to crouch lower in the grass. It was its second mistake in less than a minute. A true shot from Mike made sure it was the last. As the light began to fail, Mike walked back to the Ranger with two more bunnies for the bag. Instinctively, he carried them with their backs facing forward. 'It's something you see so often,' he said, as we made our way back to his cottage for a final cuppa and debrief. 'People walking out on a hunt with the rabbits' white bellies shining forward. It's no wonder the others get scared off.'

In the kitchen, while we discussed what we had seen that evening, and what we had not seen, a large grey rabbit came to sit on the middle of

Mike's lawn, looking in through the patio windows. 'Oh that,' said the keeper, 'that's the safest rabbit on the estate. It escaped from a hutch, so it's practically a pet. Nobody can touch him. We used to have a family of wild guinea pigs in the woods too, but I think the foxes will have picked them off by now.' Which just goes to show in life. It's not about what you know, but who you know.

21. Terrier racing

As a boy, the local agricultural show in Aberfeldy was a highlight of the summer holidays. While I probably enjoyed the morning less – it meant an early start to get the ponies in order, followed by the wrong colour of rosette because I had failed to remove some mud from its belly, canter on the right leg, or jump every obstacle – the afternoons were a boon time. It's funny which memories you retain from your childhood, but I especially remember fantastic quiches my mother would bake the evening before; and ice cream, no doubt bought for as little as ten pence a cone. The afternoon also brought the tug of war tournament, which was taken very seriously in our locality. Next to the annual raft race down the river Tay, in which teams would try to navigate their DIY vessels from Kenmore to the Wade Bridge in Aberfeldy with varying degrees of success; the tug-of-war was the big opportunity for the lads to show off to the lassies. The teams usually hailed from pubs in the area, made up from young farmers coached by wily old farmers. Each side would line up eight warriors, dressed in their battle tunic of hob-nailed boots, jeans that slipped over the backside and a rugby shirt with their pub name on. The big lump at the back, known as the anchor, would wrap the end of the rope round his torso, which was usually padded in thick rubber foam, and all sixteen would 'take the strain'.

When the cry from the judge came to 'heave', both teams would do exactly that, digging at the earth to get a footing as they dragged the opposition in their direction. Like a coxswain in a sculling match, both teams had a motivator, presumably the smallest, mouthiest regular in the pub, who would scream exhortations to make his or her team bust a gut.

The most drilled teams would not so much tug as walk backwards in a steady rhythm, building a momentum that their scrambling adversaries could not cope with. Collective discipline would win over brute force every time. If both teams were drilled, then a stalemate could ensue, which would only be resumed once one team slipped or ran out of puff. It also depended on whether they had warmed up in the beer tent or not.

My parents and their friends were careful not to swear in front of me as a child, but the tug-of-war (as well as sheep clipping time when I was the 'tar boy' daubing oil on any cuts to keep the flies away) were my opportunity to learn new vocabulary, which would serve me better in later life than any algebra equation or chemistry formula.

After the tug-of-war came the terrier racing, which was the pinnacle of my day. My father would usually have a couple of terriers entered and would often help set up the event or provide the fox brush for the dogs to chase. The course was the same as it tends to be throughout the land, with a small starting box or trap to ensure a fair start leading down a series of small hedge hurdles to a pile of straw bales that hid an upside down bicycle, which would be used to wind in the tail. The best dogs would tear out of the traps in a desperate attempt to catch the fox brush (would you be allowed to use one nowadays?), skipping over the tiny jumps like steeplechasers, before crashing headlong into the bales just as the tail disappeared. There would be a couple of heats and then the grand final, which usually involved those dogs which had since returned to their owners. Of course, the fun of the event was less in watching the winning dogs, which had probably been schooled throughout the summer. It was the amateur also-rans that attracted the crowds, as they would either cower in the trap until their embarrassed owner pulled them out, or they would go in search of the three things that are most important to a terrier: food, fighting and, well, you can add the third 'f' yourself.

We had a large Lakeland–Jack Russell bruiser called Dougal who was a past-master of all three. When he could be bothered, Dougal was a fine racer, but more often than not, and especially in his later years, he preferred to cut corners. If a slighter, more agile terrier was moving past him, he would chose to forfeit the race for both of them by grabbing the unfortunate dog by the throat. Or ear or leg, whatever gave him purchase. It would be like Michael Schumacher's alleged block on Damon Hill in the 1994 Adelaide Grand Prix: if I can't win, neither can you. There would be a yelp from Little Rosie's owners as Dougal sunk his teeth into their darling pooch. Little Rosie would quickly find her true terrier spirit, receding her lips to reveal a shiny set of sharp canines that she would deposit in Dougal's rear end. At this point, another terrier would usually bundle in from the side, leading with his mouth open, landing a cheap shot while the other two were otherwise occupied. From then on, it was every dog for itself.

When, nearly two decades later, I was asked by the editor of *Shooting Times* whether I would write an article for him during the summer (I didn't realise it at the time, but he was vetting me for the job), I replied that I could do a piece on terrier racing, because it was about the only subject I truly had a measure of. The next week, I was on my first assignment for the magazine at Chatsworth Country Fair, covering the races held by Adrian Francis and his Terrier Road Show. Adrian is a great pro, instantly recognisable with his kilt and microphone, who can whip up a crowd in no time.

I must have done a half decent write-up, as the next month there was an advert in the magazine for a staffwriter 'who could cover all manner of country subjects from pheasant shooting to terrier racing'. I like to think the editor was trying to tell me something!

Having since been to countless game fairs, where terrier racing is common fare, I still haven't tired of watching them. They say that the true cricket fan can not walk past a game without watching a few deliveries, even if it is three lads with a tennis ball and walking stick in the street. I'm sure the same goes for terrier racing.

22.

Horse riding

'You know, it's usually the man who controls the beast,' said our guide Maud, as I sheepishly retook my place in the line. Maud was blonde and petite with wide blue eyes and a wider smile that made my legs turn to gooseberry jelly. She was Brigitte Bardot in a hard hat. Some men can cut a dash on a horse, but I don't count myself in their number. Yet, I had wanted to impress her (is it not expected in France that you will flirt with the instructor?) and so had asked for a horse with a bit of va va voom. I had ridden a fair amount, I told her; I could handle whatever she threw at me. She relayed this to the groom, who started to giggle mischievously. My dopey looking grey was given to the journalist next to me, while a replacement was sought for the cocky foreigner. My new mount, a pretty-faced bay called Bibi, was also a feisty lady who preferred to jog sidewise than trot. She had been itching to find some open ground from the start, so when it arrived in the shape of a big green field, she was off, whether I liked it or not. As we overtook the lead riders and careered towards Belgium, I tried desperately to remember the French for 'slow down!' I could have shouted it in Mandarin for all the good it would have done.

Monsieur Guy, owner of the *La Rose des Vents* equestrian centre in St Jans Cappel, was grinning from tufted ear to tufted ear as if he had known all along that Bibi was going to make a bid for freedom. He had cheeks as ruddy as a ship's boson and a hooked beak that curved down from bumblebee eyebrows. Guy has been running the farm all his life, as his father and grandfather did before him. 'Does she ever tire?' I asked hopefully.

'Bibi? Never. But you will!'

We were in Flanders, which is perfect riding country, with its flat open fields and quiet winding lanes. From sixteen hands the rider can see for miles across the hedgerows into the highest part of French Flanders, Little Switzerland as the locals like to call it, with its three small hills, which poke out of the green farmland. For a few weeks in April, before the spring leaves block out the sunlight, the hills turn blue with hyacinths. It was the perfect early summer's day, save for the fact I was riding a monster.

The press trip was to highlight the accessibility of north France from Britain via Eurotunnel. We left London at seven thirty, crossed the Channel, ate a three course lunch and were saddled up by three o'clock, local time. Our ride took two hours, including long trots through woodland paths, which further reduced my poise, as Maud tucked in behind me. I doubt my rising trot was a collector's item. I narrowly avoided a mud bath when Bibi got over-excited by a wooden bridge, lurching forward onto her neck with the inevitable painful result. The trail also took us into Flemish Belgium where a village butcher offered horse sausages. I threatened this to Bibi, but she feigned indifference. Maud didn't seem to find it funny either, replying curtly that she would never eat a horse. I wound my neck in again.

As an aside, I have only ever once eaten horse flesh and it was entirely by accident. It was on a trip round the Beretta gun factory in north Italy: another press jolly, this time courtesy of GMK, the UK's supplier of the Italian weapons. The Beretta family have been crafting guns in the area since 1526, making it the oldest gun manufacturer in the world. We were treated like kings throughout the two-day trip including a visit to a local multi-star ristorante. The choice of meat was beef or horse, Carpaccio or stew, so given I come from a fairly horsy background, I went for the thin slices of rare steak. Very good it was too and I helped myself to more when it arrived. Of course, it turned out the Carpaccio was horse and the stew was beef. Mind over matter and all that.

Back in Flandres, I was eventually released from Bibi. Moody Maud dismissed me from her presence with a roll of her tea-saucer eyes. I suspect she is now tormenting a husband with her Bardot gaze. Lucky chap!

We visited a town called Bailleul, famous for its brewery for the *Hommelpap* beer, a favourite in the area. It is also the only place to find the magnificent *cheval de Flandres*. The breed died out in Europe over fifty years ago in the wake of modern farm machinery. These heavy horses, the size of Shire horses but less rough round the edges, were also a casualty of the First World War. The farmer and brewer, a Monsieur Beck, restarted the bloodline in France eleven years ago after discovering that it remained pure in an Amish community in the US. He explained that it would have been lost forever if the Amish had not lived in seclusion for so long. Four enormous chestnut mares in the field were due to foal in the next week, ensuring the continued resurgence of the breed.

That evening, we were hosted in the local *estaminet*, the traditional Flemish bistro and hub of the local rural community. The Estaminet Het Blauwershof had a typically Celtic vibe, with partisan Flanders flags on the wall and bagpipe music in the background. For the beer lover, it is heaven on earth. The local brews are very hoppy, on account of the fields of hops grown nearby, and can be either very bitter or smooth, as you prefer. There is beer with raspberries, beer with cherries, beer with vanilla… and the house speciality is beef cooked in – you guessed it – beer. Food plays an important role in the area. For lunch earlier in the day, a local auberge served a sample menu that included delicacies such as *Oeuf cocotte au foie gras*; crab and leek flan; stuffed pig's trotter; and the piece of least resistance: a tournedo of lamb slow-cooked for over seven hours. After a wickedly good *tarte tatin à la banane* it was no wonder Bibi was so keen to rid herself of the excess weight.

The next day we went on to a riding school in Hardelot near Calais for a gallop by the coast. There is something a bit exhilarating about hitting fifth gear on the beach with your eyes shut. Dolly, a chestnut *cheval de selle*, was determined to catch up with the huge grey gelding in front, ridden by our instructor Gaylord. Dolly seemed unfazed by the constant spray of sand in her face from the charger's hooves. That her rider was in the same firing line was clearly an irrelevance. Again, any attempts at 'whoa, there!' were met with a mouthful of sand, so all I could do was sit back, shut up, close my eyes and pray that Dolly went in a straight line. Any sudden sidesteps and I would have been sent tumbling forward, doubtless into the rock pool she had tried to avoid. Gaylord proved to be a humorous individual with an obsession with Arsenal Football Club. His great ambition was to move to North London and buy a season ticket. I tactfully tried to explain that his fellow supporters might be amused by his name and even become childish or spiteful. Perhaps I was being over-sensitive and was doing the North Londoners a disservice. Either way, Gaylord was offended.

'I was named after a great crusader who showed great bravery in battle. I would never use a different name.'

I eventually made it back to Blighty, albeit with a smaller ego than when I left. And I struggled to walk for days. But then it never hurts to be humbled from time to time.

JANUARY
FEBRUARY
MARCH
APRIL
MAY
JUNE
JULY
AUGUST
SEPTEMBER
OCTOBER
NOVEMBER
DECEMBER

23.

Cormorants

Life coaches talk about seeking out a happy place, where we feel most at ease. In these familiar surroundings we can find contentment and inner peace far from everyday stresses and strains. It may be a physical setting such as the silence of a childhood forest, the whistle of widgeon above a foreshore hide, the kitchen table, the bath, a fishing boat or an Alpine restaurant. It need not be a question of leisure: some yearn for the anonymity of a packed tube carriage or the cocoon of their car in a traffic jam. It might be somewhere convivial, such as the arms of a loved one or the local pub with old friends. Is it the banter of the beaters' wagon, the hot seat on the Home Drive, or walking a dear dog along the crest of a hill as the sun rises? There are intangible comfort zones too, such as retelling an old yarn (some do this more than others), the story of a favourite book, daydreaming, the taste of your mother's rhubarb crumble, or doing the crossword on the loo. It is the place or time when nothing else matters.

We all have them, several if we are lucky, and the more often we find time to visit them, the happier our lives will be. And if some external force starts to destroy our cherished destinations, then we react with frustration, annoyance and even anger. So it was for the members of a fishing club in Yorkshire when the cormorants came to eat their fish. Ravenfield Park coarse fishery near Rotherham could have been the setting for a 'gritty Northern drama' that was the rage a few years ago with films like *The Full Monty*, *Brassed Off* and *When Saturday Comes*. The ponds and woodland in Ravenfield were bought by British Steel for its workers as a recreational outlet in the mid-Seventies when the industry was on its downward curve. The steelworkers did not know whether to laugh or cry. Sure, the ancient waterways were a wonderful resource, but they were in such bad condition after years of neglect and vandalism that only the most optimistic would have envisioned the slice of paradise it is today.

One of those dreamers was Martin Read, who has worked a career in the steel industry in his native Yorkshire. He and his fellow fantasists devoted twenty-five years of toil, sweat and love to transform the park into a place of rare beauty. The volunteers rebuilt fourteen hundred yards of stone walls and planted eight hundred yards of hedgerows. Some of the ponds were only three feet deep and the weed was so thick that fishing in mid-summer was impossible. As a result, in 1981 the water was pumped out and the fish – most of which were carp – were removed to clear the silt. Some two years later with the depth increased, a monk sluice was added to allow for future drainage and the ponds were refilled and restocked with roach, bream, perch, rudd, crucian carp and tench. Fishermen can now cast their line from clean jetties into still, opaque waters. Green tiger beetles and greener grasshoppers are found in the uplands of the park while the adder, which is becoming increasingly rare, is not known to exist anywhere else in Rotherham. The open grassland is a good local example of unimproved acid grassland, comprising of wavy hair grass, red fescue, sheep's fescue, crested dog's-tail, rough meadow-grass, plicate sweet-grass, creeping bent, heath bedstraw and creeping cinquefoil. The wooded areas are particularly good for birds with a variety of tits, finches and thrushes. The tree pipit is a regular summer visitor, while siskin can often be seen feeding on the alders in winter.

'I think everybody needs a refuge,' Martin explained as we walked round the trimmed banks of the Great Pond, one of six ponds in the facility. 'That quiet special place where you can get away from it all.' Martin looked more like a timid maths teacher than the fist-waving campaigner that I had imagined. But there is steel behind the gentle eyes and courteous manner that burns into molten fire at the mention of cormorants.

In the early Nineties, this wonderland, along with countless other fisheries in the country, found themselves under attack from an aerial threat that was beyond their control. As pound after pound of their fish was snatched from under their noses, the dream ended and the nightmare began. 'I have fished for forty years and when I started you simply did not see a cormorant,' said Martin. 'Whether it is lack of fish at sea that has driven them further inland or the easy pickings of fisheries, I don't know, but they are now a very real force. But when we started making noises, nobody wanted to listen. We were told there was nothing we could do about it. That there was no such problem with cormorants and just to stop complaining.'

Of course, the law was on the cormorants' side as the voracious seabirds were protected. For the time being, Martin's hands were tied in red tape. And when something you love – in this case the peace, quiet and satisfaction of fishing at a pond you have helped build – is being taken away and you are powerless to act, a natural reaction might be to disobey the law?

'The very worst thing we could have done was to start hammering cormorants,' Martin said, watching a fisherman return a small roach into

Martin Read on the right has led the fight to save Ravenfield Fisheries from the cormorants.

the clear water. 'You only get progress by sitting at the same table with the lawmakers and putting forward a reasonable case for change. As soon as you start breaking the law, then all the good you may have done is lost. Legitimacy was the only way to win.'

So rather than adopt the sledgehammer approach, Martin decided to learn everything he possibly could about the feathered felon. Know thy enemy! He poured through web pages, books and scientific exposés, as his obsession increased, so that he could present factual evidence at every turn. Martin's extensive research into his nemesis took him out at first light to witness cormorants feeding, not a sight he would recommend to any fisherman with high blood pressure. 'I've seen them in groups of twenty birds and each will leave with a kilo of fish,' he recalls. 'Sometimes they are that laden down with fish that they will have to spit them out so they can take off. And it is not just the fish they catch that suffer. They will hound the others to the edge of the pond until some are jumping out onto dry land. There are always plenty that will die from stress. I've watched coots spend many a happy hour picking up the dead fish that the cormorants left behind.'

There were spats with bird charities, governmental departments and quangos. Ravenfield jumped every hoop in their path to gain a culling licence, but progress was always barred. Martin was often disappointed by set-backs, disillusioned even, but family and friends kept him strong. At times, he felt he was fighting a one-man losing battle. Were the articles he wrote in the local press, or the letters sent to anyone with influence, simply a waste of time? Was he being dismissed as an old fool with the same old rant?

In 2001 he found out emphatically that he was not alone. Thousands upon thousands of anglers, including many big names from the world of fishing and beyond, added their signatures to a petition calling for a solution to the population explosion of cormorants. Eventually the Government cottoned on to the groundswell of unrest, not to mention the scientific evidence, and admitted that the population of cormorants had risen by seventy per cent since 1989. In 2004 Ben Bradshaw, the then Minister for Nature Conservation and Fisheries, and one of the good guys as far as Martin is concerned, announced changes to the licensing system which would make it easier for fisheries to gain a permit, allowing them to shoot ten marauding cormorants a year, as long as scare tactics had proved unsuccessful.

Working to the Government guidelines, Ravenfield has been able to quell the impact of cormorants. The site has also developed a series of effective fish refuges – tubes of wire that allow the fish somewhere to hide. Nowadays the only avian threat to the fish is from herons and kingfishers, but Martin could never begrudge them a meal.

The fight still goes on, however, and Martin is willing to help other fisheries with similar problems. His experience with red tape and paperwork can help save them making the same mistakes he made. He can inspire them that no task is too great if means saving your favourite spot of peace and quiet.

24.

Big cats

There are not many opportunities to fulfil tabloid urges whilst writing for *Shooting Times*, but one recurring subject does offer some room for sensationalism. Since I arrived at the magazine, and no doubt for many years before that, there have been regular articles on big cats with some claiming concrete evidence of their existence in this country and plenty of others telling the believers to get their eyes tested. There are pages upon pages of web material with 'proof' that leopard, lynx, puma, bob-cats and bright-eyed black panthers are prowling the British undergrowth, yet still the dispute continues.

Doing my best to keep an open mind, I set off with PQ for Rutland – one of the big cat hotspots – to prove once and for all whether these creatures are indeed breeding and thriving in our countryside; or whether this countryside is full of cranks who can't recognise a black Labrador at dusk. You may be starting to work out where my sympathies lie…!

We started by interviewing David Spencer, one of the leading worshippers in the big cat cult and owner of Bigcats.org.uk, which he runs with his son Nigel. David had his brush with what he calls an ABC (alien big cat) in January 1995. 'It was just after 7 a.m. on Friday the thirteenth of all days,' he recalled, serving us tea in his living room, 'and I was leaving the garden to walk my dog. The first thing I heard was the sound of pounding feet coming down the hill opposite the house. I thought it was a horse and seeing the field gate was open, I was about to cross the road to shut it, when I saw it was not a horse, but a black creature, as big as a black Labrador dog, but lower to the ground. I just stood there in shock.'

The narrator's eyes blazed with conviction. I was in no doubt that he truly believed he had seen a panther. 'The animal continued to bound down across the frozen field and through the gate towards me as if I was not there. Time just stood still. I was shaking like a leaf.' As the panther gained on David, he raised his hands and yelled 'rah' in an attempt to frighten it away. But the cat paid no heed until the last second, when it leapt away at right angles, skimming past David's face with its long, thick, fluffy tail flashing in front of his eyes. And then it was gone.

Compelling stuff, no? Indeed, David is credited with having the closest encounter with a wild big cat in Britain for about two thousand years. His senses were so alive that morning, David swears he remembers a strong whiff of cat ammonia as the beast passed him, sure evidence that this was a male. Since that moment, the Spencers have sunk time and money into proving David's story received due respect and publicity. Both are convinced that panthers and pumas (also known as cougars and mountain lions) are breeding on this island.

But here's the rub. While I've no doubt that David believes he genuinely saw a black panther on Friday the thirteenth, I still don't think he did. My reasons are subjective and short of evidence, so let's just call it a hunch. David didn't inspire confidence. Shuffling around in his bedroom slippers, his eyes darting sideways above grey cheeks, he was desperate to show he was not a crank. He reeled off a dozen facts about panthers, all learned after the event, that he claims bolster his story. He believes the beast he met was a young panther, maybe less than two years old, on an orbital prowl using scent trails to navigate. A panther will cover up to ten miles a night as though sleep-walking, which explains why it only swerved at the last moment. Yet I couldn't help but wonder whether the story evolved to fit the science, as David grew into his role as ABC 'expert'. For example, David is convinced that pumas remain unseen in the countryside because they have huge territories and pass throughout the land via disused railways lines. Of course, these forgotten thoroughfares provide a ready supply of the puma's favoured food, bunny rabbits. Again, the idea is plausible, even romantic, but it is at best a hopeful guess. It was near to one such railway line that David found yet more proof of the spread of big cats. A giant mirror carp weighing twenty-two pounds was found half-eaten a full eighty yards from its pond. Whatever had poached the fish had hauled it across a river and then devoured ten pounds of meat. Only the head remained.

'There is very little doubt that it was a big panther-like cat that had taken the fish,' David confirmed. 'They can easily leap over ten feet and could have cleared the river. It can't have been an otter.' But rather than freeze the head for scientific examination or DNA testing, it was thrown out. It could have been a big cat, I wasn't there, but it might just as easily have been a fisherman who had put his prize catch down for a call of nature after an afternoon of warm lager, and forgotten where he'd put it!

'What a cynic!' you may be thinking and I make no apology. But whenever I meet someone who has seen a big cat, there is usually something fishy if you ask enough questions. Like the wildlife warden we met later that afternoon at a nearby pub. Here was a credible witness, or so we thought. 'I was out following the local hunt with some pals,' he told me, smoothing down his beard before wiping his hand on his overalls. 'And I saw a big cat in the woods. And then it disappeared, likely up a tree.' What time of day was this? 'Well, now. In the afternoons, the pub opens at 11 a.m. and shuts for a while at 3 p.m., so it must have been gone 3 p.m.' Case dismissed. Why is it that any photo of an ABC is grainy and out of focus? Where is the CCTV footage? The road accidents? Where are the dens? The cubs? The woolly carcases hanging from a tree? Surely one of the hunts would have caught one by now, or a keeper would have lamped one unawares. Why is the black panther (a melanistic leopard), so rare in its native lands, but so much more common in Britain than its spotty cousin? Over the years, I must have asked over one hundred keepers whether they have seen a big cat or not and while some claim to have seen something strange out the corner of their eye, none hasany confirmed sightings.

True, some lynx and puma have been shot and killed in the last forty years, but they were escapees. There have been no verified black panthers. It is certainly conceivable that a big cat could live out its life unnoticed in parts of Scotland, Exmoor and Yorkshire, but living and breeding wild amongst us? I am far from convinced.

The proliferation in big cats is traced to the Sixties and Seventies when a leopard or jungle cat in a diamanté collar was a desirable fashion accessory. In 1976, when it became illegal to own a big cat without a licence, many of these pets were released into the wild (along with lions and alligators, but where did they go?). As these cats live for about twenty years, the class of '76 have either died out or started breeding.

Forget the conspiracy theories about Government cover-ups and let us consider for a second that the reason there has never been any proof of wild big cats in this country, is because they are simply not there! As a society we need monsters and unexplained phenomena – UFOs, Nessie, Yetis, crop circles, vampires, Jack the Ripper, the beast of Bodmin – which we expand in our own imagination. Roaring cats and howling dogs have long put the wind up the superstitious and the secretive leopard is top of the international scare list from Tibet to Timbuktu. Some might argue that this collective fear can be a powerful and valuable social adhesive. Yet in today's enlightened times, the things that go bump in the night have lost their sting. Maybe it would be a shame to prove once and for all that mysterious black cats with flashing eyes and sharp teeth are not prowling the countryside. What would take their place in the shadows?

25.
Mink

Mink hounds had been a subject that had eluded me for at least three years, despite various invitations to come watch them at work. Of course, in the UK the packs are no longer allowed to operate against mink on the rivers, following the Hunting Act, so they chase rats, which, photographically at least, would still make for a fantastic article.

The mink hunts were unfortunate collateral damage from the foxhunt ban, given the public are wholly in favour of mink control to save the endangered water vole. It does baffle me, however, that it can be deemed cruel to hunt a mink, hare or fox; but less cruel to chase a rabbit or rat. It was an unenviable task trying to cobble together legislation for that issue, but they didn't half make a botched job.

However, the banning of mink hunting has helped field sports gain a public relations victory. The charitable Game Conservancy Trust, which works tirelessly to showcase the conservational benefits for habitat managed for sporting interest, has perfected a raft that will live trap mink. I went down to Wiltshire to see a raft in action on a chalk stream where the water vole was once a common sight. Through the release of mink from fur farms, often by animal rights campaigners, these voracious killers terrorised the water vole colonies like a scene from the director's cut version of the *Wind in the Willows*. Pollution and riparian damage have also contributed to Ratty's demise, but the unavoidable truth is that where you have mink, you don't have water voles.

'Come look! These are beautiful! I've never seen so many here!' Dr

Mike Short cried, almost falling in the stream in his excitement, waving for PQ to join him in the water. I ran down the bank, caught up in the moment, as PQ pushed his waders as fast as he could against the current to see what had set the biologist's face alight. All day he had been quiet, laid back, measured; but now Mike was splashing about like a kid in a paddling pool.

'Look at the footprints!' he continued, twisting the homemade mink raft out of the water so we can see the clay tread pad. 'It's covered in water vole prints. This is great news!' At the time, the journalist inside me was a little disappointed at the mention of water voles. I wanted the deeper, uglier imprint of a predatory mink that we could then catch the following week. It would have made a much better story and much better photographs! But that was to miss the point entirely. The area had already been cleared of mink, and the indigenous water vole, once estranged from these banks, was making a come-back.

It is not difficult to see why Mike and the GCT's mink raft team get so excited about their project. Of all the progress that the trust has made in recent years, whether in grey partridges, moorland predator control, woodcock research or river regeneration, to name but a few; none have enjoyed the all round success of the mink raft. This is not just because it is a very effective means of locating and trapping mink, although that helps. But there are enough examples of effective predator control that have received much less acclaim. It is the method of capture and the mink itself that have made it a hit with an audience far wider than landowners and shooters. In short, it has been a public relations masterpiece, especially in comparison with other gamekeeping practices, which are wise to shy away from a media, Government and public that are quick to find fault. By finding a humane method of controlling an alien species that was pushing close to extinction a much-loved icon of the British countryside, the GCT has been invited to sit a while at the top table, where it is much easier to get heard on other matters. 'There is no doubt that the plight of the water vole, a national favourite after Ratty in the *Wind in the Willows*, has brought positive publicity to the project,' said Mike. 'But that has put pressure on us to get results. And it is not just about the water vole. In the Scottish Hebrides, the mink is being removed to protect rare waders and sea birds. For game birds too, the mink can be a voracious, frenzied killer. But the water vole has provided the headlines.'

I did finally manage to see mink hounds in action, when PQ and I visited Ireland. Of course, the Irish are allowed to hunt mink, although they are still bitter that it is no longer otter hunting. The pack was originally named the Kings Otter Hounds, founded in 1880 to hunt the Bride River, a tributary of the famous Blackwater in County Cork. Now, they are called the Bride View Mink Hunt and they have switched their sights onto the sleek black assassins.

We had arranged to join the hounds and masters on a thin iron bridge that straddled the Bride. It was the perfect meeting point for an illicit union in a romantic novel. Swifts darted overhead in the early evening sunshine chasing insects, while a brace of teal flared up from reeds below us. But instead of some flame-haired Irish beauty, I had to make do with thirty wet mink hounds. We were there primarily for a photo opportunity

Huntsman Pat Murphy with a hound from the Bride View Mink Hunt.

Hound in water.

rather than a full-on hunt, so we were never likely to see a mink. Again, there would be no story for me to work on, but PQ was in his element, splashing about with his camera in the water.

I watched one of the lead hounds, a bruiser called Sergeant, as he lowered his muzzle to the water as though about to drink from the clear streams, but he stopped his nose just short of the surface. While the other hounds thrashed back and forward, searching for signs of mink, Sergeant stood still, sniffing the ether for traces of the odour that would send him into frenzy.

'Oh, he's a good dog, that Sergeant,' laughed the Bride View Master Billy Fitzgerald, transfixed by the movement of the pack in the river. With a beer-barrel chest, plum-red cheeks, hands like a badger's spades and eyes as bright as a blacksmith's forge, Billy would have looked little different from the original followers who started this hunt 127 years ago. 'If there's a mink in there, he'll find it all right. He can smell them on the water, old Sergeant.'

Sergeant looked like he could look after himself in the kennel too. His face was a mosaic of scars from previous campaigns, while there was a deep welt at his rear end. Half an ear was missing. 'He's certainly had a colourful life,' confirmed Billy with affection. 'We never thought he was going to make the grade because he was forever scrapping with other dogs in the kennels, but he has come good in the end. He's one hell of a strong dog too, lots of stamina. Nothing stops him when he gets on a scent.'

Barry was my translator for the session, as I struggled to understand a single word said by the huntsman Pat Murphy and his whippers-in, who had joined their charges in the water. Wearing no more than a pair of trainers, cotton trousers and a sweatshirt, they were soon all up to their belly buttons in the cold, dark water. PQ was better prepared (or less tough), donning chest-high waders before he took to the depths, and he captured some truly excellent shots as the water droplets sparkled off the bounding hounds. 'Pat's wife has to find his bollocks with a tooth pick after he's been in the water,' chuckled Barry.

If one hound catches sight or smell of a mink, it will give tongue and the hunt is on. Often, the fugitive mink will make for the nearest tree, whereupon every dog will do their best to scale the bough after it. 'It's mayhem after that,' said Billy with a big grin. 'We'll usually send one of lads up the tree after it in the end. But it's that sound of the dogs that does it for me. I couldn't live without that. There's no better music in the world.' And is it usually the same dog that finds the mink? 'Often, yes. Sergeant is good. That bitch there too, Drifter. But that's what's so special about this hunt. Everybody knows all the dogs and their individual traits. Like us, they have good days and bad. In the pub afterwards we'll all be talking about how such-and-such a dog had a great hunt or how so-and-so was on good form. At the end of the day, it's all about the dogs.' After the outlawing of mink hunting in Britain, the Irish packs are not being complacent. 'We lost the right to hunt otters with these hounds in 1989, which none of us ever thought would happen, so you can't assume anything,' said Billy. 'We just have to educate people that we are a community group that helps control a non-indigenous species. I hope we do it for many years to come, because I, for one, could never survive without hearing the music of these dogs.'

26. Shotgun wedding

The descent of a sweet, fun girl into a mean, glum woman once the ring is firmly attached to her finger, has long been exploited by comic illustrators. Before and after shots show the happy couple on their wedding day, her all coyness and radiance, him with chest-out assurance; transformed over five years into a snarling dragon with a snivelling worm at her side. Should you ever visit a supermarket on a Saturday morning, then you'll see these fire-breathers striding the aisles, their trolley like a battering ram before them, while the meek husband trots in behind, waiting for the next order to obey. His eyes scream, 'I didn't sign up for this!' while his lips mutter, 'yes, dear'.

The same could be said in reverse for shooting men. The caring, attentive suitor showers his lady with time and gifts, chatting for hours on long walks through flower filled woods, ignoring his pals to woo her all weekend. Yet, no sooner has the honeymoon ended and it's 'sorry, love, but I promised Norbert I'd help him with his pheasant pen,' or 'sorry, love, but I always shoot with the college boys on the third weekend of every month. Didn't I mention it?' So the shooting widow is born and, more often than not, she's delighted to see the back of him on the third weekend of every month. Of course, many shooting wives know exactly what they are getting themselves into. Indeed, almost all muck in, given they often come from the same stock. The clever husband might also have the foresight to produce a pup for his bride, which will sign her in for the next decade at least.

However, it is a tolerant lady indeed, who will let her man go shooting on the day of the wedding itself! It is not uncommon for the groom to play nine holes of golf with his ushers or smash a few clays on the morning of the Big Day to take his mind off bigger issues. But only the most resigned bride would allow her man to don full tuxedo and cravat, and tour the woods round the church with gun in hand. I have been invited to some quirky days through the magazine, but the Shotgun Wedding in Yorkshire was the furthest off the wall.

When we met the groom on the morning of the wedding, he was sitting down to a plate of fried breakfast. His best man and head usher, Darren and Andy, had given him a monumental send-off the night before. Judging by Malcolm's pallor, it had only just finished. His face pulsed from grey to green as the large plate of fried eggs, greasy bacon and gloopy baked beans was set in front of him. All three of them looked nervously at the coffee, sausages and mushrooms that sat between themselves and recovery, no doubt ruing the decision to invite a reporter and photographer to join them vermin shooting on the morning of the ceremony. All three were dressed in hired morning suits, complete with pin-striped trousers, white silk waistcoats, pressed white shirts, black penguin jackets and red cravats. At least they had swapped leather brogues for rubber wellies. But, as the condemned man ploughed through his last meal, his cheeks began to resemble his tie more than his shirt. By the time the final grilled tomato disappeared he was positively bubbly. 'The plan of today,' Malcolm explained, removing the protective napkin from his throat, 'is to have a go at whatever we can find on my dad's land near the church. There is a rookery above the church itself which we can have a pop at and the fields are wick with pigeons. Hopefully we'll make it round the hedgerows and woodland edge to be in church for the service.'

The rooks had set up a very successful colony above the twelfth-century building and took no notice of the men in morning suits as they unloaded weapons and ammunition from the back of their vehicle. 'It's my wedding, so I get the first barrel,' said Malcolm, fully recovered and excited, as the three friends lined up underneath the trees. When he was ten years old, Malcolm used to run over here after school with his father's air rifle, the start of an enduring relationship with the rookery. It was a pressure shot, but after waiting for the most impudent bird to swoop down, Malcolm soon had the bag going. Sadly for the best man and usher, the other rooks did not hang about for another shot, but took off to warn their buddies that the scourge of the last fifteen years was back.

With their tails and ties, the trio looked almost Victorian in appearance, though the wax jackets and wellies added a contemporary feel. To start off with, at least, they made every effort to remain neat and clean despite the showers and muddy fields. Malcolm led the way, choosing to cut the string on a gate rather than clamber over as usual. The fields and woods had been his playground as a kid, where he had learned all he could about rabbiting, ferreting, falconry and running lurchers. As the shooters walked up through a nearby village, looking like three desperados in a Wild West one-horse town, a local man cleaning his car hardly batted an eyelid. I wondered what else he sees in this part of the countryside!

Just through the village was a prime spot for pigeons where Malcolm and his father had spent many a fruitful afternoon. 'They can come over in their droves,' said the groom, as they knelt in one of the three pigeon hides to pose for a photograph. As if to prove his point, three woodies appeared on the skyline and made their way in our direction. 'Get yourselves hidden,' ordered our guide. 'They'll come right over us. You watch,' he barked, pressing himself against a tree, no longer mindful he was wearing his wedding suit.

Best man Darren, who works alongside Malcolm at a local butcher, placed a couple of cartridges in his side-by-side and stared wide-eyed at the pigeons as they made their approach. Darren had only picked up a gun two weeks earlier in preparation for today and though he had done well with some clays, this was his first opportunity in the field. Malcolm did his best to encourage him. 'Get yourself ready, kid. Steady, now. Let them have it,' he cried, leaping out of hiding and firing both barrels. Andy did likewise, but Darren remained frozen to the spot, leaving the other two to it. All three pigeons flew on unharmed. 'Well, the theory was right,' grinned Malcolm. It was hard to ignore the daub of mud on his left shoulder.

We walked to the next wood, each in silence as the reality of the situation sank in. Within hours, they would be stood at the altar, standing for pictures and making speeches. I wondered whether the loud banging had tipped their hangovers over the edge.

'Aw, bugger it!' said Malcolm as we crossed a deserted lane. 'Only gone and forgotten the bloody buttonholes, haven't I. Tina will murder me if I don't go get them before the service. I guess we'll have to cut this short.'

It still left time on the way home for the groom to show his prowess with gun in hand, as he brought down a pigeon and magpie that flitted through the trees. The magpie especially was a terrific snap shot. Each time a bird fell, Malcolm would hitch up his tails and vault the barbed wire fence to retrieve the spoils, knowing that any slip could end in tears and tears. At least he managed to avoid wiping his bloodied hand on his threads after holding out the magpie's wings to admire its brilliant tail feathers, similar to the swirling blues and greens of spilt petrol.

'Don't suppose I could use those as a buttonhole?' he joked, as he tucked the bird in his cartridge bag. Andy joined the party by stopping a bolting rabbit in its tracks. 'A rook, rabbit, pigeon and magpie – not a bad mixed bag. All we need now is a big old dog fox. That said, I probably should have got married during the winter and then we could have gone after some of those pheasants.'

Every so often during the paddle round the fields, Darren would pat his inside pocket to make sure the ring was still there. It would be a long walk back, retracing our route, if it had fallen out. 'It's more than your life is worth to lose it,' warned Malcolm. 'Tina's not done much shooting, but she would track you down and she wouldn't miss!'

By the time the three sportsmen had climbed the final incline to reach the church, they were muddy, bloody, sweaty and out of puff. But in good spirits. The groom had just enough time to nip home for the buttonholes, catch his breath and composure, before the first guests started filing in.

When everyone had taken their seats, the beautiful bride arrived with her father in a vintage motor. With the church full to the gunwales, any extras, such as journalists, were left outside. But we were at least able to witness the best man sprinting to his car mid-service to fetch a bottle of Lucozade. The remedial effects of the fried breakfast had worn off and Malcolm was swaying alarmingly!

The energy drink did its job, as, the 'I dos' done, the next person we saw was the groom's father dashing out of the church to fetch some string to tie the yard gate, a tradition in this part of the county. Nobody is allowed to leave until the string is cut by the groom, when the children will throng the gate to receive coins from the congregation. But as the official photographer (looking jealously at PQ's expensive camera) herded up the family and guests for group photos, the steady drizzle turned into harder rain. With everybody corralled in the church yard, there was no escape through the tied gate, until Malcolm remembered he still had his shooting knife in his pocket.

The groom cut the string and the guests fled for their cars. 'One thing you can always rely on,' said Andy, pleased that it no longer mattered whether he looked wet or not, 'is that whatever situation, Malcolm will always have a knife in his pocket.'

JANUARY
FEBRUARY
MARCH
APRIL
MAY
JUNE
JULY
AUGUST
SEPTEMBER
OCTOBER
NOVEMBER
DECEMBER

27. Stickmaking

Ever been to the Forest of Dean? It could be one of those places you have heard of, but never really found the time to locate on a map, let alone visit. There's no shame in that, indeed it is the relative isolation of this onetime royal hunting forest created by the valleys of two great tidal rivers, the Severn and the Wye, which gives it charm. I certainly had to look it up on the atlas when given an assignment to interview a stickmaker in the hills above the 27,000 acre national park. Go to Cheltenham and head west: you can't miss it. The area is famous for its craftsmen who tap, whittle and roll throughout this ancient Kingdom; a forgotten land that offered inspiration to storytellers such as JRR Tolkein, JK Rowling and Dennis Potter. It is all too easy to imagine dwarves and trolls hidden away in the dark, gnarled forest. And if Gandalf ever wants his staff re-shafted, I could advise the right place to go!

Paul Nicholls may be in his forties, but he is still in his stickmaking infancy. The really top draws in the business, heavyweights like John Penny and Gordon Flintoff who challenge yearly for the top honours on the stickmaking circuit, have at least a couple of decades more experience than Paul, although this new kid on the block is already starting to turn heads.

'At least I am now competing with them,' explained Paul next to his trophy display which is draped in first prize rosettes that he won whilst on the novice circuit. Competition is that much tougher though in the Open section, but every year Paul is improving and learning new techniques and skills to bring him closer to the big boys.

'The great problem is that being so much younger, and having to hold down a full-time job, with a young family too, I don't have the same amount of time as the older gentlemen. They are very helpful though and I am learning a great deal from them.'

Looking at various examples of Paul's work, it is astonishing to think that he has only been in the stickmaking game for six years. Before he started, he was similar to many folk in thinking that to make a stick you need to find a straight piece of wood and attach a horn or carving to the end. Simple as that. But as he read more on the subject and learned the trade secrets, so he developed a fascination for the craft that has taken him around the country and introduced him to many new friends.

Paul works as an estate worker on the magnificent Courtfield estate in Herefordshire, which has been in the Vaughan family for many centuries. Overlooking the Forest of Dean, the estate is heavily involved in stewardship schemes and one of Paul's primary tasks is maintaining the stone wall dykes that run through the property and provide a refuge for voles, shrews and their predators. 'Working here has given me an insight into the traditional countryside skills such as wall building, hedgelaying and gamekeeping. Stickmaking is another of those old art forms,' said Paul, in his garage which is filled to the rafters, literally, with sticks that are in bundles to dry out and mature. Over the years, Paul has developed a sixth sense for finding potential walking sticks and he struggles to walk anywhere without keeping half an eye out for sticky delights.

'I go beating on the estate shoots and I am forever getting into trouble for looking at hedges or searching for sticks. People always think I am running off for a pee because I am disappearing behind thickets. Often the best sticks are made of hazel or blackthorn, because they tend to grow quickly and straight towards the light, while other trees, such as ash for example,

Paul Nicholls' competition sticks are judged on their straightness.

will grow slower and have more twigs.' But there is plenty of variety when it comes to wood, and Paul has made sticks from sycamore, yew, holly, American walnut and hawthorn, as well as the wonderful spiral effect caused by honeysuckle growing round the shank. Was I alone in thinking that those twisted sticks favoured by wizards and hobgoblins were carved by hand?

By laying the sticks flat for twelve months, moisture will be released slowly from either end, resulting in a seasoned shank. 'If you cut a branch and tap it against the floor it will make a dull thud and won't bounce,' Paul explained, 'because it is full of water. A seasoned stick will make a crisp noise and spring up when it is ready. I also coat the sticks in tractor grease to stop them cracking.'

Although several dozen will be seasoned each year, only the very finest will progress to the next stage and be attached to a head piece. In his Aladdin's cave of a workshop, Paul demonstrated the steps that are painstakingly required to produce such fine quality walking sticks. First of all, the seasoned shank must be straightened out. Some stickmakers use steam or a boiler to heat sticks twelve at a time, but Paul prefers to warm the shanks evenly with a heat gun, before bending the wood over his knee. The fibres in the wood will then fix in their new position and the shank is ready to have a head fixed.

'But don't leave the shank in a warm place or next to a window, as there is a good chance it will bend back into a bow. It is something I learned through bitter experience. The first thing a judge will do at a show is to pick up a stick by the end and look down the shaft from every angle to make sure the stick is perfectly straight and perfectly aligned,' said the stickmaker, proudly exhibiting one of his show sticks that was straight as a ruler. 'Sometimes they will bend a little with time, but it doesn't take much to put them right. Of course, a stick can always be re-shafted if it has a special head piece.'

The classic designs for the head piece are the horn crook as used by shepherds; the thumbpiece for roe deer stalkers and ramblers; the knob, ideal for boncing a burglar; or the carved decoration pieces, which are waggled by dandies. Paul has mastered all of these styles and his workshop is filled with the necessary tools and machines needed for each.

The process of fashioning a horn for a crook is a great test of skill and patience. The malleable ram or tup's horn must be moulded round a horse-shoe shaped 'jig' to precise dimensions. The horn – the best ones

Paul Nicholls in his workshop.

come from Welsh or Scottish sheep apparently – is first boiled for twenty minutes to give it elasticity, and then flattened under an eight-ton jack, before being sculpted round the jig. The artisan will then decide whether to give the horn a hook at the tip, which again involves more careful heating and bending.

'The dimensions of a stick are not for aesthetics but for their practical purpose in the field,' said Paul, showing a beautiful 'leg cleek' that would traditionally have been used to catch a sheep by the leg to check for foot rot. 'The cleek has to have an inner diameter of a two-pence piece as that is the ideal dimension for catching a leg. The 'market stick' is smaller still for close work in a market stall, while the traditional shepherd's crook is longer and stronger so that the shepherd can catch sheep that are travelling quickly. The hook is there to stop the sharp point piercing a sheep's eye and so that the shepherd could hang his lantern whilst lambing in the field. While the stick must look good, it must be workable to if you want to win.'

Good quality ram's horn is becoming increasingly more difficult to acquire and so Asian Water Buffalo horn is fast becoming the favoured material for the crookmaker. Carving wooden head pieces is a developing passion for Paul, whittling away with fine chisels to create lifelike sculptures of wildlife such as trout, dogs and pheasants. During the winter especially, Paul will stand for hours chipping away to create works of art for clients and friends. Once the head of the stick is completed, Paul will drill into both the head and shank with an 8 mm bit, and attach the two with a threaded metal bar before gluing tight. Once polished, the stick is ready to start walking. 'The join must be perfect if the stick is to win at show level and it can be an art in itself. The judge will always hold it to the light to check for any gap. You could also add a metal ferrule to protect the base of the shank, but as the judges do not require you to do so, it is just one more thing that can go wrong! But when all goes well there is nothing better. It is a very satisfying feeling to make a product that is both practical and ornate.'

Paul demonstrated how the groove of a thumbstick fitted the shape of his hand. 'You must always think about how the stick is going to feel in someone's hand. A thumbstick may look great but if you can't get your thumb in, then it is pointless. And the length should be measured to allow the owner to have his or her elbow bent at right angles for maximum comfort. You have to visualise the stick being used, when you make it.'

The stickmaking trade can rejoice that the traditional skills have been handed down to the next generation, and it has unearthed a new talent that will only improve with age. But time is not something that worries Paul. 'You have to be very relaxed and patient if you want to be a stickmaker. Things can go wrong – after all, it is natural fibres that you are dealing with – and you have to be prepared for set-backs, many of which open up new possibilities.'

Maybe we could all learn from Paul's laid back outlook. He seems to be on the same wavelength as the trees he relies on: take your time and you'll get there eventually. Before I left, he showed me a new walking stick that he had carved and painted to create a perfect cock pheasant's head. 'The piece of wood came from an old oak beam that I salvaged from a house,' he said proudly. 'The original tree must have taken one hundred years to grow; and then it was part of a house for another hundred years; so this here is a two-hundred-year-old stick, despite it being brand new. And there is no reason why it can't be a walking stick for another hundred years at least. I think that's rather special, don't you?'

28.
Pamplona

There have been San Fermin celebrations in the streets of Pamplona for at least seven centuries, although the first running of the bulls officially took place in 1591. By the middle of the eighteenth century, the fiesta was already a favoured destination for foreign tourists to the extent that local clergy were bemoaning its more irreligious focus, including the 'the abuse of drink and the permissiveness of young men and women'. The bull-running reached mainstream notoriety in 1926 when the American writer Ernest Hemingway related his own experiences of San Fermin in his novel *The Sun Also Rises*.

I visited the festival with four great friends from university, flying to Bilbao on the Atlantic coast and taking a hire car east to the small town of Pamplona below the Spanish Pyrenees. There are risks involved, but statistics are on your side. The bulls do injure a few unfortunates every year, but it had been a full six years since anyone had actually been gored or trampled to death! The Pamplona bull run takes place at 8 a.m. every morning from the seventh to the fourteenth of July. Six bulls will dash 825 metres from the corral at Santo Domingo to the bullring where they will fight that same afternoon. It takes an average of three minutes for

Friends from university in the traditional garb.

these enormous creatures to reach the arena, as they are funnelled along the fenced-off streets of the old town. While the bulls cannot escape into the crowd, neither can the runners!

Even if you have no desire to do the run itself, Pamplona is still worth a visit during the San Fermin fiesta. The ancient, winding streets are packed with excitable revellers, all dressed in the traditional white trousers and white T-shirts, with a red handkerchief tied round their neck and a red sash in a bow round their waist. This uniform acts as an international leveller, bringing every visitor under the same banner. If ever you wanted to disappear into a crowd and people watch, then this is your place.

Of course, 8 a.m. brings with it new challenges. If you do not want to stay up all night in the numerous bars and open-air clubs, then you will have to stay in the outskirts of town or the surrounding countryside. The reason is simple. The noise is non-stop! Throughout the day and night (there is a small hiatus about lunchtime when you can catch two hours' sleep on a bunk house floor lined with mattresses) the streets swell to the beat of brass bands and lively processions led by local groups that have been making a heady din for generations. Unless you are stone cold deaf, you will not sleep a wink during the night in Pamplona.

This was not a problem for five lads in their twenties and we quickly threw ourselves into the spirit. Indeed, we were still going strong by 6 a.m., when the town starts to gird its loins for the bull run. Spectators line the track, climbing up the tall wooden fences to get the best viewpoint, while the runners crush into a holding pen under the clock tower in the main square. And then you wait. For the next ninety minutes, you are propped against each other, wearing yesterday's clothes, as the sun rises hot in the sky and your hangover kicks in. You can take nothing with you, not even a bottle of water, so you just sit there and wilt.

It does give you a quiet moment to wonder what it must feel like to have a half ton bull's horn driven through your stomach, trapped on the cobbled street as a crazed animal thrashes down on you with the crowd cheering on. We had been warned that if you slip on the stones in front of a bull, each of which is at least four years old and weighs 460 to 600 kg, then stay down as the animal will be unable to spear you with its horns. It might stand on your back, but that is preferable to a spike in the guts. Many of the fifteen people to have died since 1924 were caught amidships by the bull when trying to get back onto their feet. It would be like standing up in front of a barbed VW Beetle.

You are either a runner or a walker, depending on your nerve. The runners take off well in front of the bulls with an aim to reaching the bull ring before them. Those that succeed are locked into the arena, where the organisers will release a series of young bulls with corks on their horns, so any amateur matadors can play with them in safety. The walkers stay in the street for the bulls, dodging their charging horns and smacking them on the rump with rolled up newspapers. The greatest risk for them comes when the bulls turn the corners of the narrow streets, as some will slip over if they take a turn too sharply. If you are between the bull and the sturdy fence, then it gets messy. Ordinarily, the bulls will simply follow a team of large bullocks down the track without incident. But when these angry cannonballs get turned or left behind, they will start wrecking whatever gets in their path.

We were in the runner camp. This was partly to do with a fear of adding my name to the list of casualties, but also because it is a blast to get into the arena with the small bulls. At five minutes to eight, any thoughts of a hangover or dry mouth are banished, as the tension mounts. At 8 a.m. on the dot, a rocket was fired to confirm that the gate has been opened at the Santo Domingo corral. It is like the red light turning to amber. A second rocket announces that the bulls have left the corral. We were then released with a two hundred metre head start.

It is a genuine thrill edging down the twisting route of the bull run with the real possibility that one of these monsters will appear from behind at any moment. Sheer weight of numbers mean that you are unable to reach anything more than a jog, but given I spent much of the time looking back over my shoulder, I would not have gone much quicker. Crowds line the route, cheering down from windows and balconies, whooping if a bull comes close. At least two of the six black bulls passed me as I ran, cutting through the sea of runners like a zip opening a tent door. There was no way I was ever going to get in its way or play the macho hero! Our group reached the gates of the Plaza de Toros as the last two dark shapes were propelled down the steep entrance and off to another corral to await their fate in the evening.

We followed the bulls into the sand-filled arena, which was a circular amphitheatre, at least twenty-five metres in diameter. The mini-bulls are still cow enough to cause plenty of damage to anyone who gets in their way and they easily tossed the foolhardy with their bulging necks. It would have been a bloodbath if their horns had not been blunted by corks. At

Watching the bullfight. Compellingly brutal.

one point, a bull caught a beautiful Spanish blonde by the edge of the arena and threw her high into the air like a rag doll. She landed head first on the sand and there could not have been a red-blooded male there who didn't feel the urge to run to her aid; but before we could move, she was up on her feet, smiling and dancing as though her dearest wish had come true. Compare that with the 'I slipped on an orange peel, give me £10,000' brigade!

That evening, we were back at the bullring for the main event, *la corrida de toros* or bullfight. 12,500 spectators in their red and white uniform cram into the stadium to welcome the six fighting bulls and the various showmen who combat them. Seats become more expensive the closer you are to the action, but in a twist of hierarchy, those behind are allowed to throw sangria-soaked fruit at the wealthy below them. We were seated midway, so were able to throw fruit and be targeted throughout.

There is no getting away from the gruesome bloodiness of bullfighting. It is violent, savage even, but compellingly entertaining. The preconception of those who would have it banned is that the crowds lounge about revelling in the slow death of the bull like decadent Romans in the Coliseum. This is way off the mark. It is an unfair fight, say the antis, accusing the *toreros* (or *matadores*) of cowardice, because the bull is weakened first. Again, this is misguided piffle. I saw nothing but heartfelt respect for the bull from the crowd and a dazzling display of skill by the *cuadrilla* (team) in the arena.

It is impossible not to feel sorry for the bull as a mounted *picador* pushes his lance into the bull's muscular neck, but adrenaline would mask any pain. Blood fountains from the wound, lowering the bull's blood pressure, so that it does not have a heart attack in its enraged state. The bull will try to lift the picador's horse with its neck muscles, which also helps tire it out. As soon as the picadors leave, then three *banderilleros* arrive, each armed with two *banderillas* (barbed sticks) to drive into the bull's flanks. These further weaken the enormous neck and shoulder muscle through loss of blood, spurring the bull into desperate lunges.

Finally, the matador takes centre stage alone with a small red cape (*muleta*) and a flashing silver sword. The bulls are colour blind, but the cape still tempts the bull to run at it as though hypnotised. From my seat, it was easy to forget the real danger that the matador faces from the bull as he manoeuvres it around his body, often making very small movements at the last critical moment. Finally, once the bull is on its last legs, the matador will edge into a position where he can perform the *estocada*, thrusting the sword between the shoulder blades, killing the bull instantly by piercing the aorta or heart. This is the most dangerous moment as he must reach between the sharp horns to stab accurately.

On one occasion, a novice matador fluffed his lines on five consecutive attempts, missing the vital organ with his sword. The crowd quickly turned on him, yelling abuse and booing until he finally put the bull out of its misery. To me at least, it demonstrated the high esteem for the bulls among the crowd and the fine balance between glory and ignominy for the matadors. While the spectators appreciated a fine kill, they also rooted for the bull if it got close to snaring a member of the *cuadrilla*.

There was no cruelty here, although I did not envy the picadors' horses that bore the brunt of the bulls' early anger, despite their padded flanks. I was in awe of the bulls' strength and stamina, but I did not feel outraged at its death. Far from it, in fact. Theirs is a wonderful life, pampered like kings, surrounded by open fields that are far from meddling humans. Until the end comes, of course. There is something very artistic about the *corrida*, as though you are watching a dance rather than a duel to the death. Hemingway says it better than me in his 1932 book *Death in the Afternoon*: 'Bullfighting is the only art in which the artist is in danger of death and in which the degree of brilliance in the performance is left to the fighter's honour.' It is cultural, traditional, community-led, colourful and exciting. And yes, it is great fun. I left the stadium on a high, covered from head to toe in sticky sangria.

29.
Bugs

The world is getting warmer, so we are led to believe. I am not going to quibble with that, indeed I once had a very long chat with a leading member of the Royal Scientific Society who gave some very convincing arguments as to why it is we humans who are causing it. That was good enough for me. While the manner in which the Government and any number of private companies are cashing in on this new green wave appeals to my cynical side, I don't buy into the theory that it is a conspiracy theory juggernaut without any brakes.

That said, it is approaching hysteria in certain parts of the media. Every time there is a hot spell or an extended deluge, it is blamed on the over-heating atmosphere and we the public are given another rap on the knuckles. There is some truth in it, over and above the need to fill column inches, although there must have been hot Aprils and wet Junes before. I was born in the summer of 1976, which I'm assured was a scorcher. I wonder what reasons were given back then. Don't get me wrong, I do agree that we all ought to do our bit to help. The recycling revolution has been swift and absolute. Woe betide anyone who mixes cardboard and paper at my local dump! However, it seems almost futile in the face of

Oriental development. I know that is the wrong attitude, but the facts are stark. Researching an article on the rising price of lead shot in cartridges, I was amazed to read that China alone produces nearly four million cars a year. All of these need lead for their batteries, which has put the commodity's price through the roof.

While that may be one cause of global warming loosely related to the shooting industry, what are its other effects on country sports? As I write this in the summer of 2007, the skies are grey with rain as they have been for the last month and half. Some pheasant farms have been washed away, while others have contracted nasty diseases from the damp conditions. Grouse on the moors have struggled, which has been a great shame given the high hopes for a turn around in fortunes. If ever they needed an unseasonably hot spring and summer it was this year. It may just be a blip, who knows? However, it has been noticeable for the last few years that British winters have lost their sting. As a boy, it was fairly common occurrence to get snowed in and miss school, although perhaps that is selective memory.

These mild winters do seem to have affected the insect life in Britain, which has led to an explosion in the number of biting bugs in the countryside, a development that could feasibly eat a hole in the fortunes of the shooting industry. For eight thousand years, Highland man and Highland midge have bitten and slapped each other in Scotland, but in recent years their booming populations have caused even the hardiest of locals to seek refuge at altitude or indoors.

If you haven't ever been attacked by midgies, then I envy you. The secret weapon of the midge is that you never feel the first one as she lands on your bare skin and crawls along your naked flesh searching for a capillary to tap. Mrs Midge, for it is only the females that bite, silently pierces your epidermis with her razor sharp mandibles and inserts her tube shaped mouth into the wound to suck up one ten millionth of a litre of blood. Like her cousin the mosquito, the crafty midge uses your advanced immune system against you. She injects a minute dose of saliva, triggering your immune system to pump histamine that will prepare the scene of the wound for antibodies. But this histamine will also keep the blood flowing for the three or four minutes needed for our midge to take her fill, before your white blood cells arrive to patch up the damaged area. Still unnoticed, as you cast your line on the water or reach for your whisky and soda on the veranda, she will withdraw her jaws and fly away with blood to feed her developing eggs. Only then, too late, do you start to feel the effects of her attack. A small, angry, red bump appears on your skin as the white blood cells get to work, causing the spot to itch for a couple of minutes. No big deal in itself, but popular Mrs Midge has friends – thousands of them. As she takes off, she emits a pheromone which alerts this monstrous regiment of women to the unwilling donor and within seconds they are swarming round you like the prize-winning rhubarb pie at a WI fundraiser. The initial, bearable itch starts to spread as the black cloud descends on every exposed patch of your hide. Midges are crawling up the cuffs of your shirt, creeping under your collar, behind and in your ears, over your top lip and deep into your hair. Heaven only help you if you are wearing a kilt. A prickling sensation starts on your ankles, rising up along your legs, across the back of each hand, it climbs your spine, penetrating the scalp and before you know it you are scratching like a crazed baboon.

'The extended summers have allowed the midge a second generation,' explained Dr George Hendry, author of the bestselling book *Midges in Scotland*. 'Eggs laid would usually emerge as flying adults the following year, but it has been confirmed that eggs laid early in the summer can develop quickly enough for a second flush of new adults to arrive for the start of the grouse and shooting seasons.'

The lack of deep freeze in the winter has also meant that no juveniles are killed in the soil. This subterranean reprieve has worked wonders for the tick population too. A voracious parasite, there is a very real danger that the tick will start driving folk off the Highland moors if their numbers continue to rise unchecked. The flightless tick needs to be rather more patient than the midge. It has a three-year cycle, moulting first from a larva to a nymph and finally to its adult form, when it can produce up to ten thousand eggs before it dies. For all three metamorphoses to work, it must take a blood meal each time: the larva feeds on a small mammal like a mouse or rat; the nymph upgrades to a rabbit or hare; while the adult will gorge itself for up to ten days on a bigger mammal like a cat, dog, deer or human. Birds such as grouse or lapwings are also a favoured host. Once bloated with claret, the debauched female tick will search the living blood bar for a mate; get herself knocked up, before falling to the grass to set the cycle back in motion. Of course, ticks have been in Britain for as long as we have, but this recent boom is gathering worried looks like never before from people on the ground. Deer are being found literally crawling with them.

One Highland keeper told me: 'There are times when I'll come back from the hill to find over twenty ticks on my legs and back. We've got two small kids and my wife won't let me in the house until I've left my breeks and jacket at the door – then it's straight in the shower. It is just something we have to deal with and it may just be a phase, I don't know. But there's no getting away from it. I am forever removing the things from my dogs. I've seen grouse chicks with their heads covered in ticks. It's not just the game either – stoats, foxes, lapwing – they're all suffering.' The tick has the added curse of being a disease carrier, passing on louping ill to sheep, grouse and humans and the truly horrible Lyme disease, which is becoming an increasing problem among Highland keepers especially. Many will visit their GP for a Lyme disease test every three months as a precaution. Flu-like symptoms can appear up to twelve days later and may be cured with antibiotics. However, in some cases, the afflicted may be unaware he is infected for many years. Advanced Lyme disease can cause extreme pain in the joints and a debilitating lack of energy, similar to ME or chronic fatigue syndrome.

At the time of writing, members of the Scottish Gamekeepers Association have voiced their concerns that tick-borne disease may turn into a serious epidemic, even seeking assistance from the State. If a tourist or schoolchild contracts a potentially lethal disease in the Highlands, it could drive the many thousands of visitors away. Only the media would remain, tutting from a safe distance.

30.
Stalking by bicycle

At the age of seventeen, Ashley Dean was no different to the other kids in his class. Fit and agile, he was a keen scrum-half, opening batsman and tennis player. As a country lad from Monmouthshire, he was learning all he could about shooting, hunting and fishing and spent much of his holiday time out in the fields around his home. It was a lifestyle he would have surely continued for the next fifteen years, had tragedy not struck. Sharp pains began stabbing at the back of his legs as tendonitis set into his hamstrings. As the affliction worsened, so the doctors became increasingly baffled by the serious nature of the condition and the standard treatment proved ineffective.

As a result, Ashley struggles in any movement which involves raising his heel, in particular walking, running or jumping. Nowadays, he can walk no more than one hundred yards before pain and exhaustion take over. With a sixty minute recovery time, deer stalking by foot is just not feasible. However, Ashley has learnt to substitute wheels for heels, as the cycling motion does not inflict the same pain as walking. Anywhere his mountain bike, which he straps on the back of his car, can go, he can too. For more urban terrain, the thirty-four-year-old also owns a collapsible bike that will fit in the boot of his car, so his professional life is largely unaltered. Fishing, which involves minimal walking, has become a great passion and in the last few years he has fished for trout and salmon along many of Britain's finest rivers.

But shooting, and in particular stalking, has been largely off limits. Driven pheasant and partridge, on flat dry parkland or near a track, is manageable. Sitting in a pigeon hide by a wood is also possible, although cycling over stubble or a ploughed field puts a stick in the spokes. Highland or woodland stalking was simply a case of idle day-dreaming. 'I often cycle through woods and you see plenty of deer,' he told me in the pub one evening. He lives near me in the Cotswolds and we often meet for a yarn and a pint. 'Indeed, I've been able to get very close to a few as they don't seem to get scared of the noise of wheels. Maybe it is a more constant noise than walking. But I'll never be able to stalk one.'

But is it such a fanciful notion? Surely, if Ashley could cycle to within fifty yards of a high seat and be in place for dawn or dusk, then there was every chance he would see a deer. The only

Ashley Dean and Steve Bowers en route to the woods.

issue was to find the right man with suitable woods, who was prepared to entertain the idea of taking a disabled person on a stalk. 'I know just the person,' I thought out loud. 'If he's up for it, then we'll get you that deer.'

When I woke the next morning, head a little heavy, I cursed my bravado. It was indeed possible that Ashley could cycle to a high seat and shoot a deer if it appeared. But it was also likely that the whole thing would be a disaster. If he struggled to get to the right place at the right time, all it would serve would be to reinstate his disability. Besides, with my two fully-fit legs, had it not taken me over a year to shoot a roe?

First I had to secure my miracle maker and when it comes to weighing up a sporting situation, few are as astute as Steve Bowers. A rifle manufacturer and engineer of rare talent, the forty-three-year-old has been shooting constantly since the age of six. As a professional stalker with thousands of acres to manage, most of which he has worked for decades, his knowledge is unparalleled in this area of Gloucestershire. Built like an ailing stoat, his lean stature belies fantastic strength, while his senses are closer to those species he hunts than anyone I've met so far. 'As long as he can get to the high seat quickly and quietly, then he will definitely see deer,' he said. 'But getting a shot is a different matter. If he can prove to me that he is an accurate shot, then I see no reason why this won't work.' I was starting to breathe a little easier now. The two of us made a recce of the wood the week before and sat on the high seat, waiting for the light to fail. The woodland floor was alive with bluebells, criss-crossed with occasional deer runs. Steve cuts back the vegetation during the summer months to increase visibility and provide corridors for the deer that will bring them to where he wants.

'Depending on the wind, the deer will usually appear in the middle of the ride, to the right or left of the high seat. As long as you are patient, they will eventually end up in front of the seat, no further than one hundred yards away.' For a Rifle of Steve's ability, that is a formality, but how would Ashley react when 'buck fever' took grip?

As dusk fell on our recce, we moved down the ride into a pasture field. Steve knows that when it is dark in the wood, there will be twenty-five minutes of light left in the field. 'It is pretty much the perfect field for stalking deer,' he enthused. 'Apart from anything else, there are almost always deer there, especially if it's a warm evening.' Its bowl-shape provides a safe background, while the woodland edge and the long grass give fodder for the deer and cover for the stalker. Steve led the way across the field downwind towards a young buck he had spotted. 'Lift your knees higher as you walk,' he whispered, as I crashed through the grass behind him. The mature does were producing fawns, so this buck was one of last year's generation that had been sent out into the big bad world. 'They'll be chased on by resident bucks until they congregate together in little pockets,' the stalker explained later. 'I call them coffee bars and they are a good place to remove the lesser bucks.'

Creeping forward as the deer put its heads down to graze the fresh grass, we edged to within thirty-five yards. 'Perfect for a sitting shot,' Steve grinned, shouldering an imaginary rifle and allowing the buck to see us in the grass. Its head lifted high in an effort to identify us as friend or foe. 'You watch as he runs round in a circle to work out what we are,' Steve said, pre-empting the deer's movements. Sure enough, the roe buck trotted round in an arc, eyes wide and ears cocked. Every so often it would stop and stare, providing ample time for a shot if we were armed. 'He's about to wind us….now,' the engineer predicted, as the deer winced like he had been slapped in the face, before steaming off into the woods like a late train.

No matter how well Ashley could move on a bike, Steve was not going to let a novice loose on a deer without proof that he could shoot straight. It would be Ashley's first look down a telescopic sight, but he was in good hands. Another feather in Steve's cap is that of Deer Commission instructor. In tight woodland, where the deer will be no further than one hundred yards away, Steve swears by his Marlin 30.30 Winchester. The short, light rifle allows for a quick draw, especially if riding a quad bike. 'It is just perfect for close quarter woodland stalking, as it is not overkill, but will stop any deer at one hundred yards. In the US there are more deer shot with the 30.30 round than any other, although the lever action does mean I get accused of looking like John Wayne.'

Ashley had mugged up on roe deer stalking by reading the definitive *Roe Stalking* by Richard Prior, part of the *Shooting Times* Library. 'I have to admit though,' he said, as Steve pinned up a paper target one hundred yards away down a range, 'that there is little about deer management. It is mostly etiquette. And he doesn't mention stalking by bicycle!'

Steve gave his charge a quick lesson in how to relax when shooting. 'You sometimes hear people say you should breathe in and hold your breath before you fire. That's rubbish. That will only give you a few seconds before your eye starts ticking and your body shakes. You will be too tense. Ideally, you should take a deep breath, so your lungs are fully aerated, before exhaling. Then you can hold your breath with your body relaxed.'

The first two shots grouped nicely, but high of the round 'kill zone' that Steve had drawn on the paper. A few clicks on the sight and the next shot slammed through the centre, leaving both stalker and guest feeling rather pleased with themselves. The next two proved it was no fluke and the test was passed. Before we set off for the high seat, there were just a few more lessons to learn. Drawing a miniature deer on a filthy window of his truck, Steve demonstrated where he wanted Ashley to shoot. 'Above the foreleg, one third up or two thirds down – a bit lower than you might think.'

He then showed him how to carry the rifle, when he was not cycling. 'So often you see people carrying a rifle with the barrel facing up,' he said, ensuring that Ashley held it barrel down. 'If the rifle fires then it will go up in the air, instead of into the ground, and you never know where it will come down. Also, when walking down a bank, the rifle can be nearer horizontal and the bullet will shoot off at high velocity towards someone who is maybe walking down another hill in the distance, or even right behind you. Another tip for safety, is that I only ever take five bullets with me – you're unlikely to ever need more than that. It means that I know how many I should have when I leave. If there is one missing, then first thing, check the chamber. Then you may have to retrace your steps. But if you go out with a load in your pocket, you never know how many there are.'

Time was not on our side, so we set off towards the woods, Ashley peddling furiously in a low gear to keep up with Steve across the soft steep ground. Once in the trees, the cyclist was able to direct the wheels between ruts and sticks at low speed, making no more noise than the rest of us. Given there were five in our party (stalker, Rifle, nervous reporter, photographer and dog), I was left unsighted at the foot of the tree with Willow, Steve's eighteen-month-old German shorthaired pointer bitch, who used me as a climbing frame, while the other three surveyed the woods from above.

After ten minutes, Willow froze to the woodland floor. Twenty seconds later, a terrible rifle crack made me jump four foot in the air. A jubilant Ashley later explained what had happened. 'The deer appeared very quickly and skirted the area where I would have had a straightforward shot. It was all a bit of a blur, to be honest, as my heart was thrashing about in my chest. It then doubled back and stood with its head and neck between two trees. Steve whispered that I should take a neck shot and that was that.'

Steve was equally delighted. 'When you're stalking in woodland, you might only get one opportunity, and he took it well. Didn't hesitate at all. It was the right deer to take, as he's the old boy of the woods. One of its antlers was probably damaged in velvet and you can see where one point is growing down into his cranium. That must have been extremely painful. I've never seen one quite like that before.'

The stalker quickly paunched the carcass and Willow, who had been allowed to 'track' the animal, was presented with slices of kidney, so that she would learn to associate the smell of deer with a tasty reward. Ashley led the way on his bicycle as we carried his first roe buck from the woods. 'It will be a while before I wipe the smile off my face,' he said. 'The only problem is, I've now got a taste for it!'

Steve was pleased that we had achieved the result we had hoped for, but stressed that Ashley's unique condition was not proof that stalking is available for all. 'We would not have been able to stalk an animal on foot and Ashley certainly could not have tackled a beast on his own. We were fortunate too that the ground, weather and density of deer were in our favour.'

I was just relieved that it was successfully over. Once the relief subsided, I felt marginally peeved that on a balmy evening in July, it had taken Ashley ten minutes to achieve something I had struggled so hard for. Fate, whoever she is, works to her own agenda.

31.
Game fairs

As mentioned earlier, country shows were one of the highlights of the summer as a boy. Alongside the local town show at Aberfeldy, I would visit the county show in Perth and finally the national Royal Highland Show in Edinburgh. My mother is a leading breeder of Highland ponies, nurturing a bloodline of pretty, well-boned animals that have earned a reputation for high quality (I'm not just saying that because she's my mum!); so the agricultural shows were a three line whip for all the family. Often, I would be entered into a class or two myself aboard an unfortunate beast and we would languish together at the wrong end of the line. The rest of the time, when I was not watching the tug-of-war or terrier races, was spent visiting the array of trade stands on the hunt for freebies. To a ten-year-old, country shows are enormous. Tents and marquees tower above you, dwarfed by gleaming ploughs, threshers and combine harvesters that could gobble you up like a half-penny sweet. Even the stand owners – usually huge farmers standing like gorillas in a checked shirt – loomed over you from the top step of their cabin. 'Have you got any hats, stickers or badges?' we would chime hopefully. More often than not, they would, and our fingers would soon be cut by the weight of so many plastic bags filled with unwanted literature and a treasure trove of key-rings, plastic rulers and pens. The very best destinations, usually a leading tractor manufacturer such as Ford, CASE or John Deere, would hand out good quality cotton caps. It didn't get better than that and they would necessitate a second visit later in the day in the hope they had forgotten your face.

I also remember peering into the smoke-filled beer tents where most punters would eventually congregate, especially if it rained. Being a farmer can be a lonely life and these shows would provide an opportunity to see old faces and let off steam, which (so I learned later) would sometimes result in romance or confrontation.

Fast-forward twenty years to the modern day and country shows have not changed a great deal. There are still the same livestock shows, trade stands and beer tents, but now it does not seem so other-worldly. Every year for the past half decade, I have been to the CLA Game Fair, England's largest country show, as well as a few others dotted throughout the land. There is always a groan in the office when the CLA approaches, in recognition of being another year older, but it is usually a fun weekend. On a business point of view, it provides the opportunity to catch up with contacts and plan new features for the coming year. Instead of hats, stickers and badges, I trawl the stands searching for stories.

On one hot summer weekend, I visited the French Game Fair at the astonishing Chateau de Chambord near Paris. It is a smaller cousin of the British version, but none the worse for that. Indeed, it is altogether more manageable. Added to that, the French have a more relaxed attitude to fieldsports. For them, it is something that just is, rather than something that must be protected and defended. I doubt, for example, that the CLA would ever get permission to host a moving target range for high-powered sporting rifles. Likewise, children are encouraged to try all the weapons on offer, from shotguns and rifles to crossbows, blow-pipes, throwing knives and spears. I tried them all myself with mixed success, although I did break the show record for battle axe hurling. Everyone has a gift, I suppose, but it's just a shame mine isn't more mainstream! The French Game Fair does not boast the wide array of eats that one might imagine. Of course, most game is out of season in June, so there is none of that on offer. But if you go armed with a baguette, a lump of *pâté de campagne*, some *cornichons*, a bag of apricots and bottle of something cold and dry, then there are plenty of fine trees to lean back against that overlook the chateau. The hounds have gone to sleep, the shooters have stopped for lunch, the eyelids are growing heavy and it's time for *le snooze*.

If you can rouse yourself in the afternoon, the castle is well worth a visit. It was designed under the orders of Francis I in 1519 to be 'the most beautiful castle in the world'. When asked why he would start such a big project when he had no realistic chance of seeing it finished, the young king answered, 'if one is too occupied by the completion of anything, nothing would ever get started'. Quite. The location is relevant to the game fair, as the Parc de Chambord was originally a favoured hunting ground of Francis and the woods still run with deer and wild boar. It seems that Chambord was primarily a whim for the king, as he planned to use it as a hunting lodge. Yet at 8,700 square metres, with 77 staircases, 282 fireplaces and 426 rooms, it is not your average hunting lodge!

While it is easy to marvel at the opulence of the castle, I could not help thinking it was a little over-the-top. For all its beauty, there is a bit of the white elephant about it; a demonstration of power and wealth with very little practical purpose. Indeed, if you close your eyes on the staircase, you can almost sense the Fops flip-flopping about on the smooth steps in a cloud of perfume, powder and lace, all feeling rather clever about themselves. With every year that Chambord grew, so the gap between Have and Have-Not in France was widening, culminating in the bloody tipping point a few centuries later.

With unabashed hypocrisy, however, I was delighted to take my seat at a silver service dinner that accompanied the Saturday evening entertainment, while many thousands of other spectators sat on grass banks at the other side of the main ring. Fine wine accompanied a seafood starter with salmon, prawns and crab stacked on two chunky scallops. Pork chops with an exquisite veal and truffle vol-au-vent came next, topped off with goat's cheese and a gaudy chocolate tart. All I lacked was wig, 'kerchief and tights!

Various hunting acts are played out while you eat, peaking in a fireworks display. And what a display it was too! By that stage of the

At 'the most beautiful castle in the world'
Chambord in the Loire Valley.

evening, the sky is black above the chateau. It was the two hundred and fiftieth anniversary of Mozart's birth and his operatic works accompanied the barrage of screamers, explosions and multicoloured phizzers that rocketed above the old building. Often with fireworks there is an impressive beginning and a quick climax before the show quietly peters out to gentle applause. This was altogether different as wave after wave of pyrotechnic brilliance assaulted the eyes and ears. It just kept on coming at you until you wanted no more. I dare say even King Francis would have been impressed.

JANUARY
FEBRUARY
MARCH
APRIL
MAY
JUNE
JULY
AUGUST
SEPTEMBER
OCTOBER
NOVEMBER
DECEMBER

32.
Hedgelaying

Frank Malin paused to mop his brow, resting his sharp billhook on top of the umpteenth hedge that he had cut and laid in his eighty years. A mouthful from his tea flask, then his nimble hands were back on the job, slicing into the hawthorn pleachers with a trained eye. 'I've been doing this since I was a boy,' he said in a snatched interview, as all the competitors were working against the clock, and lost time can mean dropped points. 'Well over sixty years now. I suppose it is the clean nature of hedgelaying that I enjoy, and it's good exercise too. Keeps me out and about. There's a great deal of job satisfaction at the end as well.'

Frank was in the running for the veteran prize at the fifty-seventh running of the annual Yelvertoft and District Hedgelaying and Ploughing Association competition at Watford Gap farm near Daventry. Although some see the Watford Gap as the boundary between North and South, there is no such division in the hedgelaying world and all competitors are welcome, just so long as they adhere to the local rules.

My guide for the day was Tony Carter, chairman of the Yelvertoft branch and the National Hedgelaying Society, and a five times national champion who had competed on the circuit since 1950. When he started there were no chainsaws or hedgeclippers that are the staple in most garden sheds nowadays, but simply his pushbike, axe and billhook.

Tony suffers from arthritis in his hands and so can no longer mix it at the highest level, but today the Carter family were represented by his son Nigel, second at this year's national championships; the dynasty continues. This year there were 137 competitors at the national championships, held on HRH Prince Charles' Broadfield Farm in Gloucestershire, so interest in the pastime is still high. Even if Tony had known his passion would have led to the condition he now has, would he have reconsidered at the beginning? 'I wouldn't have changed a thing. I've that many good memories from hedgecutting. It is all about the characters you meet and the friends you make, because it is not about winning huge amounts of money. The winner will only ever get £25 or so. No, hedgelaying is all about the people, and there's non-stop ribbing, believe me. It's always "you could drive a bus through that" or "that's so rough, I could hang my coat on it". You meet some great characters. There was a kind old soul called Nelson Russell, who passed away last year at the age

of ninety-one years old. He left his body to science – what he thought they'd learn from it I don't know! At his wake, he made special provision for twenty gallons of cider, so we could have one last party on him. That's the way it is amongst hedgecutters.'

As we walked up the line of sixteen cutters who were each allocated a half chain (eleven yards) of worn-out hawthorn hedge to regenerate in three hours, Tony explained what was going on. The hedge was to be bound in the local style, known as Midland Bullock, originally designed to keep heavy bullocks in their field. This style is mainly found in Leicestershire, Northamptonshire, Oxfordshire and Warwickshire – traditional beef rearing areas – and has its stake sides facing the road or ploughed land. The brush is on the animal side to stop them eating new growth and the hedge slopes towards the animals. It has a strong twisted binding of woven branches below the top of the hedge, so that bullocks cannot twist it off with their horns.

As the hedgelayers are providing a good service for the farmer at a lower cost than contractors, there is no entry fee for competitors and the farmer provides stakes and binders to hold the new hedge in place. In this case, these were fashioned from pliable and durable hazel. Soup, sandwiches, locally-grown apples and a tin of bitter is also part of the deal.

Eighty-year-old Frank Malin has been hedgecutting for over sixty-five years.

A hedge is basically a row of living trees or shrubs that are linked together to form a 'stock-proof barrier'. The competitor will cut each tree bough in such a way that the plant is not fully severed, but will lean horizontally and pile upon its neighbour. The cut, called a pleach, must be clean, otherwise the tree will not continue to grow and add body to the living hedge. The stacked boughs, or pleachers, are laid uphill so that their sap can drain back to the roots during the dormant season. New stems shoot up vertically from the heel or stump, and from the *pleachers*, producing a lattice of diagonal and vertical stems, to create a very solid barrier. Does that make sense? Put very simply, you end up with a stack of live trees all growing on top of each other. Hedges, of course, differ depending on the stock enclosed, the area, soil and local tradition. Big animals, like bullocks or horses, can lean on hedges, so unless the hedge is tall, about 4ft 6in, laid away from the roots towards the animals, with close, well-driven stakes and a binding on top, the hedge can be broken, or even jumped. Sheep usually push through the base of a hedge, so it may be smaller, but must be tighter. Some areas have a lot of wind, so hedges tend to be laid low. Other areas have a lot of snow, so twigs are arranged to give a smooth, rounded top, so that the snow slides off. You get the picture.

Tall hedges tend to be more unstable. They also allow predators, such as crows and magpies, to gain access and kill eggs and nestlings of smaller birds, so they are not ideal havens for wildlife. A low, dense hedge lets in small birds, small mammals and insects, but keeps out predators, as there is not room for them to go between the twigs.

Once all the pleachers have been stacked, the cutter must then finish the hedge by tightly rolling and spiralling binders to keep it all in place. The competitors will be judged on their pleaching (thirty-five points), staking/binding (twenty-five points) and conformation (twenty points), i.e. whether it is bushy at the back and smooth at the front; and a final twenty points for overall neatness.

'The good cutters will make sure they are done a good hour before the finish time, and you can then use that time to touch up and make everything pretty for the judges,' said Tony. 'Of course, an experienced hand will know ways of making things look better than they are with dead wood, but judges have a good eye for any of that. Cheating is allowed, as long as you are not caught! There is luck involved too, as the plots are drawn by lot and you may get better natural material to work with than your opponents. The best thing you can get is a couple of rough ones either side, so you look good!'

Once the hedge has been laid, it will be unrecognisable within twelve months. 'You come back next year and you'll not know we were ever here,' said Tony. 'Instead there'll be a lovely bushy hedge.'

33.
Eating game

The Glorious Twelfth is a symbol of how shooting has decreased in the nation's consciousness. Before the Second World War, there would have been very few people who didn't know about the start of the August grouse season. Newspapers would record the respective bags shot by gentlemen on each estate, while crowds in London met the trains south from Scotland, Northumberland and Yorkshire carrying the precious cargo for the dining tables of the well-to-do. People near the moors would bunk off work to join the beating line or watch the Guns. Ask someone in the street today when the shooting season starts and many will give you a blank look. Some do still have an inkling. 'It's the Magnificent Seventh, isn't it? Or the Famous Fifth.' If they do get the day right, fewer still will know the month or the species. Scottish newspapers carry an article reminding the nation of the big day, but it usually comes with a paragraph about the expense involved or speculation about raptor abuse by keepers. It certainly doesn't get the respect it once did.

The reason is simple. Fewer people care any more. The idea of shooting a live animal is a disgusting prospect to many. Those that don't object on moral grounds would probably have no concept of how to get themselves in the position to point a gun at a bird or beast in the first place. Meat is something you buy in a shop, sat in a plastic tub on a sanitary towel, so even the blood is hidden. There are no feathers, no fur, no guts or lifeless eyes. No bones either if you prefer. There is no emotional connection to the clucking, oinking, or bleating donor and that's the way the consumer wants it.

I'm not trying to lecture or chide here. Apart from anything else, if you have read this far, then I doubt you live your life entirely wrapped in cellophane. Besides, I have walked into a supermarket on many occasions and picked out a packet of bacon or pork sausages without giving a moment's thought to the piggy (or several piggies) that they belonged to last week.

So much has been done in the last decade to further the cause of game, especially by the Countryside Alliance's Game-to-Eat campaign and there are signs that tastes are changing. Celebrity chefs enjoy a massive following and many of the big names have come out in favour of wild food, including game. Some have even been filmed with gun in hand procuring meat for the table. Ever keen to join the bandwagon, I once covered a day's shooting in Perthshire with a team of budding chefs, who were astounded at the lengths it took to down a pheasant or deer. The message seems to be getting across to the public, although so much of the posh nosh on the TV remains beyond the budget of many.

Ten years ago, a carrot was simply called a carrot. It did not matter where it came from or who had sown, picked or processed it – it was just a carrot. But nowadays many shoppers and diners are much more enlightened. They want to know that the carrot that is in their basket or on their plate has been well tended from seed to fork. A small detail will usually suffice, such as 'grown in Norfolk' or 'finest Welsh' but at least it tells the consumer that somebody somewhere is accountable for the standard of produce. Often an establishment will put the name of the farm or a smiling picture of the farmer himself on the package or menu to show exactly where the carrot came from.

So it goes on up the food chain. How much less appealing is 'Sunday Roast' compared with 'tender Black-faced lamb from the Lake District with Herefordshire new potatoes with a julienne of locally-picked carrots'? And game has to join the party. Highland venison, Rutland partridge, West Country rabbit, Cotswold pheasant – the possibilities are endless – but they are all tags that can help the consumer identify with where their food has come from.

On one Glorious Twelfth, I managed to gain access to the famous Drumlanrig estate, part of the Duke of Buccleuch's property in the Borders, to write an article on the traceability of game. The idea was to demonstrate the food chain by following by this unique bird from moor to plate. There is always something just a bit special about being up on the hill at the start of the shooting season. The cloud lifted before the first drive to reveal the full range of colours across the moor. It was warm enough to make the beaters perspire as their lungs remembered the energy needed to stride across the heather, flag cracking overhead; but sufficient breeze to keep the midges from massing an attack.

I stood next to the estate manager Roy Green, listening to his radio crackle with anxious voices from along the beating line as the headkeeper and his beatkeepers willed grouse to fly forward to the Guns. 'We really cannot be sure how many birds we have, but the most important thing about today is that we are up here at all,' he said. 'The Guns know that too so there is no pressure.'

When I joined the beating line for the second drive, it was easy to see what an important role the local shooting estate can play in the lives of the community. From thirteen-year-old Kieron Allison, known as Harry Potter because of his round glasses, to sixty-plus Rab Bell who was manning the game cart, there were well over thirty folk involved in sending the birds over the Guns, and picking them up at the other side.

Jimmy Routledge, a forty-two-year-old beatkeeper who had come late into the gamekeeping world after a career working on the council roads, kept the line straight with his Sergeant-Major's rap. 'It couldn't get much more different from being in a cab all day, to working out on the hill. I've learned so much in the last five years and I am very grateful to Buccleuch for giving me the opportunity.'

We approached within 150 yards of the butts and a horn blew instructing the Guns to shoot only once the birds were behind them. A covey of eight birds sprang up from under my feet, causing me to jump, and flew hard over the two middle butts with Jimmy and Kieron flagging them forward. Four shots rang out and three birds fell to the heather. At the end of the drive, picker-up Jean Mudford sent forth her Labradors Ruby and Sally to fetch them in.

Jean's grandmother used to live in Knightsbridge and would greet the London train on the Twelfth to ensure there were grouse on her table for guests that evening. 'It was one of those things she just did. For myself, a young bird on the Twelfth is as good as it gets. Some people say you should keep it a few days but I can't wait. Just roast it in a hot oven for ten minutes, no longer, and it is sublime.'

The three birds were quickly relayed to game cart man Rab Bell who laid them out to cool. He pushed the back of each bird's head to test the softness of the skull and when his thumb met little resistance, he gave a satisfied grunt to say they were all fine young birds. 'It is important to give them plenty of space and air to cool down,' he said, carefully positioning each bird on a crate to aid the process. 'We try to get them out of game bags as quickly as possible, which are preferably made of netting. We all must adopt the mindset that as soon as a bird is killed it is classed as food, and must be treated accordingly.'

While the temptation was there to enjoy a lazy lunch and snooze a while in a heather bed, we needed to get our birds off the hill if they were to be eaten in an Edinburgh restaurant before closing time. The day had been organised by a bear of a man called Craig Stevenson, director of Braehead Foods, a specialist game processing plant in Kilmarnock. Like an ambulance with a donor kidney, Craig drove the precious cargo at breakneck speed to his factory south of Glasgow. 'Until you talk to these restaurant chefs, you don't quite realise in what high esteem seasonal foods such as game are held,' said Craig, as one of his employees worked the plucking machine that takes under thirty seconds to defrock a grouse. 'Most chefs would like to have a game dish on the menu, whether it is rabbit, hare, pigeon, venison or grouse – depending on the time of year.' Before the minute was up, the bird had been drawn and decapitated, although the lack of time spared it a hanging. Within just a few hours, all three of those young grouse that had been wild and free in the morning, were packaged in cellophane with a loud sticker saying exactly where and when they had been shot.

'So much of the game that is shot in this country goes abroad, but we are trying to address the home market, as there should be no need to export it,' Craig continued. 'The challenge we face, is that we tend to be preaching to the converted. It is not *Shooting Times* readers that need to be told to eat game. But if they were reading about the quality of game meats on the streets of Easterhouse in Glasgow, then we would be making great strides forward.'

The final stage was to deliver our babies to the Grain Store restaurant in Edinburgh, one of the Old Town's finest eateries. The Grassmarket and Royal Mile were heaving with festival goers, many en route for the castle's Tattoo. Given the scarcity of grouse this year, it was a valuable package indeed that we transported through the Capital. With such a build up throughout the day, there was the risk of anti-climax if an old boot had appeared on the table, but the chef Ben Waumsley served up a treat. 'It is always a great pleasure to cook grouse as the flavours are so unique. We also find here that all other game dishes, especially pheasant and partridge in season, are extremely popular.'

Jean would certainly have enjoyed the Grain Store House Grouse, as it was cooked to perfection, with its pink juices still running. And yes, it does taste that little bit better when you know exactly where it comes from.

My job has taken me into some privileged positions. Roast grouse cooked by a top chef on the twelfth of August counts as one of the jammiest of all.

34.
Red stags

When I was in my early teens my father took me out on the hill to shoot a deer. At the time, I thought he was going to pull the trigger, so I was pretty relaxed as we crawled up on a group of young stags some three hundred yards away. We tried to stalk up on them a couple of times, but each time they moved on and we gave up.

Only later did he admit that he would have passed me the rifle at the last moment, as he didn't want me to be too nervous on the stalk itself. It could have been a poignant moment in my upbringing, but it was not to be. In hindsight, if I had shown more enthusiasm, we would probably have gone back up again, but like a truculent teenager, I wasn't fussed, so the experiment ended there. I was showing very little interest in shooting or fishing, two pastimes which my father adores, and he understandably didn't want to force the issue.

Back then, you would have got very long odds on me becoming a shooting journalist. I probably wanted to be anything but. The future has a funny way of surprising you and some fifteen years later I was back up on the hill with my father after stags in Perthshire. This time, I had a notebook in my pocket and PQ by my side, as we set off into the hills above Loch Tay on Remony estate. There would be no chance to pass on the rifle either, as head stalker Angus Hogg was calling the shots. As a boy, I had worked as a beater on Remony with Angus in charge and I remembered him as a very fair figure of authority. But someone to be obeyed none the less. It felt good to be back there as a guest rather than a lagging employee.

Red deer stalked.

With thirty-six years of experience as a stalker and gamekeeper, we couldn't have been in better hands. My father has long shot deer in this part of Perthshire and has known Angus for many years, but there was only one person in charge of the show when the stalk was on. 'As the man with the rifle, you have to know when to follow orders,' he said. 'After all, you are often nothing more than the artillery once the stalker has found the beast to shoot. No matter how well you know the stalker or the relationship off the hill, when the stalk is on, he is in charge.'

Our day had started in the best possible weather, with the mountains lit up and Ben Lawers the only peak in the clouds. Loch Tay was like a

With my father and his stag.

sheet of dark glass, reflecting the pine-clad slopes that rise sharply from her banks. Climbing the bumpy track from the house to the hill, it was easy to imagine the sedate procession of the Victorian shooting parties that would have turned these quiet glens into a frenzy of activity all those years ago. As can so often be the case, the deer were not exactly where Angus had hoped they would be for the ideal stalk, so he quickly turned to Plan B. 'It seems they have all bunched up together, probably because of activity from shepherds gathering their sheep, so we're not going to be able to go in at them from the usual direction,' he said resignedly, pointing to a different corrie that would involve more legwork. 'They are all up near the top to get away from the flies.'

If the deer would not read from the script, Angus was prepared to interact with the herd to move them where he wanted them. 'If we cannot get access to them, I'm going to have to bring them into the wind, either

Trying out the rifle for size.

by a short whistle, a squeak on grass or tapping two stones – just enough so that they prick their ears, get suspicious and draw into the wind. That should give us a chance to creep in behind them.'

As we climbed the burn to get closer to a possible target, Angus was constructing his plan of attack. 'You have to think of it like a snooker player – you need to play your pot with a second shot in mind. Too often a young stalker will go for an all or nothing stalk, not thinking about what happens next if the deer move, as is usually the case.'

PQ and I were left to laze in the lea of a peat hag while the two senior pros, with over 130 years between them, went forward. Within five minutes I heard the deeper breathing of a photographer asleep! With so many deer about, it took Angus a good hour of hiking and crawling to find the correct beast and get in range. Happily, Valentine Senior did the rest.

The crack of the rifle brought PQ back to his senses, as the boom ricocheted off the steep slopes. Seconds later a new noise filled the damp air, causing the hair to rise on the back of the neck. It was soft at first, as though seagulls were calling on a distant shoreline, but we were about as far from the sea as you can be in Scotland. The murmurs grew quickly into a loud and constant wail, sad and haunting in the drizzle that had swept in across the hills. It seemed the whole glen was alive with a soulful, plaintive song that railed against what had just happened.

PQ was wide awake now and we shared a worried glance, both ignorant of what had happened. It was a sound I will never forget, as if the hills were alive with sobbing ghosts. Only later did my father explain. As the unfortunate deer fell, so the other groups of deer herded together in a hidden corrie, creating a gathering of up to one thousand animals. Amid the mêlée, lost calves were crying for their mothers, causing the haunting song that shot shivers up the spine.

It would be a while after that before I got the opportunity to bag my first stag. There were pleasant days spent in the hills above Loch Ness and various destinations in Speyside, as well as a trip to view hybrid red deer (crossed with Sika deer) in the Wicklow Mountains below Dublin. On one stalk, there was high drama as the paying guest shot the stag too high on the shoulder, sending the bullet through the meat below the spine. For all money, it looked as if the beast was dead, but it was only stunned, tripping forward to snag its antlers in the heather. When the stalker prodded it with his stick for a photograph, the animal leapt up, causing both snapper and stalker to scatter. Ordinarily, the stalker would still be holding the rifle and would have dispatched the stag if it moved. But because of our media meddling, he had left the weapon with the client. The stalker drew his knife from its sheaf and strode down the hill after the giddy stag that was doubtless in extreme pain. The plan was to stick the blade between the vertebrae below the neck, severing the spinal cord, much like the Pamplona *estocada*. The stag had now sat back on its backside and as the stalker made to strike, it used its antlers to toss him ten feet down a bank. Given the antler points or the knife itself could have done untold damage, our man was lucky to avoid injury. Undeterred, he approached the beast from a different angle and dispatched it. 'That wasn't supposed to happen!' he said afterwards, with a rueful grin.

My opportunity for a stag finally came a few years later on the historic Atholl Estates near Pitlochry in Perthshire. I was under the watchful eye of Sandy Reid, head honcho on Forest Lodge, one of six beats on the sprawling property. Sandy makes stalking look easy. There is no fuss or bother, just a determination to enjoy the day on the hill and a confidence that the opportunity for a shot will eventually arrive. With over forty years on the same patch, perhaps it is no great surprise.

Sandy's relaxed demeanour was inherited from old keepers such as Willie McLauchlan and Fergus Ferguson who taught him the ropes as a teenager. 'They were never short of a story or two,' Sandy recalled, as we went in search of stags. 'I learnt that you have to be so much more than a stalker. The guests who stay in the lodges here are on holiday at the end of the day, so you try and show them a good time. Too often you see young lads who are too intense and worried about getting a stag. As a result, the client is uptight. You must tell the Rifle what you plan to do and why – involve them in the process. And it never hurts to tell a few stories about the glen or a certain river or bothy, even if they are made up. For example, there is an old stone which looks a lot like a gravestone. I always tell Germans that any Rifle that misses a stag will be buried there. They hoot with laughter. You have to make it fun – the stag will take care of itself. Besides, there are many clients who will have a great day on the hill, even without firing a shot.'

We spent the morning trying to get in on a herd on a plateau, but to no avail. There is always something to see though. A pair of golden plovers screamed abuse at us, although we were unable to see any chicks. 'I won't let anyone shoot them here,' Sandy said. 'I can't think why anyone would want to.'

We also surprised a family of grouse: a cock, hen and eight bundles of fluff that were able to flutter for a few yards before diving down into the heather. 'Well done, mum and dad,' the stalker said with affection. 'You two look after them now.'

Later, we skirted an ancient dug-out in the heather that once served as a trench for musketeers, who would lie in wait for stags driven up the hill. The beasts would appear at the top of the hill to be met by a barrage of smoke and lead. Any wounded animals would be set upon by shaggy deerhounds. Today the plan was to get within 150 yards with a high-powered rifle, a much more efficient culling method, if I could shoot straight. Two ravens circled above us throughout the day, fully aware of what we hoped to achieve. 'They're not stupid,' Sandy said. 'They know exactly what's waiting for them if we get a stag. I remember once on a dark overcast day we were struggling to locate beasts, so we sat down to have

Stalker Sandy Reid who led me to my first stag.

our piece. These two ravens came and sat on a rock not fifty yards from us. They kept croaking at us as if to say: "Come on then lads. Quit hanging about!"'

In the early afternoon, Sandy spied a group of stags in a favoured lay-up and he moved round beneath them, so they would not see or wind us. Approaching from a dry burn we were out of sight and smell. As long as the swirling breeze did not change direction, we were in business. After glassing the site for what seemed an eternity, Sandy eased backwards down the bank on his belly like a crocodile in reverse. He grinned, raised his eyes to the heavens, and then motioned that I bring the rifle over to him. 'The good news is that there are plenty of stags in shooting range,' he whispered, clicking forward the bipod stand of the Tikka 22.06. 'The bad news is that the old chap with the switch antlers, who would have been perfect for you and who was standing just right for a shot; has sat down. We may get another chance though, so we'll get you in position.'

I squirmed up the bank to lie next to the stalker, poking my head over the top for the first time. There were over twenty beasts, no more than one hundred yards away, most of which were lying down. 'Get yourself comfortable,' Sandy hissed, 'you've plenty of time.' Pushing the rifle butt into my shoulder, I looked down the

My first stag on Atholl Estates.
Sadly it was not with my father.

'scope. There was a stag staring directly back at me. There was less time than we thought. 'That's your one,' Sandy whispered. 'He's seen us so take him now if you're ready.'

It was an ideal shot for a first-timer. A close, big target with no time to get nervous! Only once the shot had hit the target did I own up that it was my first stag. For the umpteenth time that day, Sandy's face lit up with a broad grin. 'Why didn't you tell me? Well, then, you know what's coming next,' he said, scooping a dab of blood from the bullet's exit wound and painting it on my cheeks.

I was delighted with the stag, but a little piece of me was still guilty that it had not been my father who had blooded me all those years before.

35.
Cockers

Cartoonists are forever having fun at the expense of dog owners, portraying them as their pets. From the hunched-over neurotic whippet lover to the shaven-headed tattooed bulldog man, or even George W Bush's poodle, it is a winning formula. If there was ever a need for the archetypal cocker spaniel owner, then the artist would need look no further than a trainer and breeder I met in Dorset for a day's rabbiting.

John Corps shares many of the cocker characteristics with his beloved dogs. Small, compact, yet charged with vitality, he carries an air of quiet mischief. (Although that could be due to his looking very similar in appearance to the comic legend Norman Wisdom.) The immaculate, preening springer spaniel owners have a reputation for looking down on their scruffy cocker cousins, but it is a stereotype that sits well with John. 'You can always tell a cocker owner from a springer,' he said, wearing a favourite old shirt and a pair of worn trousers. 'The cocker man always has muddy paw-prints where the dog has jumped up. You can't stop them doing it. It is part of their nature to be tactile and seek social interaction for reassurance.'

We were joined by his long-time buddy Lyn Randall and between them they had four of the eager rabbiters, as well as an adorable pup called Rooney, all willing to be the one let off the leash. Lyn likewise had muddy trousers. 'The Queen is a great cocker woman,' Lyn said, releasing her black bitch Molly and sending her out into a field of golden corn. 'She once saw me at a trial with a cocker jumping up and said: "oh don't worry. I've got nine at home that do that."'

'Oh, yes, Her Majesty is a true cocker enthusiast,' added John, 'and a very fine handler. She has been down at Broadlands a few times and always looks so natural and relaxed, with a broad grin, chatting about cockers.'

Molly reached the edge of the corn field and bounded in, disappearing from view. But soon, it looked as if some dark, sinister creature was swimming through the sea of gold, invisible save for the rustle of corn swept aside as the deadly predator probed the depths for signs of prey. No dorsal fin, but two curly ears would break the surface as this shark of the undergrowth leapt high to chart her progress. The movement in the crops pronounced the speed and agility of a hunting cocker spaniel. Molly the black Exocet was moving through the gears as she locked on to the

John Corps looks on as Molly bounces through a field of gold.

heat of a hiding rabbit. 'They really speed up when they catch the scent of game,' whispered John, getting caught up in the excitement. Lyn gave instructions to her dog while John stood on guard, shotgun at the ready in case a fleeing rabbit bolted from the corn.

That morning, John and Lyn had demonstrated their training routines to get the dogs in peak condition. A stretch of common heath land provides the ideal practice ground for cockers to hone their skills. John will come up here at six o'clock in the morning and evening to give each of the dogs a half-hour hunt every day. The scent of rabbit is stronger at this time and he will send the dogs out to quarter through the heather, their keen noses leading them round and over clumps of heather and thorn bushes that might be impenetrable to larger dogs.

172

'The cockers are trained to hunt within a certain range so that if the rabbit gets up I will be able to have both barrels at it if needs be. They were built for this sort of work, so there is little point in putting them out to train on a flat, open field, as it will do little for their fitness. Most of the trainers go up to Yorkshire at this time of year to hunt bunnies in the heather as there's nothing like it to get a cocker in shape. It does us no harm either, as it makes you lift your feet. You can always spot a Yorkshire 'keeper in the street as he's the one walking with his knees up.'

It was a stiflingly hot day, so the owners were careful to use the cockers in short bursts. It seems these whole-hearted companions do not know the meaning of half-cocked and will launch themselves into any task with scant regard for their own well-being. 'It is important to build up their stamina before the season starts,' John explained, as the other spaniels strained at their leads in jealous enthusiasm. 'Especially if they are going after grouse in heather as they will not be able to retrieve a bird if they are gasping all the time.'

Why cockers? What was wrong with a strong springer or a dependable Labrador? 'I don't think you choose them, they choose you,' said John. 'And once you're hooked, that's it for life. I'd also say it is because they are such fun dogs and so optimistic. That's why they will run all day for you, even when they are worn out.'

Lyn reckoned you need a good sense of humour to be a cocker owner. 'They will infuriate you at times and ignore your commands. Even the most decorated trial dog will run in or chase a rabbit from time to time, but if you can't deal with that, go for something else. They've got great heart. Real triers. Molly once retrieved a big old goose, much bigger than her. When she realised she couldn't physically pick it up, she grabbed it by the neck and pulled it towards me!'

And what makes a good cocker handler? 'As long as you are patient with the dog and don't dampen its natural instinct, then it will work for you,' said John. 'Unlike the Labrador, for example, I don't tend to do any obedience until the dog has learned to hunt. If you try to dominate the cocker pup and curb its spirit with "sit" and "stay" exercises, then it will think bugger this and you've lost him. In that respect they are very similar to flatcoat retrievers, as they will be independent and let you down sometimes, but when they come good, there is nothing better.' Swimming can also be an excellent way to build up the fitness of any animal, but spaniels in particular. 'On a hot day like this, they love it,' said Lyn earlier,

Close-up of Molly.

as Polly, a tan coloured bitch, dived off a bridge into the Itchen, scattering the minnows as she paddled towards a floating pheasant dummy. 'They are terrific water dogs anyway and it is worth getting their muscles used to this exercise. One of the best techniques is to throw a dummy over a stream, as they have to then get it, swim across, get out and come back again, dummy in mouth. This lot love going after ducks and will swim down underwater for any that are pricked.'

With age, it seemed the dogs developed a more relaxed, smooth swimming style, while the younger retrievers were more ungainly, if no less effective. Most energetic was twelve-week-old Rooney, named after the footballer (perhaps more pit-bull than spaniel?) who was dunked under for his maiden bath. He thrashed around for a while, eyes wide open in panic, but instinct soon took over and he quickly paddled to shore. 'He looks like a drowned rat, poor mite,' laughed John, as Rooney padded over for attention. 'A regular swim can do them good though, especially at this time of year when they're shedding hair – it helps keep the coat fresh. I quite often line them out on this bridge and send them off to retrieve, one at a time, while the others sit and watch. It helps teach them that not every bird is theirs.'

Back in the corn field, Molly was clearly on something. The sweep through the corn had gone up a notch in pace and there was less zigzagging. John sensed this and was ready when the first of two rabbits emerged from the thick stalks and into the sunlit ride at the edge of the field. Molly was just behind them and like us, stopped dead, waiting to see how John would shoot. She would not be disappointed. The first shot was an outright kill, sending the rabbit bowling to a standstill. The second rabbit was moving fast towards the safety of a thorn bush as John fired, and was hidden from view.

Molly waited for the signal to retrieve, before bounding forward out of the corn and diving straight for the rabbit. For some reason, best known only to her, she darted to and fro, just ten feet from the still corpse, as though she had found some new scent. Had she but looked up she would have seen her target. Instead, she looked back to her mistress, who gesticulated that the bunny was further away. Molly reacted to the signal, picked the rabbit and returned as quickly as her legs would carry her, her jaws holding the prize.

John then sent his roan cocker Kate – posh name Petronella – to investigate where the second rabbit had gone. Again, like a midget sleuth, she scoped out the area, following various leads and a couple of dead ends, before appearing from the thicket with a dead bunny. John and Lyn were delighted. 'The best thing about that was the lack of noise,' said John proudly. 'There was no barking or whining or shouting by us. It was all done by hand movements or the whistle. That's the sign of a well-trained dog.'

I left Hampshire that evening hooked on cocker spaniels. Indeed, it was a good thing I didn't have a spare six hundred pounds in my back pocket or I might have gone home with a pup in the boot. And poor old Rooney would have got a new name…

JANUARY
FEBRUARY
MARCH
APRIL
MAY
JUNE
JULY
AUGUST
SEPTEMBER
OCTOBER
NOVEMBER
DECEMBER

36.
Ploughing

The full title of my paymaster is *The Shooting Times and Country Magazine*, so the remit does have potential to cover all countryside pursuits. However, I have rarely been allowed to do an article without some sort of hunting-based activity involved, which is a pity, in my opinion, as rural Britain is riddled with quirky, colourful traditions that capture the local identity and provide ample ammunition for a feature writer or photographer. Cheese-rolling, worm-charming, eel pie-eating, to name but a few, are still on my 'to do' list.

One idea I did manage to shoehorn past my editor into the 'Country' category was tractor ploughing. Like most small boys raised in a farming community, tractors were about as good as it could get. Riding in the cab by your father or bumping about on the trailer behind made you feel important, useful and grown-up. I remember with awe the day when my father upgraded from the old Massey Ferguson and Davey Brown to buy a monster red Zetor with an enclosed cab. It even had a radio!

I could never claim to be an experienced tractor driver though and my shallow knowledge was highlighted at the annual ploughing match held by the Banbury & District Vintage Ploughing Society. Over sixty tractors with ploughs from the same era, lovingly restored and handled by proud owners, competed for the opportunity to test their skills against the very best at the fifty-fifth National Ploughing Championships.

While a handful of big guns were entered in the top qualifier class, most of the competitors were simply there for the satisfaction of running their tractors and catching up with old friends. Little did I know that I was entering into a murky world of underhand tactics and skullduggery. In ploughing, he who cheats wins!

For the uninitiated, as I was, the basic object of ploughing is to turn and aerate surface soil, thereby burying plant growth and vegetable rubbish underneath the surface where it will decompose. The competitors are judged to this end. 'Exactness is of the essence and every blade of grass and stubble on the plot must be buried within a specified time limit, furrows must be identical and straightness is paramount,' is the neat explanation in the guidelines from the Weald of Kent Ploughing Match Association. Prize money is minimal.

My guide for the day was sixty-seven-year-old Arthur Parrish, a wily old

Arthur Parrish, in the middle, explained the dark arts of ploughing.

cove who had been ploughing in the area since he was a lad. Although his competitive days are now behind him, Arthur still has an eye for a straight furrow and a nose for the dark arts of top class ploughing. 'He'd have been better staying at home to dig the garden,' he whispered, as we passed one set of grooves that did not impress. 'You see they're not an even depth and there's a kink half way up. The judges will be all over that.'

Massey Fergusons, Internationals, Fordsons, David Browns, Ford, Ferguson, County and John Deere tractors, all dating before 1960, were slugging it out as their owners craned their necks back to ensure the ploughs were kept on a steady path. Once the competition starts, no outside help is allowed, so it is all about the man and his tractor.

'The great fear you have is that you will break down,' said Arthur. 'Nobody can help you so all of these drivers are expert mechanics too. But these are old machines, and they can't go on forever, so the challenge is finding the right spare bits. You have to spend a lot of time rooting round farm sales or breakers' yards.'

While ploughing is a male-dominated sport, women have long been involved, especially as many learned the trade as land girls during the War years. Jean Basely, one of the supervisors charged with ensuring no misdemeanours take place while the judges' backs are turned, is still an active plougher, who Arthur fondly refers to as 'paraffin Jean'.

'There are a fair number of ladies who plough and we're often a lot better than the men,' she said. 'There's a few men who don't like being shown up by a girl and would still rather it was men-only, so I only really do it for the devilment.'

At the start of the day, all the competitors are allocated a plot by drawing lots. As with the hedge layers, luck can play a part. 'There are times when you don't stand a chance,' said Arthur ruefully, no doubt recalling times when he was stuffed from the start, 'but on other occasions you can be in the best place, and the pressure is then on to perform.' At one end of the field, where the top dogs were ploughing, the dry, sandy soil was easily carved, but further down the slope, it was like pushing a cold knife through treacle.

Tom Baimbridge was at the sticky end where the mud caked on his boots. 'It is just the luck of the draw,' he said cheerfully, 'and you can see that my furrows are no good at all. Up at that end though, I bet their mouldboards are still shiny, while I have to clean mine with a spade every few minutes. But there's no point moping about it. Ploughing has always been just a bit of fun for me on a Sunday morning.'

It may have been a step back in time, but these machines were once the pinnacle of modern engineering. 'It is almost impossible nowadays to appreciate the difference that the arrival of the steam engine, and latterly the combustion engine, brought to agriculture. To the farmers of the time it must have been like us going to the moon,' I was later told by Robert Oliver, chairman of the Steam Plough Club and editor of the quarterly *Steam Plough Times*. 'Prior to that it was all done by hand with an ox or horse, and it took eighteen miles of walking to plough just one acre. You never saw many old ploughmen in those days – they had all walked themselves to death.' Arthur agreed that the romantic notion of the happy ploughman, with a red hanky round his neck, leading his trusty Shire horse through the fields, was utter tripe. 'It was a hard existence. I remember it as a lad. They'd have to drag the ponies to the field. It was back breaking work. But the tractor changed all that.'

While the match was a light-hearted friendly affair, it seems that ploughing, like many motor sports, is not one for saints. After all, rules are there to be broken. 'There are rules and there are rules,' revealed Arthur with a boyish grin. 'I don't know a single ploughman who doesn't go in for a bit of gardening with his boot, when the judge's back is turned. And if you go up into Yorkshire, that lot are criminals. There's a hell of a lot of gardening goes on up there.' Arthur started to warm to his role as whistleblower, waving his hands in excitement. 'Oh yes, there's all sorts goes on when the judge isn't looking! One trick is to move the guidance sticks of your neighbour to make them plough squint. You'd only do it to your friends though. That's the thing about ploughing, you see. We all have a great deal of fun and you make smashing friends. That's what it's all about.'

Final word goes to the ladies of the tuck van (because they said they would hunt me down if I didn't give them a mention). Serena Rees and Lucy Schultz and their burger van are devoted followers of the local ploughmen, turning out in all weathers to provide sustenance for the club members. Thank you also for the apple crumble – it was delicious!

37.
Driven grouse

While grouse may be famous for the twelfth of August, it is rare that they are shot so early nowadays. Back in the past, the great Shots would have needed to have their fill of grouse before the grey partridge season started in September. Partridge would tail off in time for the pheasants in October and November. By Christmas time they would be deaf as gateposts and bloated with gout.

Fanatics will still insist on shooting a grouse on the Twelfth, just as addict salmon fishermen will brave the January chills to be out on the first day of the season. Wildfowlers worth their salt will also camp out on the evening of 31 August, excitable as school children in anticipation of the first duck of the season, despite knowing they will probably see nothing more than the moon. In recent years, with the unseasonable warm weather, partridge and pheasant shooters have been organising days later in the year, so that the trees have finally shed their leaves. Many have called for a postponement of the seasons to start the pheasants in November instead of October, ending in February and not January.

Both times (excepting the morning at Drumlanrig, as described earlier)

I have written up an account of grouse shooting, the day has taken place in September, so it makes sense in my mind to mention it now. The first was at a famous estate called Danby on the North Yorkshire Moors, one of my favourite regions in England. I stayed the evening before with a wonderful family nearby who ran a B&B on their farm. The owners were in their thirties with three small children and they took on paying guests in their spare rooms as a supplement to their income. They gave me the choice of eating in the dining room with four German hikers or taking my chances in the kitchen maelstrom with them. It was, as they say, a no-brainer. Indeed, during a particularly hectic moment, I ended up serving the Germans their pudding, pretending to be a brother of the hosts.

In the morning, I was rewarded with the biggest of breakfasts – eggs, bacon, sausages, black pudding, potato scones and mushrooms – which I nobly dispatched. It was very kind, but exactly the last thing you want when climbing steep hills! When I first arrived at *Shooting Times*, the seasoned reporter and ex-editor Tony Jackson advised me to keep off the fried breakfasts or it would be the death of me. To date, this sound advice has been mostly unheeded, I'm afraid, not least because it can be rude to say 'no thanks' when it is put in front of you.

My brief was to stick with the beaters and keepers. On the way to the first drive, I climbed into a Land Rover with a handful of beaters and introduced myself, no doubt sounding like a Surrey plum. 'Where do you live?' asked a suspicious Yorkshire voice from behind a prickly moustache. 'London,' I replied, wishing I hadn't. 'Like that Tony Blair,' the moustache continued. 'It's a good thing you're not that Tony Blair, otherwise we would have buried you on the moors.' Unable to think of anything clever to say in retort, I kept quiet. I was delighted when the action finally started.

For nearly fifteen minutes the line of beaters pressed forward towards the stone butts with coveys of grouse lifting and dropping, edging ever closer to the hidden Guns. But not one bird had yet flown the gauntlet and not one shot had been fired. It was the calm before the storm, when the mouth is dry and the breath short. All of the bluster and bravado in the vehicles to the moor was forgotten as each Gun braced himself for the action that was about to begin.

The plan was to steadily push the grouse forward, with the idea that they will fill up in front of the Guns. Once there, the line could tip-toe the last few hundred yards so the birds would trickle through at regular intervals, instead of all making a dash for freedom at the same time. 'Well, that's the idea, at least,' explained Peter Snaith, headkeeper on Danby moor. In the distance, the dark North Sea was leaning up against Whitby Bay. At least six-foot-two, broad and purposeful, Peter makes a formidable sight striding across the heather in his traditional hob-nailed boots, with Fern, his four year-old retriever, bouncing along by his side. He was also as gruff as a prize billy goat.

Peter had arrived with the Guns, so had to skirt up the side of the drive to meet the beating team half-way, barking orders on his radio to his underkeepers to ensure steady progress. The outer perimeter of the drive was marked with old white boundary stones, similar to the dreaded out-of-bounds markers on a golf course. They had no doubt kept Victorian beaters and flankers on the straight and narrow all those years ago. Nowadays the public highway provides a more permanent boundary and the first of the morning's purple anoraks were stretching their legs. Perhaps it was my Germans from the night before.

Every fifty yards or so along Peter's path, there were small, charred heather mounds, like giant cigarette burns on a tweed skirt. These were grouse picnic tables covered in grit. 'It is their knife and fork to digest the heather,' Peter said pointing out the green fronds and seeds that form the diet of these delicate game birds. 'We get through tons of it, and each bag has to be lifted by hand, mind. We tend to put grit on newly burned heather on a little raised mound, as the grouse feel more secure. The three most important aspects to grouse management are vermin, heather and gritting. A lot of people swear by the medicated grit, but to be honest, if you have the ground well managed, with enough young birds breeding, then simple grit should be sufficient.' As the other beaters drew level with Peter, he joined the line, each of the white flags dressing into pace with the headkeeper's orange flag. 'I get an orange one, so they know who's boss,' Peter growled. 'If it's waving wildly at them, they know they're in trouble.'

The temperature was cool but not cold, typical of September in Yorkshire and perfect conditions for shooting. Peter explained that Danby will rarely shoot early in the season, as the birds are not keen to play the game. 'Grouse round here really come into their own in September and October as in August they can be too soft and won't fly. It tends to be too hot then and they are too used to humans, especially with all the summer hillwalkers and birdwatchers in these parts. But by this time of year they are properly wild.'

The first covey broke cover from the heather and skimmed over the middle butts. There was a flurry of shots and three birds dropped: two in front and one behind. It was a good start and sign of the sharp shooting to come. I watched one of the Guns in action, dressed in a light brown sweater, tweed breeks and a pointed tweed cap. Throughout the drive, he never stopped shifting, stepping from side to side in his dug-out. Like a nervous English batsman waiting for the next ripper from Shane Warne, he would move about his wicket. Between each shot he marked out his crease by touching the guidance sticks on the corners of the butt that made sure he fired in a safe direction. When he was not shooting, he talked to himself, telling himself to stay alert, keep his feet moving and always reassuring himself that he was up to the challenge.

'I just adore this type of shooting,' he said afterwards and it showed. Anyone who thinks driven shooting is exercise-avoidance, they should come and see his workrate. 'You don't get much chance to see them and sometimes that is the best way. I find it is best to put the gun into position as soon as you see the bird coming, even though it is out of range, as because of the speed they are flying, they will be in range by the time you get there. Once you are trying to play catch up, you won't.'

As the whole shoot party gathered at the end of the drive, the flankers congregated to give their verdict. These old boys stand at the side of the drive, flagging the grouse back down the causeway to the Guns. Known as the terrible trio, there was little that Jim Harding, Granville Hay and Alan Snaith, father of Peter, had not seen or heard before. Jim had been walking these hills with flag in hand for the last forty years and it was clear that there was nowhere else he would rather be come shoot days. 'In these last four decades there's no bit of this ground on this estate that I've not been on. It is funny how things have changed though. A lot of people used to think that sheep were the mortal enemy of grouse, but many now admit that grouse need sheep to keep the ticks off.'

Jim is known as Superflag for his innate ability to flag at the right time. 'Alan came up with that,' he said, rolling up his beloved instrument. 'But I won't tell you what else he calls me. To be honest, a good flanker knows more importantly when not to flag. If they are flying well, just leave them be. If you stand there with your flag up, it can scare them back over the beaters' heads before they get a chance to fly forward. And I don't always get it right – you've not been beating unless you've had a good cussing.'

If you are ever out on Danby moor, then Jim is easy to spot on account of his white Labrador that lights up like a beacon on the darkest days. As is often the case, this closest of relationships between man and dog was borne from adversity. 'His real name is Rolo, but Alan always calls him the Commondale Yeti on account of his colour,' explained Jim warmly, stroking the dog's ears. 'To be honest I wouldn't normally go for a dog this white, but I was asked to take him on from a family that had neglected him in Middlesborough. I found him in a tiny cupboard under the stairs, no room to move, next to a gas meter, and he had started to eat his own muck he was that hungry. He has turned out to be a real softie, with a great nose for grouse. He knows he's in a good home, don't you boy?' he added, as the Yeti licked its master's hand.

The flankers moved on to join the vehicles, perhaps slower than some of the younger beaters, but sprightly enough nonetheless. Before they left, Jim added a warning about the next drive. 'You want to get yourself in a cosy gun butt for the second drive, if I was you, lad. We've got to climb Heart Attack Hill. Some people call it Holiday Hill because you feel you need one at the end. You want eyes up your backside going up that hill. But the views are unbeatable at the top. All my life, I've never moved far from this part of the world. There is no other place like it, where you have stunning moorland like this, right next to the sea. This is where I love to be most and if I'm honest, if I could die up here, I would die happy,' he said wistfully, before adding with a wink: 'Aye, but not yet!'

I felt my stomach gurgle in trepidation, struggling to digest the black pudding and potato scone. 'We'll take it nice and slow, Jim. There's no need to rush.'

38.
Fox
lamping

One reader of *Shooting Times* once told me that, 'I should stop bothering with pheasants and stick to writing articles on foxes. That's what we're all interested in'. I ignored the advice, but accepted the point that many country folk are at their most content when tackling the fox. Charlie has his fair share of admirers from mounted foxhunters to terriermen to gamekeepers, all of whom revel in his demise. I am not trying to be callous here. Foxes are a nuisance and a constant threat in areas where lambs, poultry or gamebirds are a priority. While many land managers see them as a worthy adversary that will outsmart them on occasion, the aim is always to protect their stock from these handsome pests. I have no problem whatsoever that it can be enjoyable and satisfying at the same time.

I tend to cover at least one fox lamping article a year and I look forward to them immensely. Apart from the fact that the lamplight allows PQ to capture some terrific shots, the keepers are invariably good company. They all have their tales about strange sights they've seen in the dark from young lovers in the back of a car to strange flashing lights in the sky. Most will talk at length about their rifles and the varying ballistics with endearing affection. There must be many a long night when it is the only companion they have!

The first time I went out was with a trio of young keepers in Cornwall, when we beetled about country lanes in a souped-up golf buggy. One drove the vehicle, another held the lamp, while the eldest shot a large vixen. Another time, up in Perthshire, I was out on fields after midnight with three likely lads called Andy, his father Jim and their friend Colin, ('you'll not put our surnames, will you?') who offered local farmers an effective fox control service. We met in a lay-by after dark with only a car description to work with, like punters on a promise from some kinky website chatroom. All three were dressed in realtree camouflage jackets, trousers and baseball caps, with wide grins above unshaven chins. A quick shake of hands and small talk, then we were off into the fields after foxes.

Having worked in the area for years, they knew the lie of the land as well as any fox and it would take a sharp brain or a minor miracle for a night prowler to escape when they got close. But one succeeded! If it knew what it was doing, this fox was as cunning as its reputation suggests. With Andy in the prone position, steady and confident of a kill with his well-tested Remington 700, the pest was certainly in grave danger. But as Colin held the lamp still and true over Andy's shoulder, its eight thousand candlepower keeping the bright round eyes of fox in place, there was no expected crack and thud of the bullet leaving the rifle and finding its target.

'We'll no get a shot with those hooses behind,' explained Colin in a whisper. The buildings were a good five hundred yards further on across the field, their pale orange glow a reminder that most normal folk were enjoying the warmth of their living rooms or kitchens on a cold, windy night. Taking a shot was not an option, so Colin extinguished the lamp in the hope that the fox would move somewhere more accommodating. Of its four options – back, forward, left or right – the first three would keep it protected by the farm buildings behind, where, with neat irony, it would be indirectly saved by the farmer who wanted it killed.

But if it moved right, towards fields that had earlier been alive with rabbits and hares, and towards a wood that held the promise of a pheasant breakfast, then the fox would have made the wrong decision. With a clear backdrop for miles behind, it would probably be its last. 'Just wait, lads. It'll go right,' hissed Jim assuredly. How could he be so certain? 'They may be sneaky and intelligent and all,' he explained later, 'but they are also very curious. It has likely no idea what we are, and given it wants to find out, it'll try and wind us. By moving to the right, it can get downwind.'

When Colin switched his lamp back on, the fox had indeed moved twenty yards right and into the kill zone. But again, fate intervened on its behalf. While foxes are curious, it seems the farmer's dairy cows also take an active interest in what goes on in their field at night. The fox needed a miracle, and it came with four legs and an udder. Again the lamp and rifle were lowered. Whether the fox or vixen did indeed wind us, or whether it decided to count its blessings and take off behind a wall, we will never know.

The trio took the rub of the green in their stride and were quickly back on patrol, crossing the fields towards a pond that attracted mallard, teal, duck shooters, and no doubt foxes. As we approached, two mallard took off with a disgruntled squawk, their flight illuminated by Colin's lamp. 'You'd usually get far more ducks than that at this time of year,' said Jim, holding his son's rifle as he nipped over a barbed-wire fence. 'It's just there has been that much rain that the fields are sodden, so there are splashes everywhere for the ducks to get into. They're very spread out, so it makes flighting very difficult to predict.'

It was not just the ducks out at this time of night, as sky larks and peewits flitted overhead, wary of the threat of owls. The lampsmen had learned from the earlier fox, moving in a deliberate arc to stay upwind of any other foxes that were trying their luck on the pond. Within moments of Colin swinging his lamp back into action, a pair of guilty eyes shone back at us from the gloom. Andy fell to his knees and instinctively found a comfortable position to take aim. Knowing the lie of the land, the safety factor was deliberated and cleared, and in less than twenty seconds the shot was taken.

'Aye, good shot, lad' confirmed Jim, with a tinge of pride at his son's

Nick Corbett with his custom-made fox rifle.

accuracy. At ninety yards, Andy would have been surprised to miss, but as the dog fox was lying down, facing the light, the target area was smaller than it might have been. Either way, it was a clean kill. The dog itself was a monster. It had to be a good four feet from ear to tail, with a large belly and a big white tag on its chest. Andy struggled to lift him back over the fence to have its picture taken.

'I've not seen many bigger than him,' said Andy, taking a look at its teeth that had surely accounted for a good many pheasants, rabbits and maybe the odd lamb in the past four or so years. Many of the other foxes on this stretch of land would probably have come from litters he had sired.

'I suspect he was sitting up having just eaten. He must be about twenty-eight pounds or thereabouts,' continued Andy. 'With the wind this strong, he'll not have heard us, and he was upwind, so he'd not have had a clue we were there. I had an idea there might be a fox in that part of the field – after a while you get a knack for knowing when and where a fox will be working.' 'It didn't take long, did it?' said Colin, looking pleased. 'Put the lamp on him, Andy goes down on his chest like a sodger, and that's that. But it won't be long until another one takes his place,' he added gruffly. 'Foxes are just like drug dealers – get rid of one, and another moves into his patch.'

Yet another fox lamping excursion took me back out after dark with a vermin controller from Buckinghamshire called Nick Corbett, who had commissioned the 'ultimate fox rifle', custom built by the engineer Steve Bowers who had set up the bicycle stalk. On paper, the rifle sounded very impressive: the action sends a 39 grain bullet from a .20 PPC round through 22 inch barrels, which have a three-rifling groove one-in-eleven twist format, at 4,000 feet per second with 1,385 foot-pounds of energy. But for those of us who aren't fluent speakers of ballistics, what does that mean? I was sent to find out if the thing actually worked.

We went out twice in a week, as the first trip returned a blank. One-nil to Charlie. We were no closer to finding out whether this bespoke fox rifle could do the job it was designed for. Perhaps therein lies the paradox that faces anyone who goes in pursuit of the fox – you do not want vermin on your ground, but if it does not turn up, it is slightly disappointing! Undaunted, we met a few days later at a different farm in Buckinghamshire where Nick helps the keeper Eric Cross with fox control. Again, the estate comprises a decent acreage of fine arable land with stubbles that offer a hunting paradise for the red peril. It was on the higher ground though that we started, overlooking the vale beneath us. These steep hills offer ideal grazing for livestock and natural height for pheasants to fly over Guns below. Of course, the pheasants are also highly palatable to Fantastic Mr Fox.

We sat on the stage of an enormous amphitheatre whose sides reached up steeply, providing a natural background for a shot. The trees wrapped round the slope like a curtain and as the sun began to set, we scanned the woodland edge for signs of life. Nothing stirred. In the distance we could hear a patient dog owner putting her retriever through training exercises, but there was no movement in our immediate vicinity. The shadows continued to lengthen until it was too dark to see suitably with the naked eye.

'You're turning into a bit of a jinx,' Nick said, unloading the fat, stocky cartridge from its chamber and holding up the single-shot rifle for us to see it was empty. 'That's clear now. We'll see if we have better luck tonight with a lamp.'

Two-nil to Charlie. We retreated to the farmhouse, tails between our legs. Happily there was a large pile of freshly baked scones waiting for us. We devoured the lot, seeing off a pot of tea and the entire contents of a pot of homemade raspberry jam. We waited for darkness to fall. As it happens, we would have waited all night. A round high moon shone from a cloudless sky, illuminating the fields like a spotlight. Even at 11 p.m., we could have played eighteen golf holes without difficulty. This only added to our run of bad luck.

'I'm afraid these could hardly be worse conditions,' explained Nick, phlegmatic as ever. 'It is so still that any sound we make will carry. You ideally want a dark night with low cloud and a bit of wind to hide your noise. The fox is in the same boat, of course, as he is out hunting too. He can be bolder on a dark, windy night, as his prey will not see or hear him. Tonight he will be edgy, if indeed he comes out at all.'

But it was a good night for photography, if not a lot else. For the best part of an hour, Eric kindly drove us about the fields, forsaking a deserved bed after countless early mornings feeding his birds. Both he and Nick came armed with a lamp, but there was nothing stirring. Nick did once manage to light up a pair of eyes, but they quickly disappeared over a wall. It could very well have been a local farm mog out on a forage – we would never know.

'We'll try one last set of fields,' Eric offered, eating further into his brief shut-eye. 'They are three huge stubbles by one of my release pens. There's often a fox or two by there. Indeed, I lost about forty pheasant poults in one night to a fox that wriggled in. It was a massacre.'

En route, Nick explained why the rifle had been such a success. 'First of all, it is entirely customised to fit me, so it is extremely comfortable to shoot. It is a heavy gun, which can be a burden, but that means it doesn't shift at all in the shoulder, and I can see the bullet hit the fox. The accuracy is unbeatable. I zero it in at two hundred yards and at anything up to three hundred yards, you need only aim at the engine room and it will be effective every time. I use a light 39 grain bullet, which shatters on impact. The insides of the fox will be practically liquefied and it can be like picking up a bag of sand. The sole purpose of the rifle is to kill vermin – it is nothing to do with harvesting an animal for the table – and this is the most humane method I have come across. The fox simply has no idea what hits it.' Added to the accuracy is an absolute confidence that the aim will be true. Home-loading, bench-testing and repetition have reduced any variables to their minimum.

'Nearly always I am out lamping on my own, so there is no glory in taking long distance shots or showing off by aiming at the head. It is all about doing a job for a farmer or keeper. I enjoy it, of course, but most of that enjoyment comes from doing a job properly.' Crows often provide a stiffer challenge than the foxes, as they can be harder to approach. Nick will shoot them up to four hundred and even five hundred yards away with little difficulty, although there will be adjustments made for wind speed, humidity and gradient where necessary. 'You need to know your terrain and your rifle intimately if you are going to be successful at that range. Again, the .20 PPC is extremely accurate. But I have to get it right first time. A rabbit will stay put if a bullet passes over its head, but a crow is clever enough to sense something is wrong, even though it cannot see you.'

Tonight, we were after foxes and the final whistle was fast approaching. Nick and Eric shone their lamps across the middle field. Bingo! A pair of eyes shone back. Wordlessly, they switched the lamps off. It was a fox out mousing. Nick gestured with an outstretched palm that we get down. He led by example, setting the weapon down on its bipods and crawling in behind the stock.

Eric sent the beam of his lamp over to the hedge and the eyes lit up again. I waited for the phizz and thump of the bullet, but it never came. The fox had not settled but had moved onto the other side of the hedge. Nick dared not attempt a shot through vegetation as the bullet would disintegrate on impact with the smallest twig. Yet all was not lost and, as though acting on telepathy, keeper and fox controller were quickly on their feet again, skirting along the bottom of the field to reach the hedge.

Nick was again on his belly and we followed suit. Eric lit up the other side of the hedge, before scanning across the field. Our fox was still there. The light went out as Nick eased himself into position. A quick nod and Eric revealed the target once more. Nick has the trigger set to a hair's weight and will wait to have the fox lined up on the reticule before simply resting his finger against the trigger. With that, it was over.

Or was it? Eric knows from experience that one fox can often bring two and sure enough a second pair of eyes shone back near the top of the field. It was a longer shot, but Nick made quick work of it. He would come back the next day with a rangefinder and confirm them both at 260 and 308 yards respectively.

'It is rare that I would take a shot as long as that when lamping,' he said, as Eric retrieved the bodies. Both had been killed instantly to shots that entered a couple of inches behind the shoulder. 'The slope gave a natural backstop and it is almost like daylight out here. Such is the accuracy of this rifle I needed only to aim where I wanted the bullet to go and it did.'

For Eric, the venture had been well worth halving his sleep allocation. 'They're both youngsters, possibly from the same litter, and there's every chance they both got into my release pen. It explains why there was so much carnage in there. I'm delighted to see the back of them.'

39.

Beating

As I mentioned in the introduction to this book, I did not take to shooting as a boy. I didn't mind beating though, because it was a regular wage, good exercise and it could be fun in the right team, especially if there were kids of the same age. Grouse beating on the estates above Loch Tay in Perthshire was genuinely enjoyable, scrabbling over burns and high heather or skidding over the peat hags to keep in line.

But there is the odd bad memory jumbled in with the good ones, which still bear their scars. Some days were pretty miserable, although this had nothing to do with the cold, wet or terrain. There were certain pheasant shoots where the beating team formed marked cliques that were aggressively inward-looking to the extent you found yourself sitting alone on your bale during the lunch hour, desperate for the in-jokes and snide remarks to end, so you could return to the neutrality of the woods and pheasants. Having left the local primary school for a place at an Edinburgh private school, it was perhaps inevitable I would meet disdain as the 'posh kid'. The fact I spoke like the paying guns rather than my one-time schoolmates, probably didn't help. It was nothing too vicious – I'd put it in the character-building bracket rather than open bullying – but compared with other inclusive shoots, it was an eight-hour trial. The keepers and underkeepers are invariably pleased to see you, because they need bums on seats for the shoot to work. But they were soon off driving the trailer, marshalling the Guns or positioning flankers. You were on your own to sink or swim. There are some who are not fazed by this situation. They muscle their way in with a loud observation on the weather or a lewd reference to one of the Gun's wives. Soon, they are passing round a hip flask or discussing the finer points of pigeon magnets. As a teenager, I didn't have a hip flask and I knew nothing about pigeons. All too often, I sank.

Leaving for university in Nottingham, I thought my beating days were behind me. During the holidays, I got my pocket money working as a tour guide at a whisky distillery and although a Scottish accent would have helped, I fitted in well. By the time I reached the mean streets of London, slogging through woods after pheasants was nothing more than 'something I used to do'. So it was a walk down memory lane when I went back to Perthshire to do an article on partridge beating. I felt all those past anxieties return briefly as I climbed into the beaters' wagon on the Pitcastle shoot near Aberfeldy, but it was soon clear it was going to be a good day. Some of the lads shuffled along the bench to allow me a seat and I was soon shaking hands and trying to remember names.

The forecast had said it would rain and there had been a cold deluge the day before. Like most of the beaters I had dressed accordingly. But the sun shone from a cloudless sky and by the end of the first drive the beating line resembled the final scene from the *Full Monty* with jackets, jumpers and waterproof trousers being shed in unison.

The beatkeeper was generous to me on the first drive, putting me out in an open field to flank the line, safe from the head-high bracken whose tangled stalks gave way to hidden troughs and ditches. Maybe he had seen the pale London grey in my cheeks and chosen not to throw me in at the deep end. Maybe he feared I would lag behind and disrupt the smooth running of his well-oiled machine. It did at least give me a vantage point to view the forward manoeuvres being performed. It was immediately evident how much a beater's worth increases if he comes with a dog in tow. Or the other way around! No matter your level of fitness, volume, agility, speed or experience, there is no substitute for a four legged nose that will meet any game at floor level, penetrating deeper into the undergrowth and filling in the inevitable gaps. Those with dogs were spread evenly down the line as the owners moved cautiously through the bracken, flags waving and cracking overhead, forcing the red-legged partridges to trickle forward towards the waiting guns.

So it went on throughout the day, sloshing through bogs (wishing I was wearing Wellies and not ankle-high boots) and tracking the hand-cut rides through forests of broom. Lunch was a riot, with various members of the team taking turns to tell shooting stories that had doubtless been told many times before. I jumped in with a yarn about a keeper I met in

Dorset who once found a young couple in flagrante whilst fox lamping. 'They didn't stop,' said the old keeper. 'They could now see what they were doing!' It raised a couple of titters, but given I butchered the punch line, I think they were being polite.

That afternoon, the heavens opened. We were on a different beat and, like most of the others, I had left my waterproofing elsewhere. There was nothing else for it but to carry on in short-sleeves and keep moving to stay warm. I was now under the instructions of another beatkeeper who had no qualms in sending me into the thick stuff and I soon found out what everybody else had been up against all day. It was not so much the wet tangles of bracken towering above my head that was the problem, but what was hidden beneath. Slippery logs and boulders, stone dykes and rusting fences, streams and bogs all vied to snare ankles and graze knees.

Too much flagging left you lagging behind as it was hard to keep abreast of the seasoned beaters, the sweat on my brow being washed off by the downpour. There would be a brief pause to regroup and catch the breath as a squadron of partridges took their chances over the Guns, before it was ever onwards, scrambling up a steep bracken bank, grasping the weed's strong roots to pull myself up, while its fronds' pungent smell invaded my nostrils. Five partridges got up from under my feet, rising over the bank and four shots rang out, although I could not see whether they connected. As the whistle sounded to signal the end of a good day, I rather hoped they had made it through unscathed.

I left Pitcastle feeling invigorated, as though I had confronted past demons and slain them with my plastic flag. For that I am extremely grateful.

JANUARY
FEBRUARY
MARCH
APRIL
MAY
JUNE
JULY
AUGUST
SEPTEMBER
OCTOBER
NOVEMBER
DECEMBER

40.
Rough
shoot

I need to go to Wales more often. I've only been there three times in my life and each time I leave, I vow to come back again soon. Somehow, it just has not worked out like that. One of those visits, on a clear day in October, I will count as the most quirky of all my *Shooting Times* adventures. All I had was a name, an address and the brief that I was to do a report on a chap who had won a gun in a *ST* sponsored competition.

The plan was to stay in a B&B the night before, arriving at the competition winner John Williams' house off the A5 towards Bangor. As you leave Llangollen the Welsh outback reveals in every turn of this twisting road and it can be difficult to concentrate on the road in front with all that scenery on either side. Wonderful sign names like Glyndyfrdwy, Gwydedelwern and Cerrig-y-drudion appear in the land that vowels forgot, clear indication if needed that this is a place with a history and its own way of life.

We were advised to look out for a church in the prescribed village and I presumed John lived nearby. Not a bit of it! He had converted the church into a very cosy abode, although it was still clearly an old church. The varied skins and heads on the walls made me glad I wouldn't be left alone in there at night! But John fitted his dwelling perfectly. A short, heavy set man with a thick black beard that had two white stripes on the chin like converse piano keys, he would have looked equally at home in a Grimms fairy tale. He soon proved himself to be a fascinating individual and a natural storyteller, only too keen to relate the local nature and folklore in this mystical region. 'You saw that gorge as you drove up here,' he said, not waiting to see if I had or not. 'Well, they say that one year a coach and horses came down that hill out of control and tumbled off the bridge into the river below.' He drew himself closer to me. 'Everybody was killed. And the gorge has been haunted ever since.' That did it. I was not staying here tonight!

With his pals Richard Evans and Joey Scott, John has been shooting in this valley for many years and the trio have created their own slice of paradise. They were quick to stress from the start that this was not going to be a big bag day. 'If we get a few rabbits or a hare and a couple of pheasants, then we've had a good day. That's the way we've always done it and that's the way we like it. We call ourselves the Forlorn Hope, named

The team from the Forlorn Hope in North Wales.

after the vanguard regiment who were in the first wave of attack. Sometimes we see nothing at all.'

'It is basically ours to do with as we wish,' added Richard, who sported a thick moustache and goatee. 'Sometimes we have theme days with hammerguns, side-by-sides, over-and-unders or black powder.'

Joey made up for his lack of facial fur with a pair of reflective aviators that, with his tatty camouflage jacket, made him look like an extra from *Apocalypse Now*.

We started on a hill opposite the church, where John hoped to find a few snipe or maybe a hare. I was given a spare over-and-under, seemingly made of lead, and a pocketful of cartridges. The destination was a collection of standing stones at the top of the steep hill, which we were assured was once the meeting point of druids. It was a decent hike up with some hard-going marshland and plenty of fences, so it was something of a lottery if you would be loaded or not when quarry presented itself. It did not.

The view back down the valley made up for any lack of wildlife, as John traced the route that the Welsh hero Owain Glyndwr used to evade English captors. He was supposed to have passed by the exact spot where we were standing. 'They say he strapped horseshoes backwards on the soles of his feet to make the English think he was going the other way,' said John gleefully. Whatever his manner of escape, it worked, as he was never taken alive. Indeed nobody knew when or if he ever died and the legend goes that Owain Glyndwr still waits in a cave, ready to lead the Welsh again in the face of English invasion.

By the time we reached the druids' stone circle, we were in need of a rest. Richard was wheezing hard and admitted that this would probably be the last time he would visit the place he loved. Sitting on these rocks, he was saying goodbye to a part of his youth, which was touching to see. I don't want to sound morbid, but I got as far as mentally rehearsing my CPR, as he turned a greyish colour and looked set to cash his chips in right then and there. Happily, after a good rest, the colour returned to his cheeks.

John seemed relaxed enough and began telling stories of the druids who would have worshipped their pagan gods on this hilltop. It was a little unsettling to imagine the rites, incantations and sacraments performed there centuries ago. Dominating the circle was a smooth, flat stone presumed to be an altar for libations and perhaps sacrifices.

'We were once up here having our lunch,' recalled John dramatically, 'and we put a hare on the altar stone. When we got up to leave, the hare had disappeared. But there was nobody there!' This was another place not to visit in the dead of night.

After lunch, the barrels of our guns still shiny clean, we were taken up the other side of a different hill (by 4x4 happily) in the hope of better fortune. The wind had picked up and there was a cold wind to meet us at the top.

'Do you see this?' asked John, pointing at a spring of water gushing up from the grass. 'This is called the Well of Tears. They say it was the spot where the wives of local soldiers fighting in the bloody battle of Llanwrst in 945 BC sat and watched their husbands being cut down.' In the distance rose the peak of Mount Snowdon ablaze with the setting sun. The shooting was now a sideshow and we concentrated on the local folklore. 'There's always something strange going on in these parts,' said John, in case I hadn't been listening all day. 'One time, with snow on the ground, we came up here and found a Buddhist chap meditating. I don't know who was more surprised!'

'And then there were the UFO sightings in the Berwyn mountains over there,' added Richard. 'That got the press going for a while.'

Our minds were in galaxies far far away, when a lone jackdaw flapped over John's head. Remembering that he had his prize gun to hand, our host swung hard at the retreating corvid. The shot echoed round the hills, growing ever fainter until it disappeared into the past like all those heroes, soldiers and druids before them. The jackdaw barely noticed and swooped off down the hill none the worse.

'You'll have to clean your gun now,' crowed Joey, delighted.

John broke his gun open and retrieved the smoking cartridge. 'I fear that's the closest we'll get today. Another blank for the Forlorn Hope.'

'More like no hope,' chuckled Richard. With that, John ordered the 'Officers of the 24th Foot and Mouth' to fall in and we made our way back home.

Before I left the church, John pushed a bottle of brandy into my hand as an early Christmas present. There was no reason for him to do it, but it struck me as typical of the generosity of shooting folk. So many in the last four years have invited me into their house and offered genuine hospitality, well aware that they will receive nothing in return. It is the range of people and their kindness that makes this job uniquely enjoyable.

41.
McDougal

The modern day MacNab – a stag, salmon and brace of grouse in a calendar day – adapted from John Buchan's timeless tale of poaching high jinks, is well enough known, though few nowadays get to achieve it. Not only will the attempt cost you a tidy sum to stalk a stag, shoot a brace of grouse and catch a salmon; but the odds of catching your salmon are not as short as they once were. Nowadays, the ghillie in charge of delivering his client a MacNab will get them out there early on the salmon as the other two can be 'caught up' on later.

Its distant cousin, the McDougal, however, is rather less spoken of, though it can be every bit as testing and considerably more affordable. The Ashbourne McDougal, to give it its full title, was conceived by a Scotsman named Douglas Chalmers, owner of the East Sussex estate of the same name. The ground has a variety of mixed woodland, home to a few hundred pheasants, and a pair of lakes, where both brown and rainbow trout swim. A keen angler and shot, Douglas was keen to maximise the sport on his little corner of England.

'The concept is very easy on paper,' he explained, as the three contenders took coffee in the fishing lodge before the challenge began. 'In the morning, you have to shoot a cock pheasant. Over a good lunch and a glass of claret, you will be shown how to tie your own fly from the cock's feathers. Once you have independently tied your fly, the final test is to catch a trout on that fly. So, apart from the stag, grouse and salmon, it mirrors the original MacNab exactly!'

Ashbourne stands in the shadow of Tent Hill, the final camp site of the Saxon Army before the Battle of Hastings in 1066. The ill-fated King Harold would have snatched a few hours rest after the gruelling march from Yorkshire, where he had been repelling Vikings. That same night, a few miles away, a Norman archer would have been sharpening an arrow head with the English monarch's name on it. Nowadays, in the nearby towns of Hastings and Battle, it is hard to move without reminders of the famous date, more often than not with commercial gain in mind. As a parody, there is a similar brass plaque on a fence post at Ashbourne that reads, 'In 1066, on this spot, nothing happened at all.' I will add here that I spent a similarly restless night to King Harold in the nearby town of Battle in one of the worst pubs I've had the misfortune of visiting. A Spartan room I can deal with, but one with bare floorboards, rattling hot pipes and a bed on an angle was beyond the pale. The breakfast had been fried in yesterday's chip fat. They even had the cheek to charge fifty pounds!

Douglas soon restored PQ and me to good humour. Of south-west of Scotland descent, he worked for many years throughout the West Indies and was resident of Hong Kong for over eighteen years, before settling back to Sussex. A single-figure handicapper, member of the Magic Circle and manufacturer of a devilishly tasty Trinidad Hot Pepper Sauce; there are many strings to his bow. In short, the man was good company, which makes any day go quicker.

But it was not all fun and games. 'The McDougal is far from guaranteed,' he stressed, as three of his old chums spread out on one side of a lake. 'Indeed, it needs a fair amount of skill and luck to get it done. It's not simply a case of pay your money and we make sure you get your McDougal. There is pressure to hit that cock pheasant, especially if you miss the first one and panic sets in. We allow Guns to shoot hen birds and woodcock too, but they don't count towards a McDougal.' Winners get prizes, while those that fall short go home empty handed. Douglas laments the modern trend of 'everyone is a winner because they take part'.

Douglas Chalmers (left) demonstrates how to tie a trout fly from the feather of a cock pheasant.

'When I was a kid at sports day, only the fastest and strongest won prizes. If sports were not your thing, it was tough luck and you learnt to excel in other areas. But in this day and age, they don't hold the egg and spoon race, because Little Jimmy may end up a loser and that's not fair. I believe it is healthy to know the difference between success and failure, and not be wrapped in cotton wool.'

The McDougal rewards sporting elitism. If competitors are struggling – usually on fly tying or casting – then they may ask for an 'assisted McDougal', but the emphasis is on the 'assisted' and they are recommended to come back and do it off their own bat next time. Weather, as always, tends to play its part; and what's good for the pheasant, is not always good for the trout. 'It is cold today,' said Douglas, 'so the birds should fly well enough. But the fish might stay deep in the lakes.'

Groups tend to be three to five strong on a McDougal day, which allows for an intimate relaxed shoot, with every chance to throw banter up and down the line, especially if that first cock is hit or missed. Of course, a walked up day or rough shoot along hedgerows might provide the same fun and opportunities, if you are going to try this at home. 'And while the original McDougal is a pheasant and trout,' reasoned Douglas, 'you could have a Silver McDougal, say, which could be a different fish caught on a fly made from a pigeon you shot that morning.' The permutations are endless, so long as the bird's feathers catch the fish.

'The key is to still be in the running at lunch,' the host warned. 'That keeps morale up. The fishing isn't quite so exciting if you are not using your own bird. Then again, the pressure is off, and you can sit back and enjoy the claret instead!' While Douglas is in charge of hosting the guests, teaching fly-tying and cooking lunch, Roy Foster makes sure the birds fly and the fish bite. A true countryman of the old school, he can turn his hand to almost any pursuit, whether it is dog work, deer stalking, falconry, vermin control, clay shooting, rifle marksmanship or fly fishing.

'It is just the perfect job for me,' he said, as we passed an old oak tree that had recently been split straight down the middle by a bolt of lightening. 'I love being outside. I have done all my life. As a kid, I used to love watching Jack Hargreaves' programmes, with his horse and cart, and it's a shame those times have gone now.' Despite living so close to London, Roy never goes into the city, saying that foxes and badgers, not humans, are supposed to go underground. He did watch the recent Remembrance Day ceremonies at the Cenotaph at Whitehall with great pride, however, as both his sons were on parade with the Army Air Corps.

As a younger man Roy had plenty in common with Buchan's trio of rascals who joined to form the shadowy figure of John MacNab. 'We would only poach for the devilment,' he admitted, as eight fallow deer trotted through the trees ahead. 'It was all about seeing what you could catch by using your fieldcraft, rather than making any money from it!' Now turned keeper, he and next door Ashburnham headkeeper Mark Saunders worked their dogs through the undergrowth to send numerous birds forward over the three Guns. But it was only heavy rain that fell from the sky. Chris Long-Price managed to pull down a cock on the third drive, keeping his McDougal alive, but come lunchtime, that was the only success. The other two were out!

Preceded by smoked salmon and champagne, Douglas' excellent venison stew, potato/celeriac mash and hot pepper sauce quickly raised spirits and the trio were soon being taught how to tie their first fly: a pheasant tail nymph. Expertly, Douglas set the hooks on a vice with the spool of thread hanging below, and demonstrated how to set the head, twine on the thorax and wing casing, before tying off with what he called a 'nerdling pole'. Then, like the *Generation Game*, the pupils had to follow suit.

'The only help you get is on the tying on and off – apart from that you're on your own if you want to get a true McDougal. It's a bit like sailing – the key is to always stay attached. If you can tie a second, then do; because your first one may fall off. If that happens with the light fading, you'll lose your chance.'

One of the contenders got himself all tied up. 'Mine looks more like a bumble bee!' he wailed. As Chris was the only 'McDougaler' with a chance of success, all eyes were on him as he began to flog the still waters of

Kingfisher lake. Having never fly fished before, it was vital he learnt to cast quickly, as he would have to play the trout himself, to avoid the 'assisted' prefix. Roy outlined the basics of casting, effortlessly throwing the fly a magnitude of yards to the other side of the lake, before drawing the line back in with practiced ease. Understandably, Chris' first attempts were not so precise and there was rather more time spent untangling than angling. 'The rules are tough, but I'm afraid that if he did get a fish now, it would probably have to be assisted,' Douglas decreed. 'We can't just give McDougals away! Successful participants receive a commemorative disc, a bottle of champagne and a special box to take their fish home. We believe it is the little extra details that count.'

There is a 'catch and keep' policy on all rainbows caught at Ashbourne. 'The water is extremely clear here and so there is never the muddy flavour you might get in other lakes. There are some beautiful fish in there and if you catch one, you will get a good supper from it.' The brownies are less numerous and are harder to catch, preferring to sit closer to the bottom at this time of the year, although if hooked give a very powerful account of themselves. Douglas will put these fish back, unless they are too well hooked for easy release.

I was allowed a go and managed to attach myself to a weighty rainbow trout, but it slipped the hook just as the net was being pushed under. By the time the shadows had lengthened across the lake, the only trout had been caught by PQ, although it had been hooked on Brian Everall's impressively tied pheasant tail nymph. So it really can be done! Yet, today there would be no newcomers on the McDougal role of honour. Everyone retired to the lodge for tea, but no medals.

42.
Punt-gunning

It was eight-fifteen in the morning and I was feeling decidedly nauseous. This was nothing to do with the full Scottish breakfast served by the Nith Hotel in Glencaple, but simply a case of good old-fashioned butterflies. These were big butterflies too and not so much fluttering as having a full-on jamboree in my belly. Maybe it was the mysterious aura of punt-gunning, always talked about in hushed tones behind closed doors, that was getting me nervous. Or the fact I might soon be aiming a small cannon at rather a lot of birds from an extremely light looking vessel. At certain times, I have been guilty of finding myself in over my head for lack of research. This time, I was beginning to wish I had not read the tales of punt-gunning adventures as many are filled with mournful obituaries to the most experienced of tidesmen, hard as teak, who fell victim to their love affair with this challenging sport. Long before the days of base jumping or sky diving, the adrenaline junkies got their fix holding the lanyard of a one-and-a-half inch gun in some of the most treacherous waters and weather conditions in Britain. They are the wildfowling equivalent of Special Forces. When it goes badly wrong in the cold mud of the estuary, then it's the coastguards if you're lucky and the evening news if you're not.

The key to being a successful punt-gunner, and part of the attraction no doubt, is exactly what makes it so dangerous. You and your boat partner have to be on your own in filthy conditions and strong tides; otherwise you will not be able to creep up on wildfowl. The ideal stalk will allow the punter at the back of the low-slung canoe to sneak silently over the shallow water on the mudflats, using poles of varying lengths to navigate the currents. If it is blowing a gale and raining hard, the ducks will flock together on a mud flat with their heads under their wings. They won't know what's coming until it's too late. Once in range of the widgeon, mallard or geese, the gunner (me) would aim the ten foot cannon just above the heads of the flock and fire at the first sign of movement. Twenty ounces of shot would then create a pattern of about thirty feet in diameter, bringing down anything in its path.

The gun is lashed to the punt with thick breeching rope that keeps the single barrel straight as it recoils. This recoil can be as much as five inches, enough to break a nose or smash teeth if you sit too close. The gunner will 'cock a snook' by pressing the thumb against his nose and extending the hand to the butt of the cannon to measure a safe distance from the end of the cannon. I was once told that this is related to the derivation of the insulting nature of the gesture, as British gunners would do that towards the enemy before firing, but while it is plausible and apt, I have since found no evidence to back it up!

The naturalist and wildfowler Basil Hasler, a great authority on the Norfolk Fens, once told me he often found the most enjoyable part of the day to be the few hours before the action starts. Anticipation can be better than reality. Reading and research, preparing equipment, packing the car and heading to the destination will all set your senses alight. The familiar sights and sounds of an old patch with all the memories they embody; or the novelty of arriving in uncharted territory with its promise of new experiences is as valuable as the day's sport itself. Sometimes even more so.

However, this was scant consolation as I stood outside the Nith in too-big waders, awaiting my host and skipper Steve Cooksley, feeling like the last ripe fruit on a plum tree. Happily, this hotel is a favoured watering-hole of wildfowlers, so I would have looked more out of place in a suit and tie. It was already a clear, bright day and the early morning geese flighters were returning for their breakfast empty-handed. Clouds of pinkfeet were laughing down at them from a couple of hundred feet up, enjoying the mild weather. A little bit of me was delighted that we too would struggle to get close to birds in these benign conditions and so avoid the drama of letting rip. But enough of me still wanted to test my mettle on the mudflats, so I was a little confused when I saw a silver punt ghosting down the estuary in front of the hotel. I ran as fast as my waders would carry me to the edge of the channel to get a closer look, but the punt was soon gone. Punt-gunners are renowned for being secretive, shy creatures, few in number, so the chances of getting two on the same day are slim indeed. I did not know what Steve looked like, so had to presume that my ride – and story! – was rafting its way down the tide without me.

Further up the Solway, however, I saw with some relief that there was a second punt being launched, a Land Rover backing it into the grey seawater. Jogging along the main road, my waders acting like a Thermos flask, I got there just in time for both sailors to confirm that neither was called Steve.

This was good news, in a way, but it did mean there would now be three punts on the water, an extraordinary coincidence, but hardly conducive to successful hunting. 'A total waste of time,' was Steve's rough translation when he arrived with the punt. 'If you had not been a journalist I would have just kept the engine running and turned round.' As a fourth punt arrived at the make-shift jetty, now a crowded car park for Land Rovers and boat trailers, Steve started to laugh. 'You can go out many times a year, for many years, and you will never see another punt,' he explained, handing me a sky-grey jumper and woolly bonnet to make me blend in with the water and punt. 'Indeed, it is the last thing you want as the ducks will never settle. Another punt is tedious to say the least. Four is just unthinkable. I can safely say we will not get a shot today.'

The butterflies began to slow their merry dance in my stomach, even when I took my place behind the safety-ed cannon. Indeed there was very little to be nervous about – on this trip at least. Prostrate in the punt, both punter and gunner are almost invisible in the water. Like a pantomime horse, the front man becomes the eyes of the double act, while the back legs creeps the craft to within firing distance. But every time Steve poled us into position to begin a stalk, the ducks would move on, no doubt confused that their causeway had become a thoroughfare for boats. For me, it was an extremely serene way to see this wild environment. With no chance of a shot, I was blissfully redundant as Steve made the hard yards across current or against the tide to keep us out of the way of other punts.

'To be honest, punt-gunning is generally a lot of hard work for precious little reward,' said Steve, as we drifted back to the jetty after a four-hour tour. 'You must never gauge success by the number of birds shot. If it was all about that, I'd be better off shooting them with a twelve bore from the bank. It is about the fieldwork: knowing the tides, perfecting and maintaining your gun and punt, working with a partner, learning about the birds and just being out on the water in such a wild place far away from anyone else.' He unloaded the gun. 'Usually, that is.'

43.

Bassets

Treacle reacted like he had just put his paws in a light socket. His nose, thousands of times more powerful than our own weak snozzles, had caught the smell of fresh hare in the turnip field. With nearly five hundred years of specialist breeding coursing through his veins, he knew instinctively what to do next. Don't be fooled by the earnest, almost gloomy look in a basset's eyes. The comical floppy ears that trail along the ground may look Disney-cuddly, but this is one finely-tuned killing machine. Forget cartoon Fred, when a pack of basset hounds is on the hunt, there is no hare alive that wants to be on the receiving end.

For the past five minutes, the twenty-six hounds had spread out across the field noses to the ground to draw the field, weaving forward to the instructions of the huntsmen and whippers-in. Treacle edged forward as though being pulled by a cotton thread on his nose. The scent of the hare grew stronger. Of course, insensitive human that I am, I could not see, let alone smell, the hare lying down in its form. Indeed, how many near heart attacks have been caused by a hare springing up from beneath a beater's feet? But for Treacle, it was standing out like a bill board with H-A-R-E written in bright neon letters.

The hare is also fully aware of the peril it faces. Plan A in its survival manual is to sit still and hope the danger passes by. A hard wind was swirling over this part of Worcestershire, enough that hats blew off and the voice of the huntsman was lost to all those save the keenest of followers. Individual bassets are renowned for their 'independence of thought' (it's called disobedience in retrievers) but a pack will operate as an extremely effective unit. The wind gave them an added excuse to read from their own script.

The theory was a good one for our hare, given its scent would quickly be lost on the breeze, unless a hound stepped upon it or was downwind at the critical moment. As Treacle had done. With the hound locked on, it was the hare's nerve to break first, realising with sufficient foresight that it would lose this particular game of chicken. The bassets may have half a millennium of experience in their tank, but old brown hare has been hunted far longer, even before the Romans introduced him to Britain for exactly that.

Switching to Plan B – high speed evasion – the hare abandoned its scrape and set off across the field as though its life depended on it. Treacle immediately spoke to the rest of the pack, his rich, deep voice echoed by the other hounds as they took his lead. Trooper, Trigger, Trotter, Tracker, Trinket and Treasure all joined Treacle on his chase across the turnips, their short legs going like Homer Simpson after an ice cream van in pursuit of their quarry.

At first glance, the odds seem stacked in the hare's favour. Given it can escape the poise and speed of a greyhound, what chance does the ungainly, low-slung, heavy-set basset have? Tortoises only ever catch the hare in fables. But that is the whole point, no? A fit and healthy hare, capable of turning on a sixpence at high speed, will always outrun a pack of bassets to live a full and happy life, passing on its genes to the next generation. Moreover, being a highly territorial animal, it will know every escape hatch, tunnel and natural sough in the field more intimately than its pursuer. If the hare is fit, he will survive.

However, if the hare is past its prime or carrying an injury, then our long-eared tortoise comes back into the race. The legs may be squat, but they are powerful and, driven by large lungs, strong hearts and a collective will, they can carry the basset over long distances. The foot race is usually a short sprint with the hare making good its escape, but if it turns into a long distance, cross-country flight, the basset with its quivering nose will stay on the hare's scent for as long as it takes.

Having learned from the beagles, I was not about to set off in pursuit, so stayed to watch the contest with the other spectators. The chase was at full tilt. The hare tore across the field followed by thirteen couple of hounds in full voice, the huntsmen, two whippers-in, four energetic foot-followers and a photographer. It's no wonder that townies think that country folk are weird! There were at least thirty locals and supporters of the Leadon Vale Basset Hounds who had turned out to enjoy watching the hounds at work and catch up on gossip. Those who had turned out were not there to see a hare killed, but rather to watch the hounds work. Only one in twenty hares are caught and this one proved to be too fast for Treacle and his friends, and lived to be a hare another day.

'I hope you're not going to write one of those articles that is nothing more than a social diary piece,' said a chap called Peter May, a local terrier man. He was limping after the hunt with his three terriers Parsnip, Pimple and Bucket against doctor's orders after a painful case of tendonitis had put his leg in a cast. 'It's the hounds you want to write about. Humans are boring and predictable. We all act and look the same. But each and every hound is different.'

44.

Geese under full moon

For the first couple of years at *Shooting Times*, I worked from the big IPC Media offices on the Southbank near Waterloo. It is just next to the OXO Tower if you know that part of the Capital. It made for a varied week, changing from the wilds of Scotland or the bonhomie of a driven pheasant shoot to the grimy crush of London where eye contact is deemed an act of aggression. The IPC building was itself a microcosm of that contrast. Most of the time you were surrounded by trendy media types working for successful urban titles like *Loaded*, *Nuts*, *Marie Claire*, *NME* and *Now*. There was the odd tweed flat cap, but it was always on backwards and pinned down with headphones. But travel high enough up the lift and you would reach a small oasis of calm, where the country titles worked. *Horse & Hound*, *Country Life*, *The Field*, *Anglers' Mail* and *Shooting Times* were all edited from the same two floors and it was the only place you were likely to see mustard cords, tweed jackets, Laura Ashley skirts and a spaniel.

One day in October, we'll call it a Wednesday, I bumped into Jonathan Young, editor of *The Field* for over a decade and one-time editor of *Shooting Times*. Jonathan was writing about shooting when I was still in short pants, although he is still considerably younger than many of the regular shooting scribes! He also likes to talk loudly in lifts, while I have long been of the 'stand quietly and contemplate your navel' variety.

'Off to shoot anything soon?' he asked in his Hooray Henriest voice, knowing well that it would wind up the ten urbanites crammed into the same lift. I went a darker shade of puce. 'Erm, I, erm, have to go to Scotland tomorrow. Flighting geese under a full moon.'

Jonathan started laughing. 'The Holy Grail of goose shooting? Good luck to you! Who on earth promised you that?!'

The lift reached the first floor, home of the company canteen. I wriggled out with an apologetic grin, as though I had it all in order and didn't need to answer. Jonathan continued to the ground floor and I was left to field the reproachful glare of a woman with short pink hair who evidently thought shooting anything, let alone pinkfeet at night, was a bad idea.

I'll show you, I thought to myself as I munched a granary bap in the canteen. I was still thinking it the next evening in the village of Kinross, as PQ and I waited for our goose guide to arrive. After all, what could possibly go wrong? When I had organised the trip with our man Gary at the CLA Game Fair earlier in the year, he had assured me it would be a cake walk. 'Just give me a few days' notice, as to which full moon you want to go for, and I'll take you out with some of my punters,' he had said. 'Anything you like.'

Being the trusting kind – some might call it naivety – I believed him, to the extent that I had a four-page article scheduled in for the following week's issue. I had it all worked out in my mind. PQ would get dramatic shots of geese passing under the full moon or maybe a profile of a shooter silhouetted against the night sky; while I would capture the bewitched thrall of these lunatic sportsmen. It would be prize-winning stuff, for sure. And we had a window of about twenty-four hours to achieve it.

When Gary picked us up from the hotel at half past five that morning, he did not look so tidy and chipper as he had done at the Game Fair. Indeed, he looked like he hadn't slept in three days and if he had, it was on a haystack. At under five foot six, he reminded me of the tragic Archibald Ives in the *Great Escape,* only dressed in full camouflage neoprene and a tweed cap. There were bags under one eye like a coalman's caddy, while the other sported a shiner of a recent vintage. Best not to ask, but already my bravado was beginning to wilt.

'I woke up at two and I've not been able to sleep since,' he said, by way of explanation, as we approached the ditch in a field where we would set camp. It had gone seven by now and there was a bite in the air as cold as a penguin's stare. 'Normally it wouldn't be so bad, as the pinks will be fairly predictable with their feeding habits and regime,' he said, navigating his vehicle through the muddy tyre ruts that sloshed with the excess rain of the last few months. In my mind, I heard the voice of Jonathan Young pre-empting the next word with a loud, BUT…

'But when the full moon's out, they do their own thing. There seems to be no pattern to what they do. It's almost a case of pot luck whether they come your way or not.' I nodded and smiled at him in the half-light, as though this was exactly what I expected. On my notepad I scribbled the words, 'bugger, bugger, bugger'.

My optimism had not been entirely misplaced. After all, it had been a bumper year for geese on the farmland around Kinross, with an estimated twenty-five thousand birds flocking into Loch Leven, one of the biggest turnouts in living memory. Gary with his partner in crime Colin had provided three hundred geese for guests since the start of October. The pair of rogues rallied round in the field, like Burke and Hare, setting out the hide and decoys for the two shooters who had travelled up from Devon for their first attempt at goose flighting. It was a race against time, before we were rumbled by a scout goose on a pre-breakfast recce.

We took our place in the freezing mud trench and watched the first chevrons of geese fly over the loch, a kilometre to our right. Gary gave them a speculative call, but if they heard it, they ignored it. The gooseman seemed to read my worried eyes.

'One of the great problems we have now is that the geese are under so much pressure from shooters that they have become impressively cautious. They are nervous about settling anywhere. Sometimes they give a warning cry and take off when there is nothing to scare them. Add that to the mysteries of the full moon and you can see why it becomes guesswork at times.' I added another 'bugger' to my list.

If I had done my research, then none of this would have been a surprise. For one, anyone who knows anything about geese flighting knows they go haywire under the moon. Also, an unavoidable truth about goose guides is that they don't like telling it straight. I'm sure there are exceptions to the rule, but the policy seems to be: promise the world, collect the money, then do what you can. It is a competitive business, with plenty of speculators after a finite number of birds, so scruples can be a hindrance. You will never hear a good word from one goose guide about another, indeed it is usually fairly slanderous.

The morning was not a complete write-off. One of the guests, James Baron, had brought a magnificent eight bore hammergun, made by Edward Paton & Sons of London in 1871. It was still in pristine condition and its owner was desperate to get it dirty. He had been sent forward by Gary to intercept any higher birds that flew over the trees by the loch and within ten minutes the plan bore fruit. A team of pinks flew sixty yards over and James let the old girl speak, shattering the morning silence with an almighty boom. A goose plummeted from the sky.

Gary's face was one of pure relief. 'I've never been so pleased to see a goose fall in all my life.' Another squadron of pinkfeet flew into range above James' head and again the small cannon rang out, but this time the two shots were just milliseconds apart.

'It has never double-discharged before,' said James later, still flushed as he carried his goose. 'I reckon it was because my hands were so cold that I snatched at the trigger. I was on my knees when I shot and the force of it knocked me on my back!'

While the rest of us went for a late lunch and a siesta before the evening flight, Gary and Colin spent the whole afternoon trying to work out which way the geese would fly. They reckoned to have covered 130 miles before satisfying themselves they had a vague clue what would happen. Gary was in a reflective mood by the time the moon was up. 'There's no point in me promising lots of action, when I can't be sure,' he said ruefully. 'This year, our shooters have had an amazing time, but these are wild birds after all. If it does happen tonight, under a full moon, then you'll never forget it for

JANUARYFEBRUARYMARCHAPRILMAYJUNEJULYAUGUSTSEPTEMBEROCTOBERNOVEMBERDECEMBER the rest of your puff, I promise you that,' said Gary, as we took our place behind some silage bags in a field by the Loch. 'For the chance of that alone, it is worth coming out here.'

At Gary's feet sat Hoosend. Shaped like a straw bale, with a head like a rugby ball, he was the biggest yellow Labrador I had ever seen, bigger even than the Commondale Yeti. 'There's a saying round here "to be built like a hoose end", so it kind of caught on. He is one hell of a strong dog and the only one I've seen dive down into the water after a goose. The only problem is when he tries to carry two at the same time!'

The moon, fat and happy, was now high in the sky, revealing the countryside like daylight. Now and again it was hidden by a veil of cloud to remind the worshippers below it was indeed night time, before breaking through to admire its reflection on the still, cool, geese-littered water of loch Leven. The honk of activity on the loch was increasing in volume, as though the geese were preparing to lift off for their evening feed. But the Guns' hopes rose only to be dashed as the first ribbons of mist began to rise up from the ground like spectres. The field was fast turning into a Sherlock Holmes crime scene and within ten minutes the banks of the loch were hidden. 'I'm afraid they'll not fly in this,' said Gary, waving the Guns over. I did feel sorry for him. He had worked flat out to provide a chance at the sublime, but the conditions were against us. But I felt a lot more sorry for myself. I would have to take the stairs at work for the next three weeks....

JANUARY
FEBRUARY
MARCH
APRIL
MAY
JUNE
JULY
AUGUST
SEPTEMBER
OCTOBER
NOVEMBER
DECEMBER

45.

Farm shoots

It is not often I am given a gun for the day – indeed, most of the time I have been grateful to leave it to others. As previously mentioned, this was largely because I never used to be able to hit a barn door at four paces, so it was embarrassing to be the only one firing at the clouds. Some shoots might kindly offer me a weapon for a couple of drives at the end of the day, usually with the expectation that someone who works for the *Shooting Times* will be able to shoot. As with so many sports, if your confidence has dropped, then your success rate follows.

But if someone was to offer me a day right now, I would bite their hand off. This change in attitude is largely thanks to a shoot in Dorset called Courtbury Shoot, which is set out across two farms either side of the quirky village of Shapwick, near Blandford. The owner John Chappell invited me to take a gun for the whole day and to immerse myself in the occasion. His son Paul is a good friend from university, so I had an ally in the line, and I soon found myself at ease. Too often in the past, shooting was work. OK, it is not a bad job to be involved in, but it is work nonetheless. On a shoot day, I would usually be chasing round after quotes, interviewing the keeper or flattering the Guns. I would be a representative of the magazine, on best behaviour, stiff as a garden rake. At Courtbury I was able to relax and appreciate, perhaps even for the first time, what this shooting lark was really all about.

With a mixture of flat pasture land, hedgerows, small plantations and wetland by the river Stour, it may not be the place to come for stratospheric pheasants or non-stop action, yet the team of Guns still proved the birds can take some hitting! No, at Courtbury there is ample time to smell the turnips along the way. Participation is by invitation only and members of the syndicate who muck in with the releasing, planting, feeding, foxing and general husbandry pay less than those who do not. The scenery is picture postcard; the people are pleased to meet you; and the lunch portions are generous. In short, you can keep your Taj Mahal, Grand Canyon and Uluru. There's nowhere else I would rather have been on a sunny day in November.

And was it ever sunny! Just the day before, it was as if someone upstairs had fiddled with the thermostat and switched the power shower to cold. Even the ducks were starting to seek refuge. But this morning I was delighted to be awoken early by the bright light shining through the curtains.

John is tenant farmer on the National Trust's Bishops Court Farm and gave the pre-shoot instructions before the party set off. While some shoot captains will hurriedly mumble something along the lines of 'no ground game, number left to right, move up three, good luck gentlemen', John revels in his role as both watchdog and motivator. It is a valuable exercise, moreover, as there are few shooting teams where everybody knows each other and, just like the beaters' wagon, it can be a lonely place if you are not 'one of the lads'. After all, driven game shooting is a team sport and John cleverly incorporated each member into the fold, usually with some gentle leg-pulling to break any ice that remained.

There were a few serious reminders though along the way. 'There is a very good chance that you will come across some dog walkers or ramblers who use the footpaths,' explained the circus master. 'Please tell them politely that a shoot is taking place and ask if they will wait until the end of the drive. More often than not, they will be interested in what is going on and if you explain it in a friendly manner, they may be grateful to you. You could also tell them there is the chance of a day's paid beating too! However, if they are unwilling to wait, then allow them through and inform the shoot captain or somebody with a radio, so the drive can be stopped until they are out of range.'

John also stressed the need to avoid dropping birds in other people's back gardens and eliminate the possibility of pellets falling on farm cottages. 'And do not shoot the white ducks! The final point is that you enjoy yourselves. But anyone persistently offering shoot advice unless asked for is liable to be red-carded!'

Paul was to my left and a local farmer called Martyn Tory was to my right. Both were about the only two who shot consistently well during the day. Martyn hails from Crab farm in Shapwick, the origin of which derives from a colourful episode in the village's history. The legend goes that in the late eighteenth century, a fishmonger was wheeling his barrow of wares between Wimborne and Blandford. En route, a mighty crab fell off the back of his barrow unnoticed and the merchant continued to Blandford. Now, the villagers, who were all rural folk who had never been to the coast, let alone seen a crab, were sore afraid of the alien creature with grasping claws, hard shell and wriggling legs, although no doubt it has grown in size down the generations. The local elder, a sickly shepherd, was dragged from his bed to pass judgement on the crab, which he declared to be a 'monster'. History does not relate what happened to the crab, although one story is that the fishmonger returned and took it back, making them all feel a bit stupid. Either way, the people of Shapwick were thereafter viewed as yokel simpletons.

Martyn also had a rather poignant story to tell about one of the beaters who worked regularly during the season at the Crab Shoot and nearby Dewlish Shoot. Harry Street, aged seventy-three, was a popular character in the team, who made all the flags for the beaters during the summer months. 'He had apparently already made the flags for next season and this year he seemed as fit as he had been for a long time,' explained Martyn. 'In the morning he was in high spirits as ever, but all of a sudden he went a terrible colour and began to clutch his shoulder. It was over very quickly. The Air Ambulance came immediately and the team of medics were truly terrific, but there was nothing they could do. We always joke that it would be a lovely way to go, out shooting in the field, and maybe Harry was one of the lucky few.' The syndicate immediately disbanded the day. At his funeral, the church was packed with members of the shoot and his coffin was carried through a salute of plastic flags.

Having a gun rather than a notepad does give a different insight into how a shoot works. For one, the field of vision is that much narrower. You have your patch on each drive, with a limited arc on which to concentrate. So much of the rest of the shoot, be it the hard work of the beaters, their dogs hunting through the briars, the execution of tactics by the keeper or the expert retrieval by pickers-up, goes largely unseen. There are brief opportunities to exchange small talk with beaters, especially if discussing a bird that needed picked. But more often than not, you are shepherded on to the next drive and your loyalty remains to the Guns. Perhaps that's how the beaters prefer it too – the last thing they want is some idiot in plus fours yabbering on to them about the weather or England's chances in the Ashes.

The names of the drives at Courtbury give some indication as to the terrain the beaters had to cover. Withybed to start with sent them through thick willow plantations and kale crops; while The Pit, Desperate Dung, Maize Madness and Beastly Brambles speak for themselves. I did manage to get a snippet from one beater who said they had to button up their jackets to the neck to avoid getting terrible itch from larch trees. 'Terrorist' is the best of the names, however, named after a cyclist who stopped on the road behind the line and shouted: 'What do you think you are? A bunch of terrorists?'

My most memorable contribution to the day came on the second drive Ram Lane, when I took an optimistic swipe at a high pigeon. Needless to state, as the woodie made good its escape, a woodcock flapped idly over my empty barrels. I was told afterwards that it had not been seen there for a couple of years and was the only one on the ground, so I'm pleased the option to shoot or not was out of my hands. 'Thank goodness you didn't shoot that owl!' cried John later, who had been watching from a good distance.

Sadly, Paul shot very well. He is one of those infuriating sportsmen who make everything look so easy, whether on the rugby or cricket field, and usually with no lack of flair or panache. An irregular shooter, there was a good chance he would be genuinely lousy, but it was a forlorn hope. I could only watch in disgruntled envy as he brought down birds with a flourish, a couple of which I had already missed. But, of course, that didn't matter. When you are among friends, everything is better. It was perhaps something I had forgotten in my years of being a stranger looking in from the outside. Shooting is not about anything else other than enjoying company in the outdoors. Although, when I wiped his eye after lunch, I did permit myself a small fist pump in celebration.

46. Fallow

When I first joined *Shooting Times*, I had to overcome a concern that almost stopped me from applying in the first place: how not to embarrass my father! As it turned out I need not have worried, but at the time I knew that many of his shooting pals read the magazine and given I knew precious little about what I was writing about, the potential for a balls-up was all too real. There were some factual mistakes and the odd split infinitive, which my 'critic from the North' would take great pleasure in pointing out, but by and large I got away with it. Presently, I learnt more and more about the lifestyle that he has enjoyed for decades, which has undoubtedly drawn us closer in the last four years. We all like to do well in the eyes of our parents, so hopefully one of his muckers has at some point said, 'I was reading the 'paper the other day and your son did an ok article'. That would please me a great deal.

Sentimentality aside, the job has also given me scope to visit my parents in Perthshire more often than I might have done and when I needed a piece done at short notice, my father usually knew someone who could help. But it was a double-edged sword. Mess it up and I was for the high jump!

One such emergency article featured fallow stalking with a keeper of an estate where my father picks up. We were up in the hills above Dunkeld, which is home to one of the biggest herds of black fallow deer in Scotland. Although identical in every other way to the traditional spotted fallow that one associates with parkland and stately homes, these are a dull, dark grey from head to foot.

My guide was thirty-three-year-old New Zealander Tim Lee, who has worked in Scotland for five years. Settling in to the close-knit keepering fraternity in Perthshire, where everybody knows each other, was a daunting task that put Tim under both social and professional pressure. 'It was a bit difficult at first, as it must be for anyone new, as I guess there was a little resentment that the post had not gone to a local lad,' he said, looking out towards Loch Ordie, several thousand miles from Lake Taupo where he was brought up. 'But as long as you work hard and don't upset anyone, then they soon take to you. When they start insulting you to your face, then you know you've been accepted!'

Tall and lean, with a dark complexion, Tim looks more like a catalogue model than a keeper and certainly far removed from the stereotypical short, red-faced Scottish ghillie. Like most Kiwis, he can rough it up on the rugby field if needs be, although he finds the standard much more to his liking over here. 'I played number eight down under to a fair standard and when you do well, you can expect a bit of a kicking. In my first match in Scotland, I made a good break, the full back tackled me, but I off-loaded the ball to set up a try. Instinctively, I put my hands over my head, because that is usually when some big Maori puts his size tens into you for doing something good. Instead, a member of the oppo put his hand out to pull me up and said, 'well played'. I couldn't believe it!'

The scenery, heritage and people that typify this stretch of the Highlands have made a lasting impression on Tim and he was already an excellent tour guide to the local area. As we drove up to the place he most expected to see a beast, he pointed out ruined settlements that once made up a thriving community on the banks of Loch Benachally. 'It used to be a market used by the drovers and you can see the old holding pens where they kept their sheep. That ruin is the inn and it's warming to think of the parties that must have gone on there. You have so much social history in Scotland. Do you see that crater? It was caused by bombing practice during the Second World War. We also found an illicit still in the hills, which the locals would use to make whisky without the excise men knowing. I think everyone takes this stuff for granted, but I love it – I mean, my cottage here is older than my country!' He later pointed out Grews Well, an ancient spring made famous by early Christian missionaries. The clear water is believed to have healing properties that will cure anything from whooping cough to lumbago. 'The tradition states that the waters are most effective on the first Sunday in May,' said Tim, parking the Toyota Hilux. 'I gave it a go and took a few bottles back to New Zealand, but it didn't make a great difference.'

The cultural tour was all well and good, but we were there for more pressing matters. With the low visibility, the tactics were simple: we would hopefully walk into a fallow doe and shoot it before it clocked us. There was precious little wind, so there was a chance we could get close, if only we could spot them in the mist. Our first foray drew a blank, but on the way back to the vehicle, Tim froze in his tracks. He gave a signal to crouch down into the deep ruts of the track. I hadn't seen a thing and it was only by following the stalker's line of sight that I spotted a single doe on the slope of a hillock, some seventy yards away.

Tim later explained that he rarely used binoculars back home in New Zealand as it is usually stalking at close quarters through thick vegetation, so he learnt quickly to spot deer with eyesight alone. The fallow raised its head, but soon returned to eating, satisfied that it was safe to do so. 'It looks like a calf without its mother,' Tim whispered, easing the .243 off his back. 'She is unlikely to survive the winter, so we're best to take her now.'

I was meant to be shooting, but I made no argument when Tim gestured that he was going to go it alone. My clumsy actions would have doubtless given the game away. Edging back along the wheel ruts on his haunches like a Cossack dancer, he soon reached a vantage point where he could slide onto his chest. At no more than fifty yards, any rash movement would have startled the deer, so Tim slowly released the rifle's bipods and cocked the weapon, sliding the bolt back until the bullet popped into the chamber, before pushing the action back into the firing position. He will never carry the rifle with a bullet up the spout, although he appreciates that many experienced stalkers prefer it that way. With both eyes open, Tim aimed and fired. He did a lot of rabbit shooting Down Under and taught himself to shoot with both eyes open. The calf fell. This Kiwi always begins the gralloch by turning the corpse on its right hand side and cutting out the spleen, which he finds helps to loosen the entrails. 'The winters here are pretty harsh and it is unlikely this calf would have put enough fat on to survive the winter,' Tim repeated, justifying the shot to himself. 'Our job at the moment is to cull down the number of weaker, smaller does. This season we have stayed off the bucks, as their numbers have depleted in recent years.' The mist was now clinging to the peat hags, making stalking nigh on impossible. 'The plan would usually be to skirt round the side of that gut, what you would call a corrie, to get upwind and then glass for beasts from the top of that slope,' Tim said, as a bullfinch flitted across the heather, building up its own fat reserves for the winter. 'But in this light there could be dozens of them up there and we wouldn't see them before they saw us. Yet, there still may be a chance, because even when startled, a fallow doesn't move far from its favoured ground. They can be a bit kamikaze.'

On a clear day, the stalker would be able spy beasts in the distance and take up to eight off the hill in one day. In these conditions our tactics were limited: crawl forward to the top of a hillock and peer over the other side. And just as it seemed that our luck was out for the day, Tim froze again like a pointer on a grouse covey. 'I tell you what…' he started, ushering us behind a boulder the size of a caravan that must have been there since man started hunting deer. He had spotted three deer: a doe and two young males. The pair of spikers moved away to the left, leaving the yearling doe no more than fifty yards from the boulder. She stood still long enough for Tim to rest the rifle on the stone and take a standing shot at her chest.

'That was just plain good luck, she was in the perfect position,' he said afterwards, turning the doe onto her right side. 'Had she been higher up the hill then I wouldn't have had a safe backdrop to stop the bullet. It could have ended up in Pitlochry! Did you notice though that after I took the shot, the two bucks ran on thirty yards before stopping to have a look? It's always worth waiting for that with fallow, and reloading quickly, as you often get a second opportunity.'

By the time we made it back to the truck, Loch Ordie was invisible through the mist. We would not be so lucky again. As we drove off the hill, we passed another group of fallow, including a white, spotty doe. Tim ignored them. 'We would never take a shot from a vehicle,' he said, 'As we don't want the deer to associate cars with rifles. As such, they have no fear of cars at all. Apart from anything else, it's a real pleasure just to sit and watch them as you drive along. I genuinely think that fallow are the best deer to eat and today's young beasts will be delicious. You should take a haunch away with you in a chilli-bin or at least give one to your father. Cover it in marmalade or pineapple jam, roast it in the oven and you'll eat nothing better!'

47.
Big bags/
high birds

A great many people involved in shooting love a good grumble about big bag days. 'If you can't remember every bird you shot in a day, then its excessive,' they say. 'These four hundred plus days are giving the industry a bad name.' Some would rather that every Gun is prepared to take home and eat each bird they shoot. Others are at their happiest pottering after a few pheasants and a rabbit with their dog and a pal.

'They're shooting birds that are out of range nowadays,' is another complaint heard regularly.

'These pheasants are just targets to these people. They'd be as well to shoot clay pigeons, for all they care about them.'

In my experience, that is predominately not the case, although there is the odd bad apple out there to rot the rest of us. I once watched an individual on a high 350-bird day in Wales, who was there as part of a company excursion. There was not the usual camaraderie that defines a shooting party, but rather a steely competition between business colleagues. The man I stood with for one drive kept leering to his loader that 'I've touched that one' or 'that one's pricked' as he fired at birds he had little chance of killing. Not once did he turn round to see where they landed. Happily, despite his protestations, he missed nearly all of them cleanly, although it was still a grotesque display. He was an exception to the rule.

In one week in Scotland, I was fortunate enough to watch two shoots where high birds were an art-form. The first was on an estate called St Mary's Isle in Kirkcudbrightshire. *Shooting Times* had been invited to celebrate the retirement of the keeper Willie Little, who had been employed for fifty years since the age of fifteen. If you told a teenager nowadays that he would be in the same job for the next fifty years, he might very well jump off the nearest bridge. But when Willie Little took a post as under keeper, it was the done thing. You found the right position, made it your own and worked at it until you retired. The owner Sir David Hope-Dunbar asked us to profile Willie and the high quality shoot that he has developed over his long tenure.

The opening drive was the one that sticks most in the memory. It was aptly called Paradise, although this name does not stem from the standard of birds, but rather the brilliant swathes of bluebells that will carpet the wood in spring. But if you like your birds high and fast, then this drive is a small slice of Scottish paradise. The Guns line out half way down a steep slope to the left of mature woodland from where the pheasants appear at great height and set their wings once they have reached top speed.

For the cricked neck spectator, you wonder whether these birds are going to be in range, but the first two shots by the owner's son Charles Hope-Dunbar answered that question as a right and left of cocks fell to the ground. In the glory days of shooting, crowds would gather to watch the Top Shots strut their stuff against beautifully presented pheasants and those throngs would not have been disappointed by the team at Paradise.

Willie evidently runs a tight ship as the birds would arrive in a trickle, allowing each Gun to watch as his team member did his level best to bring down what flew above him. It was high octane sport with the Guns needing to swing hard to keep up. 'This certainly gets the adrenaline flowing,' puffed Charles, as his neighbour dropped a hen at his feet. 'You need to be confident and in good touch to hit these birds. If you don't believe you are going to kill them every time, then you won't.' Charles is now in his early thirties and so grew up with Willie as the estate gamekeeper. 'He taught us all to shoot and fish when we were kids, and passed down much of his knowledge about the countryside.'

Many of the Guns and beaters had been shooting or working at St Mary's Isle for at least two decades. Everybody knew each other and had countless stories to retell. The lunch was superb. The birds were in first class condition flying fast and high, but the shooters were up to it. Like an old, mature golf course, it was a treat for those allowed to play.

The other shoot that proved high is mighty was a friendly shoot called Ardtaraig, also in the west of Scotland. If you go west from Glasgow across on the Clyde ferry, you find yourself in Dunoon. Continue in the same direction for another inch on the map and you are lost in the first of the wild Argyll peninsulas that creep like fingers down the side of Scotland. When you reach the head of the great sea Loch Striven, stop a while, because you have found Ardtaraig, a jewel in this rugged landscape. I was invited to watch a day's driven shooting with a party of Dutch Guns. The week preceding had been dogged with driving wind and snow, but by the time we arrived the weather had cleared. Rain showers would speed in from the coast, but they had little chance to dampen spirits as the southerly wind soon replaced them with blue skies and rainbows that dipped their toes in the cold waters of the loch.

Ardtaraig provides a full range of challenges for able shooters, although it is advisable to warm up with a few back exercises first. Natural contours allow the birds to gather height and pace, setting their wings as they bid to escape to mature woodland. During a day, Guns can expect to shoot high birds over open terrain as well as snap shooting in rides at pheasants that skim above the treetops. There is no shame in missing here!

The showpiece drive on the estate, called Two Hundred and Forty Eight Metres, as that is the height above sea level of the highest grain hopper, typifies the challenge to Guns at Ardtaraig. The beaters, nimble and agile, scurry up the steep slope as the Guns leisurely take their place at the bottom on the other side of the Tarsan river. These hills were once grazed bare by sheep, but the white peril have been removed to allow the heather, gorse and bracken to grow back, providing ideal cover for the birds.

The keeper Anton prefers English black leg pheasants as they grow quickly and are fit to tackle the harsh landscape before other strains. 'Of course, by the start of the season, we want the birds to be strong flyers and so I will feed them up the hill by cutting the supply of grain from lower hoppers. Eventually, they are accustomed to feeding right at the top.' These black legs were in top flying condition and they would spring forward as though they knew what would happen if they did not. Every time a small flush of birds got up, the beaters would stop to watch, ensuring that the

Another right and left of fresh air.

drive was long and action packed. The Guns took a while to find their range, but soon they were all pulling down memorable pheasants.

'That was just amazing,' said one Gun called Eric who had shot especially well. 'They come so high and you have almost too much time to think about them! It is a little easier though to miss if your colleague has already missed. There is no pressure! The highest hill in Holland is 271 m and it is only just higher than that hopper. This is why we love coming to Scotland – it is so different!'

Visiting Guns at Ardtaraig will not pay per bird as is often the case elsewhere, but rather they will pay for a day that will provide nine hundred shots. 'We believe it has to be the way forward for shoots,' said the owner Keith Chalmers-Watson. 'If the Guns shoot the birds, then fine. But if they don't, then it's tough luck. By setting a bag number, it puts a great deal of pressure on keepers and Guns alike, and it can lead to tension, which is the last thing you need on what should be a fun day out. We aim to provide testing, sporting birds here and I think we do a good job, so it was not uncommon for teams of Guns to operate at a ratio of five to one. We would then find ourselves a victim of our own success. By only giving Guns the option of buying sport by the day, rather than the bag, we find it allows them to relax more.'

Perhaps it is a formula that other shoots would be wise to follow.

48.

Moose

'Pull, London Man, pull!' shouted Veijo, a colour sergeant in the Finnish army, who was the ideal person to drive the twelve-strong haulage team dragging the four hundred kilo bull moose from the forest. 'Come on London Man, put your back into it,' he screamed, as I tripped forward on a tree root and face-planted in the mud. The troupe of local beaters in their orange bibs stopped to point and laugh at the sprawling foreigner laid flat against the enormous steaming carcase. I suspected they were glad of the rest, as it was hard work pulling the awkward creature over rough terrain. I looked up from the dirt to see Veijo grinning back at me. 'You must be strong to be a hunter,' he roared, flexing his large bicep and twisting his wrist in imitation of a swan. 'You are lucky, London Man. Often we have to pull much bigger bulls for two kilometres over bogs and hills.'

I was in woodland to the north-east of Helsinki, a guest of the famous rifle manufacturers Sako, who supply a great many guns to hunters throughout Europe and America. The moose had just been shot by a Canadian gun dealer called Allan Gallagher, who had sold more Sako rifles than anyone else in his part of North America and hence won the opportunity to join the Topenon Era hunting club on a driven moose shoot. The club members, who include locals like Veijo and several of the Sako marketing team, were delighted that one of their guests had made a clean kill and a sprig of fir was placed in Allan's orange cap, while a bottle of whisky was handed round to drink his health and honour the bull.

At this point, some readers may be getting exasperated by my use of the word 'moose', as technically the animal is called an elk in Europe. Only the Americans call him a moose. I make no apology, however, that I will continue to write moose, as that was the word every Finn on the trip used when they saw *Alces alces*, and that's good enough for me. Besides, it does sound better, no?

Every year, the Finns will halve the population of moose, culling nearly ninety thousand animals a year in an attempt to keep on top of their numbers. Road traffic accidents are the greatest threat of the moose. Their long legs mean that the bulky body is at eye-level of the oncoming vehicle, which often has fatal consequences.

Though guests of Sako, we were entirely in the hands of the local club. 'We are going to hunt like the Finns hunt,' explained Pentti Louhisola, an education manger for Sako and something of a hunting icon in Finland. What he does not know about hunting is not worth knowing. 'Hunting in the forest is seen as the right of every Finn, so it is very cheap for anyone to shoot and join a club. It is more a way of life than an exclusive sport as it can be in the UK, and each club has a quota of moose to cull each season.'

Members of the club take it in turn to be Rifles or beaters, though it is common for some beaters to carry rifles in case a moose doubles back. A good shot is a clean shot, so any range less than a hundred yards is advised. The moose are driven towards the Rifles who are lined up along clearings or tracks, often in high seats. As a result the moose will be moving at speed, so every Rifle must pass a hunting marksman test before he can take to the field.

Naturally we visitors were expected to take the test too, which we did on a nearby range. To pass, three shots from a standing position must be placed in a stationary life-size bull moose target at seventy-five yards within twenty seconds, and then three in a moving target, which runs across the range on rails. Unless these three moving shots are made consecutively, you start again from scratch until you can manage three in a row. Each score is posted on an electronic board after each shot, with 1 being on the outer ring of the target and 10 being a bull's eye. Get a 0 and you've missed, and you start again. Fail five times and you're on the next plane home.

'It is not as bad as it sounds,' said Pentii reassuringly. 'Remember to swing from the legs – like the tower of a tank – and not with the hands.

Aim at the beard which hangs from its chin and remember to follow through.'

The stationary shots were a formality with the high-powered telescopes fitted to a Sako 75 Finnlight. I was last on the list for the running shots and watched intently as all the other Rifles passed on the first or second attempt. Just aim at the beard, I told myself, and swing through. Try not to think of the consequences if you miss. The shame of telling the editor that you spent the whole weekend beating because you were incapable of shooting. The frustration of listening to the guys in the bar at night retelling their tales of conquest. The soul-crushing pain of failure. In practice I had done well. Just aim at the beard.

On the first attempt I missed the third target, so had to start again. On the second attempt, the fateful 0 flashed up again. On the third attempt, I missed all three. 'You're starting to panic,' said the instructor beside me. You're bloody right I am! If I had carried on in that vein, I would surely have failed, but I managed to make myself take a step backwards, take a few deep breaths and re-focus.

'Where am I missing it?' I asked meekly. 'You're way out in front,' came the reply. For the next three shots, I aimed just in front of the bull's eye and the scoreboard flashed up with a 1, 6 and a second 1. There was a cheer behind me. I had passed. Just. But I would hardly be full of confidence as we took to the woods.

To make me feel even more of a dunderhead, Sako's production manager Erkki Kauppi demonstrated their revolutionary bolt action by putting three shots in the moving target before it had finished its four-second course. Given my own difficulty at passing the test, I made a mental note to only shoot at stationary beasts for fear of wounding an animal. A moose shot in the guts will run for three kilometres, where it will eventually be found by the hunters' Corellian bear dogs or Norwegian Grey Elkhounds. While, I am sure, this would have added another dimension to the story, it was the last thing I wanted.

Pentii echoed my concerns, giving me an avuncular pat on the shoulder. 'You'll do just fine,' he said. 'But shoot only if you can be sure of a good hit – if not, let it go. If it is running too fast, if it is behind trees, if you are not sure of its sex or age, let it go. Any shot not taken, is a good shot.' We had an evening back in camp before the driven moose shoot itself. We were treated like princes throughout the stay, feasting on local dishes and fine wine. The evening would always start with a communal visit to the chalet sauna, where twenty of us would throw back beers in the nude, crammed into the steamy enclosure, telling stories of hunting and derring-do. All good male-bonding stuff! I had never shot a deer before at that point, so could do little more than listen and nod as if this was just yet another hunting sauna.

The next morning we were awoken by the sound of torrential rain, hardly ideal conditions for a moose hunt. That said, the previous year, temperatures had dropped to minus twenty degrees with horizontal blizzards, so we could count ourselves fortunate. Juuso Austin, Sako's exports sales manager, explained that rain will lead to problems. 'Often, they will decide to sit still and not play the game. The bulls, especially, are not stupid, and they will let the women and children go first to see if any shots are fired. If there are, the bulls try to sneak out the back door.'

In my state of low confidence, I decided to join the beating line on the first afternoon, especially as we had shivered in the rain all morning. A drive is usually about fifteen hundred metres in length with about eighty metres between each of the fifteen or so beaters. Each beater has their own call to push the moose forward, a sort of 'hey-ho' sung in their preferred way. To my left was a rich baritone and to my right a deep bass and there was something a little magical about walking through these ancient forests listening to the eerie melodies of the hunters. I didn't see any moose on my journey, but the odd capercaillie shifted off its perch as I passed. When we regrouped at the end, Mr Bass approached me and announced in his deep Finnish accent, 'I feel it in my fingers, I feel it in my toes.' I looked back blankly. 'It's Wet, Wet, Wet,' he said, chuckling to himself. On the final drive of the day, Allan shot his bull from two hundred yards. By this stage, I had been christened London Man by the team of beaters – I think I have one of those faces that attracts nicknames – and was quickly recruited to join in the removal crew. Again, it made me realise that wounding an animal and sending it a few kilometres to a slow death, would be a sorry mistake. If these lads had to drag it back that far, they might decide on a different name altogether.

After an another boozy sauna and slap-up meal, we were back out in the rain the following morning. Having seen Allan's jubilation, I realised it would be crazy not to give it a go myself and so took to the high seats with the rest of the team. In the morning, one of the armed beaters shot a calf that had doubled back from its mother. Bulls, cows and calves are all fair game on a driven moose hunt, but it is understandably frowned upon to shoot a mother first. Indeed, many hunters will never shoot a cow for fear of leaving a dependent young.

The afternoon was our last opportunity to bag a moose on the trip and by the final drive, my mood had changed from caution to bullish aggression. I had begun to feel a bit more confident in my ability and was willing an animal to emerge from the woods. For that final drive, I was stood in a high seat some twelve feet from the ground, which would provide a safe angle to shoot. We were lined along a wide ride in the forest, each Rifle 150 yards apart. If I didn't attempt a shot, I knew I would regret it, so steeled myself for the moment.

It all happened very quickly. To my left, a white-tailed deer came bounding down the ride before stopping fifty yards from my seat. It would have been an easy shot, even for me, and I pondered my misfortune that this was a moose-only day. Then, out of the corner of my right eye, I saw a second movement by the trees in front. It was a moose! This was a bull moose too, with a great rack of antlers sprouting from its head like a Christmas tree. A Finnish moose does not have the palmated spade-like antlers of his North American cousin Bullwinkle, but pointed tips more similar to the red or roe deer.

This chap was a monster or so it seemed as he moved across the clearing at a trot. Everything slowed down. Indeed, I can remember it in my mind's eye as though it has just happened and my heart steps up a beat just to write about it. Despite the confidence crises of the last few days and my own concerns about wounding an animal, my brain focussed immediately on the task in hand. I was going to shoot this animal and nothing else mattered. I knew it was a safe shot and I knew this was a mature male, so there was no reason to back off. The moose reached a ditch in the middle of the ride and hesitated before jumping. He was eighty yards away and an easy target with a telescopic sight on a Sako 75 Lefthand rifle.

I aimed at his chest and pulled the trigger. The animal stumbled forward, but regained its footing and trotted forward into the woods. I loaded another 30.06 calibre cartridge into the chamber, but the beast had gone. My heart felt like it was trying to bust out of my ribcage, while I was breathing like a fish out of water. For a second, the white-tailed deer and I held eye-contact, as though asking each other, 'what on earth had I done?' before it doubled back into the woods. I had missed. I was sure of it. Worse still, had I wounded it? Had I been so caught up in the moment, that I had ignored my self-doubts and taken a shot I could not convert. Unloading the rifle, I placed it on the floor at my feet in disgust. We were under strict instructions to stay in the seat until the drive was over, so I simply stood there, cursing myself out loud, and praying that everything would be all right. After what seemed like an eternity, the beaters arrived and we went to see where the moose had gone.

It lay dead in the trees. In the excitement, I had not realised that my neighbour Stephen Way, an experienced shooter from the gun suppliers GMK, had shot at the same time. We had both shot the beast in the lungs. Indeed, the entry hole of my bullet could not have been better positioned if I had done it point blank. It was testament to the strength of the bull that it had run forty yards before falling dead. At more than 450 kilos and the length of a small car, it was a humbling sight. Erkki insisted on gralloching the animal, taking great pleasure in doing a good job for a first time moose hunter. Everybody was so pleased for me, which was genuinely touching. Juuso produced a bottle of Cognac from nowhere, which brought a little of the colour back to my cheeks. Viejo, the colour sergeant, gave me a thump on the back and tensed both bicep muscles again, before placing a sprig of fir in my cap.

I certainly felt guilty in bringing down an animal of that size, but relief and later elation took over. And yes, there was a little pride that I had overcome my demons to make a clean kill. I was also exceptionally hungry and when Erkki presented me with the animal's liver at the end, I took great pleasure in toasting it on a log fire at the hunting lodge. That evening, I walked tall into the sauna. Finally, I had a hunting story to tell.

JANUARY
FEBRUARY
MARCH
APRIL
MAY
JUNE
JULY
AUGUST
SEPTEMBER
OCTOBER
NOVEMBER
DECEMBER

49.

Perfect pheasants

Over the last four years, I must have visited at least forty different driven pheasant shoots during the shooting season to document the various shooters, birds, drives, dogs and keepers for the magazine. Compared with many of the older writers, I am something of a novice, but it has still been a useful apprenticeship. Without wanting to give too much mystique away, shoot reports are not that taxing to write. If the reporter can get a quote from the shoot captain, a couple of Guns, the gamekeeper, his underkeeper, a picker-up or two, and a talkative beater; then he's almost there. Knit these quotes together with an observation about the weather, the terrain, some local history and a quirky dog; and very soon the word count reads two thousand. The rest of the day is yours! I have been asked why I bother going at all. Why not send along a snapper and piece the story together from the pictures? As long as I knew the main protagonists, surely it would be easier to write that such and such shot a fine cock pheasant, while so and so's dog executed a perfect retrieve of a partridge on the third drive. The chances are they probably did. Interview the keeper the next day on the phone; invent a couple of generic beaters who would 'rather not be named'; and fill the rest of the text with sun-sparkling cobwebs, song-filled hedgerows and soggy spaniels. From the comfort of my own desk.

Of course, this is idle talk. Truth is always better than fiction. Besides, it is a treat to be invited to so many private enclosures in Britain, ordinarily out of bounds to the public, let alone the media. However, if I was to invent the perfect pheasant day, then it wouldn't be far removed from a shoot in Cumbria named Albyfield. Few shooters will not be beaming from ear to ear on a sunny, yet nippy December morning. Streaks of fleecy cloud were all that interrupted the blue skies, while the dykes, gates and hedgerows, which divided the patchwork of fields, woods and scrubland, were wrapped in a frosty tarpaulin. And yes, the cobwebs were indeed sparkling in the sunlight!

Twenty-eight years ago a group of local farmers and school friends met for a handful of days each season to walk up the hedgerows and woodlands on their adjoining properties. Over the years the Albyfield shoot developed to include a few reared birds, strips of cover crop and new woodland. And while the shoot matured, so did the team of Guns, with the result that many of their children are now involved in the syndicate. The broad smiles and warm embraces as the vehicles arrived at the farm spoke volumes of the many experiences that had led up to this day.

The syndicate has lost only a handful of days down the years to bad weather, including the great floods in Carlisle, when nobody could get access to the shoot. The early days were very much 'hunt the pheasant', rough shooting over wide areas, but gradually they introduced reared birds. The shoot now has access to nine drives over undulating ground with steep banks, which are centred on one hundred acres. Every year they hold seven days, followed by a keepers'/beaters' day with an average of seventy to eighty birds a day.

The shoot is all about the keeper. Edwin Tailford will be seventy years old next year, but you would never guess it from the way he leads the beating line and orchestrates the Guns at the same time. Edwin has been farming and keepering in this part of Cumbria all his years and his knowledge of the area, its habitat, natural history and folklore is second to none. He is one of a fast disappearing generation of countrymen, tough as the ground they have worked all their years. Their knowledge used to be passed down, but fewer people want to listen now. Size matters for Edwin. The shoot itself is only one hundred acres, so all of the playing field must be employed to its optimum potential. 'My challenge is to show the best birds I possibly can in a limited space,' he told me, as the beaters blanked through a field of clarty set-aside which the keeper hoped might spring a few partridges. The shoot puts down one hundred partridges to mix things up, although one senses it is more of a hobby for Edwin. Only the one red-leg got up, but a pricked cock was picked, which more than justified the effort.

Like a canny squash player, Edwin uses the angles of the shoot to great effect, sending the birds from the food-rich cover crops over natural obstacles to the warm woodland where he houses the two release pens. To reach this respite, the birds must run the gauntlet of the pegs, a risky journey indeed as the Albyfield gunners are no mugs.

'In truth, I don't like to see a shoot too big,' Edwin said, tapping a hopper by a strip of kale and artichoke. A relaxed robin hopped from twig to twig on a nearby blackthorn, ignoring the commotion all around. 'I plant plenty of cover crop, as there is nothing like it for drawing the birds out of the woods. It's good soil here – red loam and clay – so they grow well. The secret for me though is big pens. I've been expanding and expanding them down the years, as you can't give pheasants too much space. It really is a simple, yet winning formula.'

Edwin puts down just over one thousand pheasants each year, bought from local game rearer Alan Sefton, who also beats and picks up at the shoot. The birds are split between two release pens, with six hundred in a 270 by 80 yard pen in the 'Big Wood' and 450 in the second 140 by 80 pen. The aim is to shoot a return of over fifty per cent, although that does not happen every year. The ground is dominated by the Big Wood on the hill, which Edwin refuses to shoot before Christmas, as he believes there are plenty of birds to keep the Guns busy until then. It also represents a safe haven for the birds in the run up to Christmas, so they are more likely to fly that way when Edwin wants them to.

'Alan has been giving us these French Black pheasants and they don't half fly well. Too well at times for the Guns, but we don't mind that,' he continued, as one cock evaded a flurry of shots to wing its nonchalant way to the Big Wood. 'We have to keep a few for the beaters' day after all.' There is no hiding the fondness that the Guns have for Edwin, who has overseen the evolution of the shoot, as well as acting as a father figure over the years. Edwin recently underwent an operation on a troublesome knee that threatened to curtail his career, and it was to great relief of all concerned that it was a resounding success.

'Ever since the shoot started, Edwin has been the glue that keeps it together,' said Miles McInnes, one of the founding members. 'And we are very pleased to give him recognition for that. He is one of the great countrymen, who knows so much about the land on which he has worked all his life. Sadly there are not many like him left. You can always tell when he doesn't agree with a proposition or idea, because he'll simply say "please yourself" and walk away.'

Now that Edwin has retired from farming, he spends his days keepering at this and the next door shoot, loading on the Pennine grouse moors or rowing as a ghillie on a stretch of the River Eden. 'He prides himself on showing excellent high birds over a remarkably small area and he is best pleased when they are too good for us!'

The third drive of the morning was being shot for only the second time and consisted of a high grassy slope dotted with a wide range of newly planted trees. The aim for the beaters was to swing round from left to right, pushing the birds high over the Guns that were lined out at the bottom of the slope. As the beaters advanced, the birds would trickle out at a steady pace to give all of the Guns a shot or two. Edwin oversaw the planting, which was funded by a forestry grant, and the mixed woodland of blackthorn, alder, oak, beech and spruce is growing well. There are also some obvious gaps in the plantation in order to provide rides and openings for the pheasants, as well as a possible lekking ground for black game.

The drive is known as Kate's Drive, named after the daughter of syndicate founder member Patrick Osborne, who was shooting alongside Kate's sister Ruth and her husband Alex Hampton. In April 2003, Kate went missing in Bali, where she had lived as an aid worker, English teacher and translator for nearly four years. Despite an agonising search by her parents in Bali, Kate is still missing and the family have accepted they are unlikely to ever find her alive. 'It is, of course, a poignant place for us all,' Patrick explained during a fine lunch of soup and sandwiches, laced with a warming shot of home-made liqueur. It was a bumper year for sloes in this part of the world and the hedges were black with them. 'The drive will look terrific though once the trees have grown and it will be a fitting memorial for Kate.'

While the Guns have been coming back year on year, so have the beaters, with the result that the whole shoot gets along famously. 'It certainly helps having folk who know the ground,' added Edwin. 'It makes my job a lot easier, as they tend to take their own bit and get on with it.' Many of the Guns' wives help out in the beating line too and probably know the coverts better than their husbands. Jane MacInnes is Edwin's unofficial deputy on the day, having stridden through the drives every year, come rain or shine. 'Give me a woman beater any day,' said Edwin. 'They take far more notice of you than a man ever will.'

Another of the long-term servants of Albyfield is Cynthia Duff, who works her three golden retrievers behind the line of Guns with great precision. Now in her seventies, Cynthia keeps buzzing back and forward over stiles and hurdles, until the last bird is picked.

However, new blood is necessary on any ground, no matter how well oiled it may run, and that day it came in the form of Robin and Joanne O'Dowd, who were beating for the first time ever. Newcomers to the local village, they had been 'nabbed' by Edwin one afternoon and persuaded to give it a go. Was it how they thought it would be? 'We were a bit worried about what we might see,' admitted Joanne, 'as you read in the papers that game shooting is a bit of a massacre, but I'm pleased to find it is nothing like that. I'm still not entirely sure where I stand on it though.' 'The exercise is certainly good,' added Robin. 'And I've learned a great deal about opening and shutting gates. They are all unique and you need to use a different part of your body each time to move them! I have found the whole experience valuable, as now that we live round here, we will be living next to many people who enjoy shooting, and I've always believed the only way to form an honest opinion is to look for yourself. I can see myself doing this again.'

The day finishes at the local pub with a late lunch and yarn or two, as it always has for the last twenty-eight years and probably will for many years to come. As the light faded and the pheasants made their way to roost in the Big Wood, the toast was to 'the best of friends'.

50. Foxhunting

This may sound a little callous, given the strength of emotion that always follows this topic, but the whole foxhunting furore was a godsend for me because it kick-started a career that was going nowhere fast. In the Autumn of 2002, I was working as a temporary hack on various trade magazines in London, when my sister Clare, who worked for the Scottish Countryside Alliance in Edinburgh, volunteered me for a relay run from John o'Groats to London that aimed to raise money and awareness for the forthcoming Liberty and Livelihood Countryside March. I grumbled and moaned at the time, but eventually worked out that there might be journalistic gain to be made from participating in such a high profile event. I put the idea of an online diary to the editors of the *Country Life* website, which they swallowed, so long as I could get the instalments to them in good time. In these situations, the only answer is to act like a goose guide and say, 'yes, no problem', before working out how on earth you're going to achieve it.

The plan was for sixteen of us in four groups of four, to each run ten miles a day in a non-stop relay, starting at the top end of Scotland. In five days, in theory, we would arrive in the Capital. It had not been so long since running the New York and London marathons, so the ten miles a day was not too scary. It was the logistics that frightened me. We would be ferried about from house to hostel, before being left at various junctures to run our stints. Given the run was continuous, we might be expected to run in the middle of the night. Would I be able to file my copy?

I will say now, in my defence, that this was in the days before widespread internet coverage. There was no broadband or wi-fi or Blackberries. We were living in a comparative dark age. Mobile phones didn't even have cameras, for goodness sake, let alone email capabilities! As it turned out, I needn't have worried. There was the odd cross country jaunt to find an internet café or a hotel with a connection, where I could type furiously what we had seen and done. I doubt anyone read it, save for relations of those running, but it made me feel like a proper correspondent.

Paul Quagliana captured an excellent shot of the protesters in Parliament Square.

Jogging into Parliament Square with crowds cheering and riot helicopters shining spotlights from above was pretty exciting. London was already filling up with country folk in for the march, so there was plenty of ego-boosting acclaim to be milked. The march itself was as vibrant as the organisers could have hoped with nearly half a million protesters in attendance. Of course, they should have all stayed at home for all the notice the Government took of them.

For me, however, things were looking up. *Country Life* gave me a full time gig on their website, where I wrote countless stories on property prices and the various developments in the hunting campaign. My editor, a brilliant Italian named Carla Passino, would send me to Westminster whenever anything kicked off and more than once I found myself caught up in the scrum of protesters. In one fracas – I think it was to do with hare coursing – the mob and the police clashed in front of the Parliament Gates. I was near the front and was pushed forward against the ranks of mounted police waiting behind a fence. There was nothing I could do as the back markers propelled us towards the barricades. Looking up, I saw the police's wooden batons raised high above their helmets from sixteen hands up. There were quite a few people who went home with bloodied heads that day, but happily I wasn't one of them.

By the time I moved to *Shooting Times*, in 2003, I was sick to the back teeth of the hunting question. Each minor development had been an excuse to fill column inches, so it was a blessing to go to a publication that obsessed on a different sport. Our news pages covered the developments, but as a feature writer, I hoped I might be spared. So my heart sank when the order came to write a piece on foxhunting. It fell further when I was told the introduction would read, 'The Arrogance of Hunting' by Ian Valentine.

Why pick such a bellicose angle? I asked. Surely hunting and shooting were on the same side? We are, came the reply, but it doesn't hurt to give them a kick up the backside from the time to time. My editor was aggrieved that various hunting folk had been hinting strongly that catching a fox with hounds was more humane than shooting it. A shotgun or rifle might injure a fox, while hounds will dispatch it instantly, they said. More foxes will be shot by keepers and farmers if you ban hunting, they warned. There were sections of the shooting community who had marched to save hunting and who interpreted this as, at best, opportunistic. At worst, it was downright selfish and further proof of the arrogance of hunting.

It was not a situation I was happy with. We ran the risk of playing into the antis' hands by squabbling with each other. Divide and conquer and all that. So I gave my stock answer, 'yes, no problem' and set about doing it my own way. First of all, that would mean a day's hunting to see what all the fuss was about.

The stereotypical view of hunting, for most people who haven't done it, is that of the red-coated, red-faced aristocrat charging where he pleases on a huge horse like he owns the countryside – which he probably once did – with local tenants tugging furiously at their forelocks. Hot on the hoofprints of m'lawd comes m'laydee, her braying voice an octave higher than the hounds as she berates some poor farm hand (who was only trying to save his chickens) for not watching where she was going, while she swigs her third stirrup cup of the morning. I was determined to prove this was not the case.

But while hunting made great strides in improving its public relations image in the fight for survival, it never did manage to shake off the Jorrocks and Wurzel motif that sits so well with the tabloids. 'No matter how hard we tried to push the right people in front of the camera,' said one Alliance press officer, 'the media always managed to find a ridiculous toff or a slack-jawed yokel to present as the face of hunting.'

It was not a difficult task either to find several horror stories of 'Hooray Henrys' with little respect for other users of the countryside. One shooter from Dorset told me a story of a day when he took his father on a drive to watch the hunt on their own farm. Coming round the corner to the farmyard, a quarter of a mile short of the meet, they discovered the road blocked with horseboxes, cars and trailers, parked at their owners' convenience, having churned up the grass verges on both sides of the road. The car pressed forward, negotiating the hunters as they gathered for the off. 'Oi, you, watch where the f***k you're going,' said one of the men from up high on his hunter. Apparently, the farm owner's satisfaction at winding down the window and explaining who they were, followed by the aggressor's bumbling apology, was ample retribution. The problem with stereotypes is that that they are easy to live up to and hard to live down.

This is another story I fielded in my research. Saturday morning: a lady demands of the man in scruffy overalls leaning against the gate that he, 'open the gate at once, man', followed by, 'didn't you hear me? Open the gate, I said!' The man does what he is told and says nothing. Monday morning: the man in scruffy overalls phones the master and informs him that the hunt is no longer welcome on his five thousand acre estate. He figured it didn't matter that the lady didn't know who he was. The point was that she shouldn't speak to anyone like that.

I spoke to another keeper who reckoned it was as much to do with perception as anything else. 'It is hard not to look down on someone from six feet up on a horse,' he reasoned. 'It is as much a problem of the hunters looking down, saying "we are loftier than thou", as the chap on the ground looking up and thinking, "look at that pillock on his pedestal". The shooting fraternity has to learn from this.'

So that would be my angle, I decided, pleased to find a positive way out of my quandary. How can shooting learn from the mistakes of hunting? It would imply that hunting had moved on from those stereotypically arrogant days and provide a lesson for shooting to avoid, for there are many who see pheasant shooting simply as the playtime of the rich and privileged. But first, I would need to prove to myself that hunting had indeed moved on.

I have ridden a fair amount in my life, but I was still anxious about joining a hunting field. There can't be many riders who haven't broken an arm, leg, collar bone or worse. Almost all of them will have banged their head on a wall or wooden rail.

I was invited to join the famous Heythrop Hunt in Oxfordshire, no doubt near the top of the antis' list of exclusive posh hunts. Annual membership, plus livery and transport can run into many thousands for the London enthusiasts who ride with the leading Southern hunts, so if I was going to find signs of arrogance this was as likely a place to start as anywhere. A colleague had kindly given me the loan of her sister's horse Blue, who I later learned has a reputation in the county for being one of the best hunters in the field. As long as I held tight, he would get me over anything. We were cubbing at the start of the season, so there was rather more standing about and chatting as the huntsmen worked their hounds through various likely spinneys and copses. No fox appeared all day, which is often the case and there is no getting away from the paradox that a low number of foxes – surely the endgame as far as the farmers are concerned – means a less fun day for the hunt. But while we did not have the opportunity to chase anything, I really did enjoy myself. And disappointingly for the story, at least, I found no hint of this stereotypical elitism.

Blue was good to his reputation, baling me out of trouble if I mistimed an approach to a ditch or fence, although given the ground was soft and it was early season, we were hardly flying over Beecher's Brook. Or Valentine's for that matter. There was so much to see from my new perspective, most of it at close quarters as you duck under a low branch. As the fabulous hounds worked through the cover, so mallard lifted from the stream and pheasants flew from wooded plantations, clucking loudly as though enjoying their day off from the guns. Judging by the number of kids among our number, school truancy is clearly not restricted to inner cities.

The hunt members seemed genuinely delighted to welcome a newcomer to their sport and it was plain that they took pleasure from my enjoyment. It was only then, listening to the passion shared for their common pastime that the injustice of the ban really sunk in. The two-and-a-half hours it took for my muscles to turn to jelly were by far the most fun I've ever had on a horse, Bibi included.

Everyone was polite and courteous. Gates were opened and duly shut. The riders stuck to paths and fields, although whether this would have changed if a fox was on the radar, I don't know. I remember one old soak who just about fitted the red-faced, aloof pastiche in the cartoons, but he kept to himself. Everybody else was young, friendly and from a variety of backgrounds. Despite walking like the bandito Yosemite Sam for the next two days, it was not exhaustive research. But it did prove to me that if hunting did have an image problem in the past, it was doing what it could to improve it. I saw no signs of haughty disrespect. In fact, I saw members of the community out enjoying themselves. If only for the social and economic benefits, there was no reason to make people stop hunting.

51. Mountain hares

Our ancestors used to be very suspicious of the hare, with its apparent ability to disappear into thin air. It was devilry, they mumbled into their pint pots. Tales swept the country of hideous witches that transformed themselves into hares to bring untold woes upon God-fearing villagers. The blue or mountain hare – able to change colour in the winter no less – was evil incarnate for the fear-mongers, especially in Scotland where witch burning became a national pastime. In our enlightened times we can be pretty sure that witches do not roam the night dressed as hares, but the beautiful blue hare remains a creature of mystery. There is plenty we still do not know about these enigmatic dancers, boxers and runners.

Hare shoots are now less prevalent in the Highlands, although they still attract the Continentals who go crazy for hare meat. I joined one such day near Kingussie, where six Frenchmen had travelled from Lyon to fill their larders. It was like an international sign language conference at two thousand feet above sea level, as headkeeper Davey Thompson tried to lay down the law to the team of Guns. Even if everybody had spoken in the same tongue, which they didn't, it would have been nigh on impossible to hear your neighbour above the wind that screamed across the desolate summit. Patrice, one of the party, was performing a dramatic mime which involved putting stones in his pockets to stop him being swept off the mountain. Denis, his pal, joined in the game by tugging his hat over his ears as though it were about to be blown to Inverness. The other four shrugged and pouted like a Marcel Marceau tribute group. None of them listened to Davey.

The keeper was not to be pushed off stage, however, and waved his carved walking stick in front of them like Moses on Mount Sinai. Having grabbed their attention, he placed the stick on the heather at their feet. 'At all times,' he said deliberately, 'we stay in a line.' With a handful of cartridges, he demonstrated where the guns would be standing. He then put one errant cartridge in front of the stick and another behind. 'Non, non, non,' he emphasised, wagging his index finger, before returning the cartridges to the stick. 'We always stay in line.'

The French party nodded extravagently. 'And we do not swing through the line,' Davey added, while he had them listening. 'Lift the gun clear of the line if the hare goes behind. Then you can shoot. Understand?'

'If not, then you go dans le Land Rover!' interpreted Andre, one of the shruggers and pouters, in his best Franglais. 'Et, it is pas bon dans le Land Rover!'

Blue hares prefer to stay out of these high winds and will be found in the lea of the hill, Davey explained to me as the guns spread out across the brow of the hill with a space of thirty yards between each. 'Mountain hares seem to run up hills if startled,' the keeper said, anxiously watching to see if his stick demonstration had been ingested by the French. 'There must be some ancient reason for it based on survival, but I can't tell you for sure why they do it.' Davey is well known in this part of Scotland, not only as a headkeeper and prominent voice in the Scottish Gamekeepers

Association, but also as a champion shinty (*camanachd* in the Gaelic) player. In his youth, he led nearby Kingussie in many a famous victory over their ancient rivals and neighbours Newtonmore, and was part of what the *Guinness Book of Records* named as world sport's most successful sporting team of all time, winning twenty consecutive league championships and going four years without losing a single fixture in the early 1990s.

It was not long before the first hares bolted from the heather and bounded over the ditches, marsh and streams that criss-crossed the slope. Like so many quarry species, it is easy to admire these lovely creatures, Britain's sole indigenous hare, as they chased over the wild terrain or sat back on their powerful haunches to spy for threats. Many had fully converted to their striking white coats designed to keep them hidden in the winter snow. Today, it made them stick out like stars in the night sky. One wonders if their evolutionary camouflage will have to regress if the global warming doom-mongers are proved correct?

'They are such a pretty animal,' Davey said with feeling as the first shot of the day accounted for a hare running brazenly in front of the guns, 'but we have to keep their numbers in check as you would lowland hares and rabbits to stop disease setting in. The hares always tend to reflect how the grouse are faring as they rely on the same moorland management such as heather regeneration through burning and vermin control, so what's good for the grouse is also good for the hare.' The foreign interest in hare shooting provides estates and local businesses such as hotels, restaurants and pubs with welcome custom in months when the grouse shooting and stag stalking is done for the year. Italians, Spaniards and, above all, the French are drawn to the Highlands in winter and while they agree that the people, scenery and sport is enough to bring them over for a holiday, it is the hare itself that gets their juices flowing. Indeed, the Guns were almost watering at the mouth when I asked them whether the hare is a favoured delicacy in France.

'Bien sur!' said an animated Michel Lambert in the lunch hut, as he refilled his beaker from the bottle of red wine he brought from his native Lyon. 'It is why we hunt the hare. When we go home, we will take as many as we can with us. Then we will invite many family and friends round to enjoy these hares, especially at Christmas time. For us, the hare is much more important than the goose, deer or turkey – it is our favourite meat!'

Denis Collange took up the baton (and a large slice of saucisson). 'You probably do not realise how fortunate you are in this country to have such a wide range of game in such numbers. In France, few species are regulated anymore and hunters have been too greedy in the past. There used to be a time when you could hunt many hares, especially in the hills, but now if you get one or two a year, you are very lucky.'

He finished by paraphrasing a quotation by King George VI that appears in the opening pages of *Shooting Times* each week. 'Many of our forefathers decided to live for the moment, rather than thinking about their children.'

I've always admired the French attitude to food and the sit-down family meal, sentiments that my own parents adhered to strictly, but I don't think any of us could match their dedication. Once they have travelled to Scotland and back, the hunter–gatherers will marinate the hares in top grade red wine (with Cognac, onion, carrot, celery, the inevitable garlic, thyme, bayleaf, rosemary and juniper) for seventy-two hours. On the big day of the feast, the ladies will spend five hours browning (with bacon and, later, mushrooms), stirring, simmering and reducing before the masses are fed. 'They wouldn't come if they weren't allowed to take the hares home with them,' Davey confirmed. Why is it that the Brits don't share the same attitude?

But while their desire to hunt and cook was laudable, Davey was still nervous about the Frenchmen's insouciance when it came to gun safety. Exuberance often got the better of prudence, and some would forge ahead of the keeper, while others lagged behind. The line was ragged enough to make Napoleon blush. I was keen not to be caught in the crossfire, especially when one gun started to compare himself to Lucky Luke, the cartoon cowboy 'who draws quicker than his shadow', and so offered to act as translator and enforcer.

From now on Davey would act as referee and would brandish a metaphorical yellow card to any first-time transgressors, followed by a red card to repeat offenders. 'There are a couple of you who are pushing too far forward. If I have to say *doucement*, then that is the first warning. If I need to say it again to anyone then I will take his cartridges for ten minutes until he learns to walk in line.' Cue howls of laughter by the French and mass waving of invisible red cards, but the penny seemed to have dropped. Nobody crossed the line that afternoon.

Throughout the day, four spaniels matched the French enthusiasm for hares as they worked like pit ponies to retrieve the heavy corpses across the heather. Each time a hare was bowled over, the line would halt to allow the nearest spaniel to sweep forward before returning to Davey carrying almost half its own weight in its jaws.

'They would do this all day,' said Davey proudly, who was careful to send his dogs out in turn to spare their energy and give the equal opportunity to show off their skills. 'This is what they were made for, hunting through the heather like that, and they would run themselves into the ground if I let them.'

The keeper's wife Fiona followed two hundred yards behind the guns in an Argocat to pick up the hares and save her husband's back. By the time we made it down the hill, the sun broke through the clouds for the first time and a vivid rainbow lit up the hills of Inverness-shire. There would be plenty of hares for a fine French feast. More importantly, nobody had been shot!

52.

Wild boar

Wild boar hunting in the north of Poland was a valuable lesson in expectation versus reality. Like the other seven Brits on the trip, I had a preconceived idea of what awaited us. I foresaw a great hunting lodge in the forest, decked out with hand-carved furniture, skins on the wall and a roaring hearth big enough to park a fire engine. There would be heady banquets every night in which local hunters would regale us with tales of the forest, pausing only to slurp back frothy lager through their handlebar moustaches. I wanted music, laughter, good food and fun. The reality was altogether different, although it was no less fun for all that.

I ought to first of all point out, before I get accused of naivety, that this was also the picture painted by the tour operator, so it was not a total flight of fantasy on my part. The party had been assured a traditional lodge in a forest that was teeming with boar. Everyone would see and shoot plenty. Always a foolish promise to make!

I should also say that I wasn't paying to be there either, so I could take a step back and watch without the same involvement. I could only imagine how frustrating it must have been for those who had saved up for 'the holiday of a lifetime'. And where there are hopes and dreams, there is always someone on hand to exploit them. There was some responsibility on my part though, as the advert for the trip had appeared in *Shooting Times*. They were a new company, with a first time rep and the offer was at a cut-down rate to attract in punters. A loss leader or perhaps too good to be true?

The first hang-up came at Warsaw airport. It turned out that the original, perfect destination had been snowed out and we would have to get a bus to another shooting area. 'Don't worry, it's not that far and it will be just as good.' So we all jumped into a minibus, evidently built by a torture expert. Nine hours later we arrived at the village in the north of the country near the German border. We'd have been better off flying to Berlin!

It was not a forest lodge. Don't get me wrong, it was comfortable enough and I really have no grounds to grumble given I was there on a freebee, but it was not what we expected. Indeed, if there are any other Soviet theme hotels in the world, then I have never heard of them! The owner, perhaps one of the few Poles disappointed to see the Russians leave in 1993, had decorated his establishment with icons of the Soviet past. Pride of place in the dining room was a montage of Marx, Lenin, Stalin and himself all looking nobly into the distance. Every night his son would appear dressed in full military garb and march round the table with a glass AK-47 filled with vodka, which he would use to load empty glasses. It was nothing short of bizarre and almost fetishistic!

The village was next to an enormous wood that once housed a Soviet military camp. These forests have a troubled history. On our way into the shooting ground, rattling in the back of an ex-military truck (emblazoned with the hammer and sickle of the old USSR), we passed the graveyard of an Anglo-French prisoner of war camp, run by the Germans during the Second World War. The Soviets then took over, using the ground as a training camp for troops. According to our driver that morning, the sentries outside the camp were positioned not for keeping the Poles out, but for stopping the Russian soldiers from escaping.

In 1993 the woods were returned to the locals, who flooded into an area that had been strictly off limits for over half a century. All they found was a ghost town, a ready supply of timber and a thriving population of deer and wild boar. With communism gone, capitalism quickly took root with Westerners ready to pay top dollar to shoot driven game.

As we tramped out to our 'pegs' on the first drive, I couldn't help but think of all those who had made a final walk through these bleak forests. The crunch of our guide's black leather boots through the frozen surface of the snow was the only sound save for the guttural choke of a raven that sat hidden amid the row upon row of black trees. Navigation would have been impossible. The temperature had long dropped below minus ten and a determined wind fought to infiltrate any pocket of warmth that remained. The times may have changed, but there was still something a bit eerie about the clunk of a round being chambered in this sinister landscape.

If you ask folk why they go hunting wild boar in Poland, there are two stock replies. For those that had not been before, 'wild boar shooting is just one of those things you have to do'. The thrill, excitement and adventure of chasing these enigmatic creatures that we do not (or certainly never used to) have in this country, with the added adrenaline rush that they may just turn round and gore you to death, is the lure. The other answer that all six gave at one point during the weekend was along the lines of 'we can't shoot driven game with a rifle at home and it is wonderful and testing sport'. The scenery, camaraderie, food, traditions and relaxation that all play a big part in a sporting holiday were all there too, but the opportunity to shoot animals on the run was the key.

In truth, it is easy to see why. While there is an attraction about creeping up undetected on a wild animal to take calm aim and shoot, to see a boar, red or roe deer come charging out of the trees at a rate of knots gets the heart beating like Ringo. And I wasn't even holding a rifle.

The Poles who provided the legwork and muscle for the driven shoot were a friendly enough bunch, always quick with a grin or a slug of cherry brandy, but their faces were as hard as their environment. Each came armed with a stick and a fierce dog, usually of questionable parentage, that would give fair warning to any waiting Rifle if a boar was coming. The beaters covered huge distances at a decent lick, tapping trees and leaping snow drifts, always to the tune of 'ay-up' at the top of their voices like an out-take from *Last of the Summer Wine*. This team also deputised as butchers, taking it in turn to gralloch whatever beast had been brought down. There seemed to be a pecking order on who did which animal, as the offal was usually taken home by whoever extracted it.

On the second day, we were joined by a couple of Polish shooters who had driven through the night to get there. On the last drive before lunch,

Maciek Rafaliski cooks the liver of his pig. Every ingredient demanded another shot of vodka.

Tasting.

which always consisted of wonderfully hearty soups and meaty sausages, I was fortunate to observe a true master in action. Maciek (pronounced Magic) Rafaliski, a bear of a man, had been hunting boar all his life, and so exuded that coolness and confidence of someone who knows exactly what they're doing. Here was the traditional Polish hunting man that I had expected, albeit without a curly moustache.

For five minutes before the drive started, he kicked out a large square in the snow, so he could be sure of a firm footing. He shouldered a few dry swings with his faithful 30.06 to decide the best places to shoot, picking gaps in the trees where the boar were likely to run. Satisfied that his neighbours, one hundred yards either side, knew exactly where he was, he stood still and listened. All he heard was my tummy rumbling.

'That is good noise,' he whispered, his eyes gleaming. 'In Poland we say that wild animals will come to you if your stomach sounds.'

'Fingers crossed, Maciek.'

'Why would you cross your fingers when shooting? How will that help?'

'It means "good luck" in Britain.'

'Oh. I see. In Poland we say "break pencils", because you can do that if you pass your exams. Now, shut up or you'll scare the black pork.'

So I did, listening as the beaters made steady progress in a small valley below us. Suddenly, to our right, two dogs began making a fearful racket, like terriers before the race. I found myself frozen on the spot. 'Shhh,' Maciek hissed. 'Black pork coming.'

The black pork came barrelling up the hill as fast as its piggy legs could take it, which was easily as fast as a fox or the dogs that chased it, nimbly skipping over the snow, branches and hidden roots. Maciek clocked it immediately and waited for it to cross the line. Once it was in the trees behind and a safe shot, there was a crack and thud. The boar cart-wheeled to a stop.

'Good pig!' Maciek cried, delighted with himself as we approached the body after the drive had finished. 'Although I think I was a little behind on the neck, no? Yes, you see, two or three centimetres.'

His pig was a yearling male and a prized catch for the table. Maciek decided that as I had been his good luck charm, it was only right that he should cook its liver for me! With great show, he eviscerated the boar and solemnly removed its liver, which he jealously stowed in a plastic bag. Back in the hotel, the successful hunter barged his way into the kitchen and quickly charmed the cook into allowing her full access to her pots, pans and larder.

He made a variation on liver and onions, padded out with bacon and apple, and fortified with tablespoons of fiery paprika and black pepper. The whole show took about an hour, filled with arm waving, lip smacking and salutations to the 'black pork'. Maciek explained the love affair that Poles have with boar and deer. 'What you have seen here is not typical of Poland,' said our translator Nathalia, doing her best to keep up with the chef's tirade. 'Where I come from in the south we do things properly. Everybody is smartly turned out, happy, friendly. There is great ceremony throughout the day, especially when someone shoots their first pig. The game is well respected and laid out on a bed of fir branches in the evening and the hunters play a different tune on a horn to honour each species. We name a King of the Forest for the hunter who has shot the most animals with a scoring system depending on the different species. I am very embarrassed that you have not seen that up here.'

Whenever Maciek said something he thought was funny or insightful, he would toast the occasion with a shot of vodka and insist I did the same.

Filled with vodka I insist on kissing the cook.

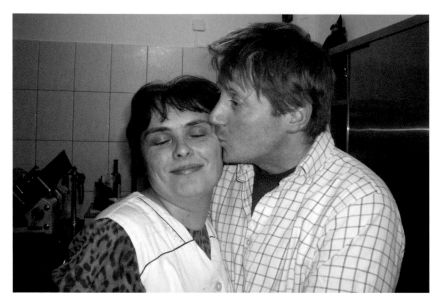

'Nasdrovia!' he bellowed time and again, slapping me hard on the back. It seemed to have little effect on him – he was loud and energetic when we started – but I was soon struggling. I'm sorry to report that I hardly remember how the liver tasted, save that it was as hot as raw chilli.

By 8 p.m. I was spent, but I was grateful for the experience. Maciek had assured me that Polish boar hunting could be what I had hoped for. The key is to make sure you go with reputable operators who share your grand ideals.

Looking back, the group had a very enjoyable trip, but it was all in adversity. While there were as many deer as anyone could hope to shoot, the boar were thin on the ground. Indeed, some hunters went home without seeing one. Yet the party bonded in mutual derision of the operators and, in a perverse way, it was all the better for that. Even when we were forced to rise at 3.30 a.m. to catch the minibus back to Warsaw, the group's sense of humour held firm. Perhaps if the trip had been as I hoped, it would not have been so memorable.

Acknowledgements

I would like to thank IPC Media for its kind permission to reproduce the photos and content that appeared in its publications. In particular I would like to thank my editors Camilla Clark, Robert Gray, Hamish Dawson and Carla Passino, and all the editorial staff of *Shooting Times*. I am grateful to so many others for their encouragement down the years, but especially my family, Ginny Brinton, Richard Butler, Holly Kirkwood and Kate Nixey. Thanks also to Quiller for backing me, my editor John Beaton and finally Charley Smith for supplying the photo on page 224.

Index